THE NAVARRE BIBLE

1 and 2 Thessalonians; Pastoral Epistles

# THE NAVARRE BIBLE
# St Paul's Epistles to the Thessalonians and Pastoral Epistles

in the Revised Standard Version and New Vulgate
with a commentary by members of the
Faculty of Theology of the University of Navarre

FOUR COURTS PRESS

Original title: *Sagrada Biblia: IX. San Pablo: Epístolas a los Tesalonicenses y Epístolas pastorales.* Quotations from Vatican II documents are based on the translation in *Vatican Council II: The Conciliar and Post Conciliar Documents,* ed. A. Flannery, OP (Dublin 1981).

*Nihil obstat:* Stephen J. Greene, *censor deputatus.* *Imprimi potest:* Desmond, Archbishop of Dublin, 9 January 1992.

The typesetting of this book was produced by Gilbert Gough Typesetting. The book, designed by Jarlath Hayes, is published by Four Courts Press, Kill Lane, Blackrock, Co. Dublin, Ireland.

A catalogue record for this book is available from the British Library.

ISBN 1-85182-078-7
ISBN 1-85182-077-9 pbk

Printed in Ireland
by Colour Books Ltd, Ireland

# Contents

# Preface

In providing both undergraduate and postgraduate education, and in the research it carries out, a university is ultimately an institution at the service of society. It was with this service in mind that the theology faculty of the University of Navarre embarked on the project of preparing a translation and commentary of the Bible accessible to a wide readership—a project entrusted to it by the apostolic zeal of the University's founder and first chancellor, Monsignor Josemaría Escrivá de Balaguer.

Monsignor Escrivá did not live to see the publication of the first volume, the Gospel according to St Matthew; but he must, from heaven, continue to bless and promote our work, for the volumes, the first of which appeared in 1976, have been well received and widely read.

This edition of the Bible avoids many scholarly questions, discussion of which would over-extend the text and would be of no assistance to the immense majority of readers; these questions are avoided, but they have been taken into account.

The Spanish edition contains a new Spanish translation made from the original texts, always taking note of the Church's official Latin text, which is now that of the New Vulgate, a revision of the venerable Latin Vulgate of St Jerome: on 25 April 1979 Pope John Paul II, by the Apostolic Constitution *Scripturarum thesaurus*, promulgated the *editio typica prior* of the New Vulgate as the new official text; the *editio typica altera*, issued in 1986, is the Latin version used in this edition. For the English edition of this book we consider ourselves fortunate in having the Revised Standard Version as the translation of Scripture and wish to record our appreciation for permission to use that text, an integral part of which are the RSV notes, which are indicated by superior letters.

The introductions and notes have been prepared on the basis of the same criteria. In the notes (which are the most characteristic feature of this Bible, at least in its English version), along with scriptural and ascetical explanations we have sought to offer a general exposition of Christian doctrine—not of course a systematic exposition, for we follow the thread of the scriptural text. We have also tried to explain and connect certain biblical passages by reference to others, conscious that Sacred Scripture is ultimately one single entity; but, to avoid tiring the reader, most of the cross-references are given in the form of marginal notes (the marginal notes in this edition are, then, those of the Navarre Bible, not the RSV). The commentaries contained in the notes are the result of looking up thousands of sources (sometimes reflected in explicit references given in our text)—documents of the Magisterium, exegesis by Fathers and Doctors of the Church, works by important spiritual writers (usually saints, of every period) and writings of the founder of our University. It would have been impertinent of us to comment on the Holy Bible using our own expertise alone. Besides, a basic principle of exegesis is that Scripture should be inter- preted in the context of Sacred Tradition and under the guidance of the Magisterium.

From the very beginning of our work our system has been to entrust each volume to a committee which then works as a team. However, the general editor of this edition takes ultimate responsibility for what it contains.

It is our pleasant duty to express our gratitude to the present chancellor of the University of Navarre, Bishop Alvaro del Portillo y Diez de Sollano, for his continued support and encouragement, and for reminding us of the good our work can do for the Church and for souls.

"Since Sacred Scripture must be read and interpreted with its divine authorship in mind,"[1] we pray to the Holy Spirit to help us in our work and to help our readers derive spiritual benefit from it. We also pray Mary, our Mother, Seat of Wisdom, and St Joseph, our Father and Lord, to intercede that this sowing of the Word of God may produce holiness of life in the souls of many Christians.

1   Vatican Council II, Dogm. Const. *Dei Verbum*, 12.

# Abbreviations and Sources

## 1. BOOKS OF SACRED SCRIPTURE

| | | | |
|---|---|---|---|
| Acts | Acts of the Apostles | 2 Kings | 2 Kings |
| Amos | Amos | Lam | Lamentations |
| Bar | Baruch | Lev | Leviticus |
| 1 Chron | 1 Chronicles | Lk | Luke |
| 2 Chron | 2 Chronicles | 1 Mac | 1 Maccabees |
| Col | Colossians | 2 Mac | 2 Maccabees |
| 1 Cor | 1 Corinthians | Mal | Malachi |
| 2 Cor | 2 Corinthians | Mic | Micah |
| Dan | Daniel | Mk | Mark |
| Deut | Deuteronomy | Mt | Matthew |
| Eccles | Ecclesiastes (Qohelet) | Nah | Nahum |
| Esther | Esther | Neh | Nehemiah |
| Eph | Ephesians | Num | Numbers |
| Ex | Exodus | Obad | Obadiah |
| Ezek | Ezekiel | 1 Pet | 1 Peter |
| Ezra | Ezra | 2 Pet | 2 Peter |
| Gal | Galatians | Phil | Philippians |
| Gen | Genesis | Philem | Philemon |
| Hab | Habakkuk | Ps | Psalms |
| Hag | Haggai | Prov | Proverbs |
| Heb | Hebrews | Rev | Revelation (Apocalypse) |
| Hos | Hosea | Rom | Romans |
| Is | Isaiah | Ruth | Ruth |
| Jas | James | 1 Sam | 1 Samuel |
| Jer | Jeremiah | 2 Sam | 2 Samuel |
| Jn | John | Sir | Sirach (Ecclesiasticus) |
| 1 Jn | 1 John | Song | Song of Solomon |
| 2 Jn | 2 John | 1 Thess | 1 Thessalonians |
| 3 Jn | 3 John | 2 Thess | 2 Thessalonians |
| Job | Job | 1 Tim | 1 Timothy |
| Joel | Joel | 2 Tim | 2 Timothy |
| Jon | Jonah | Tit | Titus |
| Josh | Joshua | Tob | Tobit |
| Jud | Judith | Wis | Wisdom |
| Jude | Jude | Zech | Zechariah |
| Judg | Judges | Zeph | Zephaniah |
| 1 Kings | 1 Kings | | |

## 2. OTHER SOURCES REFERRED TO

Augustine, St
  *Christian Instruction*
  *City of God, The*
  *De Actis cum Felice Manicheo*
  *De Genesis ad litteram*
  *Letters*
  *Sermons*

Benedict, XV
  Enc. *Spiritus Paraclitus*,
    15 September 1920

Bernard, St
  *Book of Considerations*
  *Sermons on Psalm 90*

Clement of Rome, St
  *Letter to the Corinthians*

*Code of Canon Law: Codex Iuris Canonicis,*
  *auctoritate Ioanni Pauli PP. II*
  *promulgatus, 1983*

Constantinople, 1st Council of
  *Nicene-Constantinopolitan Creed*

*Didache* or *The Teaching of the*
  *Twelve Apostles* (*c.* A.D. 100)

Escrivá de Balaguer, J.
  *Christ is passing by* (followed by
    section no.)
  *Conversations* (do.)
  *The Forge* (do.)
  *Friends of God* (do.)
  *Furrow* (do.).
  *In Love with the Church* (do.)
  *The Way* (do.)

Florence, Council of
  *Laetentur coeli*
  *Pro Jacobitis*

Francis of Assisi, St
  *The Little Flowers*

Gregory the Great, St
  *Epistula ad Theodorum medicum*
  *In Evangelia homiliae*
  *In Ezechielem homiliae*
  *Moralia in Job*

Ignatius of Antioch, St
  *Letter to the Ephesians*
  *Letter to Polycarp*

Ignatius Loyola, St
  *Spiritual Exercises*

Irenaeus, St
  *Against heresies*

Jerome, St
  *Ad Nepotianum*
  *Contra Luciferianos*

John of Avila, St
  *Audi, filia*

John Chrysostom, St
  *Ad Theodorem lapsum*
  *Ante exilium homilia*
  *Hom. on St Matthew*
  *Hom. on 1 and 2 Thess*
  *Hom. on 1 and 2 Timothy*
  *Fifth homily on Anna*

John Paul II
  Address (on date given)
  Apos. Exhort. *Familiaris consortio*,
    22 November 1981
  Apos. Exhort. *Catechesi tradendae*,
    16 October 1979
  Apos. Exhort. *Reconciliatio et paenitentia*,
    2 December 1984
  Apos. Exhort. *Salvifici doloris*,
    11 February 1984
  Enc. *Dives in misericordia*, 30 March 1897
  Enc. *Dominum et Vivificantem*, 18 May 1986
  Enc. *Laborem exercens*, 14 September 1981
  Enc. *Redemptor hominis*, 4 March 1979
  *Letter to All Priests*, 8 April 1979

Justin, St
  *Dialogue with Trypho*

Leo XIII
  Enc. *Divinum illud munus*, 9 May 1879
  Enc. *Libertas praestantissimum*, 20 June 1888
  Enc. *Providentissimus Deus*,
    18 November 1893

*Liturgy of the Hours*
*Missal, Roman*
  *Missale Romanum ex decreto sacrosancti*
  *oecumenici concilii Vaticani II instauratum*
  *auctoritate Pauli PP. VI promulgatum, editio*
  *typica altera, 1986*

Paul VI
  *Creed of the People of God*, 30 June 1968
  Enc. *Sacerdotalis coelibatus*, 24 July 1967
  Apos. Exhort. *Evangelii nuntiandi*,
    8 December 1975
  Enc. *Ecclesiam suam*, 6 August 1964

Pius V, St
  *Catechism of the Council of Trent for*
    *Parish Priests*

Pius XI
  Enc. *Ad catholici sacerdotii*, 20 December
    1935

Pius XII
  Enc. *Divino afflante Spiritu*, 30 November
    1943
  Enc. *Menti nostrae*, 23 September 1950

Polycarp, St
  *Letter to the Philippians*

10

Pontifical Biblical Commission
*Reply,* 12 June 1913
Portillo, Alvaro del
*On Priesthood*
SCDF
Instruction, *Libertatis conscientia,*
22 March 1986
Instruction, *Libertatis nuntius,*
6 August 1984
Sacred Congregation of the Rites
*General Instruction on the Roman
Missal*
Severian of Gabala
*Commentary on 1 Thess*
*Shepherd of Hermas, The (c.* A.D. 140)
Teresa of Avila, St
*Life*
*Way of Perfection*
Tertullian
*De oratione*

Thomas Aquinas, St
*Commentary on Hebrews*
*Commentaries on 1 and 2 Thess*
*Commentaries 1 and 2 Timothy*
*Commentary on Titus*
*On the Lord's Prayer*
*Summa theologiae*
Vatican, 1st Council of the
Dogm. Const. *Dei Filius*
Dogm. Const. *Pastor aeternus*
Vatican, 2nd Council of the
Decl. *Dignitatis humanae*
Decree *Ad gentes*
Decree *Apostolicam actuositatem*
Decree *Christus dominus*
Decl. *Gravissimum educationis*
Decl. *Nostra aetate*
Decree *Optatam totius*
Decree *Presbyterorum ordinis*
Dogm. Const. *Dei Verbum*
Dogm. Const. *Lumen gentium*
Past. Const. *Gaudium et spes*
Vincent of Lerins, St
*Commonitorium*

## 3. OTHER ABBREVIATIONS

| | | | |
|---|---|---|---|
| *ad loc.* | *ad locum,* commentary on this passage | f | and following (*pl.* ff) |
| Exhort. | Exhortation | *ibid.* | *ibidem,* in the same place |
| Apost. | apostolic | *in loc.* | *in locum,* commentary on this passage |
| can. | canon | | |
| chap. | chapter | *loc.* | *locum,* place or passage |
| cf. | *confer,* compare | n. | number (*pl.* nn.) |
| Const. | Constitution | p. | page (*pl.* pp.) |
| Decl. | Declaration | *pl.* | plural |
| *Dz-Sch* | Denzinger-Schönmetzer, *Enchiridion Symbolorum* | par. | and parallel passages |
| | | Past. | Pastoral |
| Dogm. | Dogmatic | SCDF | Sacred Congregation for the Doctrine of the Faith |
| *EB* | *Enchiridion Biblicum* (4th edition, Naples-Rome, 1961) | | |
| | | sess. | session |
| Enc. | Encyclical | v. | verse (*pl.* vv.) |

# The Truth of Sacred Scripture[1]

GENERAL

1. *The truth of the Bible derives from the fact that it is divinely inspired.* The Bible is the collection of divinely inspired books which the Church has received from ancient Israel and from the Apostles as a reliable source for the truth it believes and proclaims. These books are often described as "canonical" books because they provide the "canon" or "rule" of the truth revealed by God.

The teaching contained in the Bible, therefore, is not mere human teaching: it is the Word of God (as it is proclaimed to be after the scriptural readings at Mass). That is the reason why the Church believes that what is taught in the Bible is true. The truth of the Bible comes from the truthfulness of God who inspired it and who is, therefore, its principal author.

The hagiographers, the writers of the sacred books, worked under the influence of a special charism, or divine gift, which meant that while they were truly authors of the books, God used them to convey everything he wanted conveyed, no more and no less; therefore, everything the sacred writers have to say must be taken as said by the Holy Spirit.[2] That is why "we must acknowledge that the books of Scripture, firmly, faithfully and without error, teach that truth which God, for the sake of our salvation, wished to see confided to the Sacred Scriptures."[3]

From the very beginning the Church has consistently held that the Bible is free from error. This belief in the reliability of Scripture is part of the deposit of faith and it necessarily follows from the fact that Scripture is divinely inspired. The entire Bible is inspired, and the entire Bible (Old and New Testament) is true because God inspired the hagiographers. There are no two ways about this: the veracity of the Bible is an absolute truth; it is a truth revealed by God himself, a truth designed to give man access to salvation.

2. *Truth and inerrancy* God chose to teach us his saving truth by means of these sacred books. Clearly, therefore, there can be no error in them, because if there were God would be responsible for it. So, although the sacred writers all had their limitations and could make mistakes, when they were writing under the charism of inspiration they were influenced, enlightened and aided by the

---

1. This is one of a number of general introductory essays in *The Navarre Bible: New Testament*, see the full list on p. 183.
2. Cf. Leo XIII, *Providentissimus Deus*, 18 November 1893.
3. Vatican II, *Dei Verbum*, 11.

Holy Spirit in such a way that God was the principal author of these books and of the statements contained in them. It is just not possible to go to the Bible and distinguish parts attributable to God from parts attributable to man; the entire text is, at one and the same time, the Word of God and the word of man. God, therefore, must be considered the guarantor of there being nothing erroneous in Scripture.

When viewed from the angle of absence of error, the truthfulness of the Bible is called "inerrancy". Over the course of history, apologists have striven to defend the inerrancy of the Bible against those who seek to discredit the Judaeo-Christian religion by arguing that the the sacred books contain errors and contradictions and therefore are unreliable, that is, cannot be accepted as containing the truth that comes from God.

3. *Difficulties and tentative solution*  (a) *Apparent internal inconsistency* The Fathers and early Christian writers made no attempt to sidestep the difficulties raised by comparing certain Old Testament and New Testament passages, or even different texts within the New Testament itself. For example, they were perfectly well aware of the differences between the Synoptic Gospels and St John's Gospel as regards their accounts of Jesus' public ministry.

It is true that the solutions they offered did not have the academic rigour that is required nowadays; however, their faith in the divine inspiration of the Bible led them to establish sound principles and guidelines for solving these difficulties, and these principles are still valid today. St Justin, for example, replying to Trypho the Jew, who argued against the Christian faith by pointing to contradictions in Sacred Scripture, wrote: "I would never dare to think or say there are contradictions to be found in Scripture; if some (text of) Scripture seems to contradict (another), I prefer to admit that its meaning escapes me; and I shall do what I can to convince those who suspect that Scripture is self-contradictory to adopt my approach."[4]

Referring specifically to apparent contradictions in the Gospels, St Augustine wrote the following in the course of a long letter to St Jerome: "If in these writings I find something which seems to be contrary to the truth, it does not disconcert me, for I conclude that the particular codex I am reading may be faulty, or the translator may not have been able to render the text correctly, or I myself may not be understanding it properly."[5]

(b) *The biblical text and scientific discoveries*  In the course of controversy St Augustine also established certain principles which should be always borne in mind to appreciate the true meaning of Scripture: the Lord designed Scripture "to make Christians, not scholars"[6] and "the Spirit of God who has spoken to us through the sacred writers had no intention of teaching men anything other than what is useful for their salvation."[7]

4.  *Dialogue with Trypho*, 65.
5.  *Epistle* 82, 1, 3.
6.  *De Actis cum Felice Manicheo*, 1, 10.
7.  *De Gen. ad litt.*, II, 9.

In more recent times a number of difficulties arose from the fact that some biblical statements seemed to be at odds with scientific knowledge (particularly in astronomy and palaeontology). The concept of the universe projected by Sacred Scripture is not the same as that proposed by science; nor does it fit in with scientific theory about the stages in the development of the earth's surface and the appearance on earth of the various animal species. These and other questions like them led Christian scholars and the Church Magisterium to specify what it is that the biblical statements on these subjects do and do not say.

1. *The Galileo case*　In the seventeenth century, when Galileo asserted that the earth moves round the sun, some of his contemporaries saw this as a contradiction of the Bible. However, that was not Galileo's own view; in arguing his case, he quoted Cardinal Baronius to the effect that in Scripture "the Holy Spirit is trying to show us how to get to heaven, not how the heavens operate."[8]

2. *The teaching of the Magisterium*　Almost one hundred years ago, Pope Leo XIII wrote the following in the context of the evolutionary theories and archaeological discoveries of the time: "we must remember, first, that the sacred writers, or to speak more accurately, the Holy Spirit 'who spoke by them, did not intend to teach men these things (that is to say, the essential nature of the things of the visible universe), things in no way profitable unto salvation.' Hence they did not seek to penetrate the secrets of nature, but rather described and dealt with things in more or less figurative language, or in terms which were commonly used at the time, and which in many instances are commonly used at this day, even by the most eminent men of science."[9]

A classic example of this is the following. The biblical concept of the universe (its "cosmology"), like that of all the ancient world, saw the earth as the centre of the universe, with the sun and moon and stars moving round it. Science, correctly, now says that that is not the way things are; however, we cannot accuse the Bible of being mistaken on this matter—because, for one thing, it makes no claim to being a treatise on astronomy providing scientific explanations of such things; and also because the sacred writer is expressing himself in keeping with the culture and speech of his time which (as is also the case today) describes things the way they appear to the senses. In fact the senses are not wrong in what they perceive, even though science may provide explanations which are not apparent at first sight. God has left it up to man to discover how nature and the universe works. It would therefore be very silly to attack the Bible by ascribing to it defects or mistakes of this sort.

The fact that the Bible is a religious book and not an encyclopaedia does

8.　"Lettera alla serenissima madonna la Granduchessa Madre", in *Le opere di Galileo* (Florence 1895), V, p. 319.
9.　*Providentissimus Deus*, quoting St Augustine (cf. footnote 7 above).

not mean that whenever it deals with "scientific" matters it loses the divine inspiration it has when dealing with matters concerning religion or morality. Everything in the Bible is inspired by God. However, when addressing men, God accommodates himself to human language and culture (specifically, that of the sacred writers, who are really tools he uses to transmit divine Revelation); if he did not do so, the Word of God would simply not be intelligible to man. "In Scripture", St Thomas Aquinas wrote, "divine things are conveyed to us in the manner to which men are accustomed."[10]

This lowering of himself (God) to the level of man is termed "divine condescension" (*synkatabasis* in Greek).

The principle of divine condescension is very important for understanding how truth is transmitted to us in the Bible. It is a principle praised by St John Chrysostom (and other Fathers) and one promoted in our own time by Pope Pius XII in his encyclical *Divino afflante Spiritu*: "Just as the substantial Word of God became like to men in all things 'except sin', so the words of God, expressed in human language, became in all things like to human speech, except error." The Second Vatican Council also draws our attention to "the marvellous 'condescension' of eternal wisdom".[12]

THE RELIABILITY OF THE BIBLE IN MATTERS OF HISTORY

The principles we have been discussing can be applied to things connected with natural science and historical events. However, it should be pointed out that whereas knowledge of the scientific explanation of natural phenomena has no bearing on the eternal salvation of man, certain *historical events* do underpin biblical faith (this is true both for Jews and for Christians).

The events in question are all those which are bound up with the history of salvation; to mention some—the creation of the world and of man by God; the fall of our first parents; the choice God made of the people of Israel; the Covenant with Moses; the incarnation, death and resurrection of Christ; the coming of the Holy Spirit at Pentecost; and the beginnings of the Church. When speaking of natural phenomena, one can say that Scripture presents these *as they appear*, and it cannot be taken to task for so doing; however, that is not the case when it comes to statements about historical events: history based on what "appears" to happen, not what actually happens, would not be true history; as Benedict XV teaches, "History must square with the facts, since history is the written account of events as they actually happened."[13]

1. *Features of biblical history* As regards religious history, when studying the history of salvation as narrated in the Bible certain criteria apply which do not apply for modern history. Biblical history is first and foremost a religious

10. *Commentary on Hebrews*, 1, 4.
11. No. 20.
12. *Dei Verbum*, 13.
13. *Spiritus Paraclitus*, 15 September 1920.

16

history: it views events from the standpoint of faith and it includes a protagonist whose actions transcend anything historical research (in the modern sense) can explore. This protagonist is God. The sacred writers in giving their account of the history of Israel, or the life of Christ or the early Church, are not simply describing historical events; they are describing those events *and* interpreting them from the viewpoint of faith in the action of God.

The following example will illustrate what we mean. In recent times historians have done extensive research into the origins of the Jewish people; some argue that "Israel" began around the twelfth century B.C. (when the tribes were settling down in the land of Canaan); others think that the Hebrew people began to take shape earlier, under the leadership of Moses and Joshua after the flight from Egypt; others trace its roots to the patriarchal clans, around the nineteenth century B.C. The Bible's perspective is different: Israel makes its appearance in history due to a special intervention by God who wishes to create a people different from other peoples. This plan is put into effect by a series of divine interventions which goes right back to the call of Abraham; indeed, in embryo it goes back to the creation of man. So, although the Bible provides no clear answer to the question posed by modern historians about the origin of Israel, it has something very important to say on the subject: Israel arose as a people due to divine initiative, and Abraham, the Patriarchs, Moses . . . and those who were parties to the covenant of Shechem (cf. Josh 24) all played a part in the forging of the Israelite nation.

Because of its religious character, biblical history is selective in its content and is history written with a special purpose. However, that does not mean that it is any less true history. Interpreting facts in the light of faith not only does not falsify them: it gives them their true dimension, their proper interpretation, even though it emphasises and even heightens certain aspects of events—which indicates also that it is *selective* history: it does not attempt to cover everything; for it the important thing is to show in what way God has had a hand in events (which in turn provides an indication as to how he may act in the future).

2. *Different ways of recounting history*    We have indicated certain aspects of biblical history which need to be borne in mind if one is to understand it properly. However, each particular episode and the way it is narrated needs to be examined to discover what the sacred writer's intention was, that is, what he wanted to convey; for the narrative will be found to vary in accordance with the skill of the writer, his personal background and the literary genre he is using. For example, the literary style used to tell the story of the origin of the universe and of man (in the early chapters of Genesis) is going to be very different from that used for the flight from Egypt (which, as one would expect, has features of the epic).

Because historical truth is not always presented in the same way in the historical books of the Bible, Pope Pius XII makes the point that "no one who has a correct understanding of biblical inspiration will be surprised to find that the sacred writers, like the other ancients, employ certain arts of exposition and narrative, certain idioms especially characteristic of the Semitic languages (known as 'approximations'), and certain hyperbolical and even paradoxical expressions designed for the sake of emphasis."[14]

Among the events reported in the Bible are some which in principle can be checked by standard methods of historical research. These are historical events in the strict sense and it depends on historical method whether they can be checked out or not (they may be very remote in time). However, some biblical accounts of actual events can never be completely proven by historical method. It is possible to prove that Lazarus was raised from the dead, and the son of the widow of Nain; it is historical fact that Jesus' tomb was empty and that witnesses gave true accounts of the appearances of the risen Jesus. However, the person of Jesus risen and glorious lies beyond the methods available to historical science. The risen Jesus cannot, for example, be included in a census of population in the way he could have been before his death or the way Lazarus was after he was raised from the dead, for in Lazarus' case the life he was resurrected to was his old life, whereas in Jesus' case it was glorified life, a new mode of existence. These events, which fall outside the scope of historical method, are not less true for that; they are not less historical than other events but they are historical in a sense which transcends historical method. Some scholars refer to events of this kind as "metahistorical"; the Church has devised no particular terminology to describe them. Transcending the limitations of historical method, they enter the sphere of that *certainty* which faith provides; a certainty supported not only by data which are historically verifiable but also and principally by the authority of God who reveals, who has made known to witnesses chosen by him an historical fact which transcends but does not contradict purely human science.

It is this very point which causes difficulty for non-believers and even scandalizes them—how the Bible can make historically accurate statements which, however, are beyond the capacity of human research to verify. Christian faith gives the believer absolute certainty about the truth of these accounts (which are essential supports of the truths of salvation). Logic seems to require the unbeliever to respect the testimony of witnesses to these events, and to respect the Church which has conserved these testimonies. Three reasons for this might be offered—the sincerity of the witnesses; the impossibility of denying (scientifically or morally) what Christian faith asserts; and the reasonableness of the testimony offered.

On the reliability of the Gospels as history, see *The Navarre Bible: St Mark*, pp. 42-45.

MORAL TRUTHS CONTAINED IN THE BIBLE

1. *Biblical holiness*  In addition to recounting the history of salvation the Bible also contains moral teaching, that is, ethical criteria for behaviour in keeping

14. *Divino afflante Spiritu*, 30 November 1943.

with human dignity and God's plan for man's development. This aspect of the truth of the Bible is called "biblical holiness" because it has to do with showing man how to be good, and with reproving evil conduct.

2. *Principles for resolving certain difficulties*  Difficulties do arise in this connexion, particularly with reference to certain Old Testament laws when compared with New Testament morality. The basic principle is that one needs to take into account the "progressive" nature of biblical Revelation: wise teacher that he is, God never required more of mankind than it could deliver; this is another aspect of the principle of *synkatabasis* or divine condescension. Thus, for example, the *lex talionis* of the Mosaic Law ("an eye for and eye, a tooth for a tooth") must be seen as an advance on the interminable feuding endemic among the nomadic and semi-nomadic peoples of the ancient Middle East out of which Israel developed; by establishing that the punishment should not exceed the crime, the *lex talionis* was definitely an advance on uncontrolled vengeance. Also, the very restrictive nature of the Mosaic Law on the subject of divorce did a great deal to protect the status of women in society at that time. By gradually suppressing the unrestricted polygamy typical of tribal life, Mosaic marriage laws prepared the way for monogamy and equality of rights between man and woman. Thus, biblical Revelation starts out at a point when morality was at a fairly primitive stage and develops until it reaches the high ethical standard taught and practised by Christ.

It is also important to bear in mind that the Bible records the developing religious experience of the chosen people and its leaders up to the advent of Christ. However, with the exception of Christ, no man or woman is absolutely holy; only God is holy; therefore even the greatest patriarchs, prophets and kings of Israel had their shortcomings, and even sins. In the Bible God is telling us the way to holiness; he does this not only through the heroic virtue of individuals, but also by the lessons to be learned from their weaknesses, shortcomings and vices. These shortcomings are noticed in Scripture; usually they are identified for what they are or else the reader is provided with enough information to make a correct moral judgment.

One also needs to take historical circumstances into account when it comes to making ethical judgments about things biblical characters say or do; certain Old Testament characters, for example, may seem to us to be uncouth or worse; one needs to try to view the narrative from inside the culture in which it was written. In this connexion, the "acts of cruelty" which seem to be committed on God's instructions (for example, the law of *herem*, which demanded the razing of conquered cities) should be interpreted in the light of the tendency to attribute the origin of all human customs to God, and also as a way of ensuring that Israel was not contaminated by idolatrous nations.

BIBLE TEACHING ON THE NATURE OF MAN

Although Sacred Scripture is not a treatise on anthropology, in the sense that its direct aim is to explain the nature of man, it does provide the basic data man needs for discovering what he must do in order to be saved, that is, to find fulfilment. In providing this information the sacred writers naturally have to work within the cultural and literary resources available to them; but what they teach is inspired by God and therefore is of perennial value. For example, the Bible has things to say about the dignity of the human person, created by God in his image and likeness and put in the world as lord of creation; the equality of man and woman and the institution of marriage as originally designed by God; and the survival of the soul after death; and it contains other truths without which (were Revelation not to teach them clearly) man would lose his way and suffer degradation, as has often been the case down the ages.

Some of these truths were not very explicit in the early stages of biblical Revelation; some were also to be found outside Revelation. However, that does not mean that they are attributable only to a particular period or culture. Once the Bible clearly asserts them, they must be taken as truths God wishes to reveal.

BIBLE TEACHING CONCERNING GOD

The most important truth contained in the Bible is obviously what it has to say about God and his relationship with mankind. Through the sacred writings God himself is speaking to man and calling him to live in communion with him. In so doing the word of God makes use of language and cultural forms to convey its message. From some points of view the Bible speaks about God in the same kind of way that people of other religions speak of him. It could not be otherwise, if we remember the principle of divine condescension discussed earlier. This explains why human ways of thinking are sometimes attributed to God, and why we find in the Bible expressions which parallel ways of speaking of God found in earlier religions, that is, in myth.

1. *The language of myth in the Bible*    Although the language of myth may well be a valid way of speaking of God in other contexts and may even have true things to say, the Bible is very far removed from that type of language, for the simple reason that faith in Yahweh, the one true God, led the good Israelite to keep well away from the gods worshipped by other nations. The Bible's manner of speaking about God and the truth it teaches about him is completely original, as original as the way God manifests himself to Israel by actually becoming man in Jesus Christ.

The truth about God contained in the Bible is not on the same level as those aspects of truth contained in non-biblical myth (which tell us about God in a non-historical way); it is, rather, a truth which becomes present in history and which leaves marks that historical science can investigate—the Israelite nation, the figure of Christ, the origin of the Church. This explains why there is ongoing dialogue between the truth of the Bible and the truth which man can discover for himself, especially through the study of history.

2. *The Revelation of God in the Bible*   The Bible's teaching about God does not ultimately come from things that man, by his own endeavours, has been able to discover about God; it comes from God's self-revelation and man's acceptance of that through faith. The various books of the Bible, which were written under divine inspiration at particular times in history, are a record provided by God of that process of Revelation and faith; the Bible is the word of God addressed to man whereby he reveals the truth about Himself, and asks man to make the response of faith.

Following the analogy between Scripture and the Incarnate Word proposed by the Second Vatican Council, the veracity of the Bible becomes clearer if we apply to it the words of our Lord, "I am the way, and the truth, and the life" (Jn 14:6).

# Introduction to St Paul's Epistles to the Thessalonians

## THE CITY OF THESSALONICA

Accompanied by Silas, St Paul arrived at Thessalonica in the course of his second apostolic journey (A.D. 49-52) after leaving Philippi around the summer of the year 50 (cf. Acts 17:1).

That city, now known as Salonika, is situated on the Aegean Sea and was a flourishing centre of trade in St Paul's time, thanks to its port and its location on the Via Egnatia, about 150 kilometres (95 miles) west of Philippi. Founded in 315 B.C. by Cassander, who called it after his wife, a sister of Alexander the Great, the city came under the Romans in 186 B.C.; by St Paul's time it had become one of the most important cities in Macedonia. As far as religion was concerned, it was a typical pagan city. Archaeology has unearthed the remains of many statues of gods and priestesses which give an idea of the religious practices of the Thessalonians. Inscriptions discovered indicate that they were very ignorant of religious truth and had no clear notion of the survival of the soul after death.

There were quite a number of Jews living in Thessalonica in St Paul's time. In keeping with his custom, St Paul went first to the synagogue to proclaim the Good News: Jesus was the Messiah; the Old Testament prophecies had come true in him; he had redeemed mankind by his passion and resurrection (cf. Acts 17:2-3). We know that he preached in the synagogue on three successive sabbaths (cf. Acts 17:2), but he may have stayed in Thessalonica for as long as two months, lodging in the house of Jason (cf. Acts 17:6). As a result of his preaching many Jews and Gentiles came to believe, including "not a few of the leading women" (Acts 17:4). His success earned him the envy of certain Jews, who organized demonstrations and attacked Jason's house, looking for Paul and Silas; not finding them, they brought Jason before the city authorities and he had to go bail for the two apostles (cf. Acts 17:5-9).

This led to St Paul and his companions leaving the city in a hurry the same night; they went first to Beroea (cf. Acts 17:10) and later to Athens (cf. Acts 17:15).

## HOW THE LETTERS CAME TO BE WRITTEN

Paul's unexpected departure from Thessalonica meant that the instruction of the recent converts was cut short; also their situation became difficult due to persecution by Jews. This led the Apostle to send Timothy to confirm them in the faith (cf. 1 Thess 3:1-2) and bring back news of them (cf. 1 Thess 3:5).

From Athens St Paul made his way to Corinth, where he was joined by Timothy, who gave him a good report of the Thessalonians: they were persevering in faith and charity, despite still being harassed (cf. 1 Thess 3:6-9; 2:14-16). Timothy also reported that certain questions were troubling the Thessalonians—things to do with life after death, and the second coming or Parousia (cf. 1 Thess 4:13).

The Apostle wrote the first letter, which he sent via Timothy, to complete his interrupted preaching. It had the effect of reassuring the Thessalonians about the fate of those who had already died in the Lord. However, some did not understand him correctly; some so misunderstood him in fact that they began to give up working (cf. 2 Thess 3:11). When St Paul heard of this he wrote the second letter to clear up the misunderstanding.

PLACE AND DATE OF COMPOSITION, AND ADDRESSEES

Timothy and Silas found St Paul in Corinth (cf. Acts 18:5) and told him how things were in Thessalonica. Paul wrote the first letter in the winter of 50-51. It is the earliest Pauline text in the canon of Scripture. The second letter was also written in Corinth, some months later, just as soon as the earlier letter would have had a chance to have an effect.

The Apostle addresses both letters to Christians who were experiencing a considerable degree of persecution (cf. 1 Thess 2:14; 3:3-4; Acts 17:5-9).

PAULINE AUTHORSHIP

The Tradition of the Church has always regarded these epistles as written by St Paul. The first was explicitly attributed to St Paul by St Irenaeus, the Muratorian Fragment, Marcion, Tertullian, Clement of Alexandria, Origen etc. Moreover, the style and vocabulary are typically Pauline, so much so that no one has attempted to deny its authenticity.

The second letter was also attributed to the Apostle by St Irenaeus, the Muratorian Fragment, Tertullian, Clement of Alexandria etc. Some non-Catholic scholars have questioned this attribution, either because they exaggerate the differences between the two epistles or because they argue that their similarities may be due to conscious imitation by the (other) author of the second letter. However, these arguments are not convincing. The similarities between the two letters are much easier to explain on the basis that both were written by the same person within a few months of each other. The difference in content is easy to understand, for the second letter was written to develop certain points touched on in the first and to clear up doubts some people still had.

Both epistles, particularly the first three chapters of the first, bear witness to St Paul's great work of evangelization in Thessalonica—a work which is a model of how the Gospel should be proclaimed.

In evangelization the initiative lies with God and it is he who causes the preaching of the Gospel to bear fruit. The election of the Christian is made by God and proceeds from his love (1 Thess 1:4); his son, Jesus, "who delivers us from the wrath to come" (1 Thess 1:10), sustains our hope (1 Thess 1:3); the action of the Holy Spirit renders the preacher's word persuasive (1 Thess 1:5) and fills with joy those who listen to it, no matter what trials may befall them (1 Thess 1:6).

The core of preaching is the "gospel" (1 Thess 1:5), that is, the Good News of salvation foretold by the prophets (cf. Is 40:9; 52:7; etc.) and brought to fulfilment by our Lord Jesus Christ. The proclamation of this News tells those who listen to it that they are "beloved by God", specially chosen by him (cf. 1 Thess 1:4). They are called to turn to God (1 Thess 1:9), who will give the three theological virtues (faith, hope and charity) to those who accept the Christian message (1 Thess 1:3). Faith and the sanctifying action of the Holy Spirit lead believers to salvation, to attaining the glory of the Lord Jesus (2 Thess 2:13-14).

Generous commitment to the demands of his calling strengthens a Christian's faith and gives him the patience and fortitude to endure any difficulties that may arise (cf. 2 Thess 1:4). A person who really values his faith keeps the treasure of received truth whole and untarnished and entertains no ideas that conflict with the Gospel message (cf. 2 Thess 2:15). And the good example given by those who respond faithfully and promptly to the word of God helps to reinforce the effect of preaching (1 Thess 1:7-9).

The attitude of the preacher plays an important part in evangelization. St Paul makes a point of staying in the background; his word and example have their part to play, but it is the Holy Spirit who moves the hearts of his listeners (cf. 1 Thess 1:5). A person who has the ministry of evangelization must always try to have an upright intention; God reads his heart (cf. 1 Thess 2:4) and therefore the preacher should pass on the Word of God simply and faithfully (1 Thess 2:13), not putting his trust in human eloquence; eloquence may attract hearers but it can easily sully the purity of the message God has revealed (2 Thess 2:3). A teacher of Christian doctrine does not work for earthly reward (cf. 1 Thess 2:9; 2 Thess 3:8-9); he is motivated by love of God and love of others (cf. 1 Thess 2:7-8).

The Apostle relies on prayer to make his work fruitful (cf. 1 Thess 3:10; 2 Thess 1:11) and as far as possible tries to encourage and instruct people individually, showing them what they must do to live in accordance with their Christian calling (1 Thess 2:11-12).

THE FOUNDATIONS OF FAITH AND MORALITY

These letters (the earliest New Testament writings, with the exception of the

Aramaic text of St Matthew's Gospel), touch on all the main truths of faith and the foundations of Christian morality.

Written only some twenty years after Christ's death, they contain all the main articles of faith which Christian Tradition later formulated in the Apostles' Creed. St Paul teaches that God is our Father (cf. 1 Thess 1:3; 2 Thess 1:1) and the source of our salvation (cf. 2 Thess 2:14). Jesus is his Son (cf. 1 Thess 1:9-10). Salvation is brought about "through our Lord Jesus Christ, who died for us" (1 Thess 5:9-10) and "rose again" (1 Thess 4:14; cf. 1 Thess 1:10). He will come again (cf. 1 Thess 2:19; 3:13; 1:10) in power and majesty (cf. 1 Thess 4:16), to judge (cf. 2 Thess 1:5; 1 Thess 4:6) the living and the dead (cf. 1 Thess 4:16-17), according to their works: the impious will be condemned (cf. 2 Thess 1:8-9) and those who do good will be welcomed into his Kingdom (cf. 2 Thess 1:5) for ever (cf. 1 Thess 4:17). God the Father sends the Holy Spirit (cf. 1 Thess 4:8), to whom is attributed our sanctification (cf. 2 Thess 2:13) and who moves us to accept with joy the preaching of the word of God (cf. 1 Thess 1:6).

The moral teaching contained in these letters has its roots in the fact that all Christians are called to holiness: "For this is the will of God, your sanctification" (1 Thess 4:3; cf. 4:7-8; 5:9). To attain this goal we need to share in Christ's own life (cf. 1 Thess 5:10) supported by the theological virtues: we need to "put on the breastplate of faith and love, and for a helmet the hope of salvation" (1 Thess 5:8).

Our relationships with others should be founded on brotherly love (cf. 1 Thess 4:9); therefore we need to give good example (cf. 1 Thess 5:11), correct those who need correction, help the weak, support the sick and be patient with all (cf. 1 Thess 5:14).

We need to be watchful (cf. 1 Thess 5:6), to exercise self-control (cf. 1 Thess 4:5) and sobriety (cf. 1 Thess 5:6), to be always joyful, pray always, give thanks for everything (cf. 1 Thess 5:16-18), and to do our work conscientiously (cf. 1 Thess 4:11-12).

ESCHATOLOGY

Christian teaching on the end of the world and the last things is the subject which receives most attention in these letters. The matter is dealt with on two levels—what happens to a person when he or she dies (individual eschatology) and what will happen at the end of time, when the ultimate victory of the Church will be revealed, the good will go to heaven and the reprobate will be condemned (general eschatology).

Man's life does not end with death, for his soul is immortal and lives forever. Unlike those who have no hope, believers should not be saddened by the prospect of death (1 Thess 4:13). The moment the soul is separated from the body, it enjoys the vision of God (cf. Phil 1:23; 2 Cor 5:8), whereas the body must await the day of resurrection: Christ has risen and we too will rise and join him (cf. 1 Thess 4:14).

Therefore, we hope in the resurrection of our bodies (at the end of time), once our Lord Jesus Christ comes again in glory. The Apostle describes this second coming as an event of great solemnity: "For the Lord himself will descend from heaven with a cry of command, with the archangel's call, and with the sound of the trumpet of God" (1 Thess 4:16). The apocalyptic language Paul uses to describe the second coming of the Lord highlights the mystery and power of God. After the Parousia will come the resurrection of the dead. Each body will be brought back to life by its own soul, and those who are still alive on that day will, together with their brethren who were dead and have risen, go to meet the Lord (1 Thess 4:16-17); however, the bodies of both will be glorified (cf. 1 Cor 15:51) and therefore those who died before the Parousia will suffer no disadvantage compared with those who were still living at that point.

St Paul is not specific about the timing of the Parousia, for "as to the times and the seasons, brethren, you have no need to have anything written to you" (1 Thess 5:1). He simply exhorts them to be always on the watch, for "the day of the Lord will come like a thief in the night" (1 Thess 5:2), when least expected.

In the first epistle, St Paul did not go into details (cf. 1 Thess 5:1), but some of the things he said—"we who are alive, who are left until the coming of the Lord . . ." (1 Thess 4:15); "we who are alive, who are left . . ." (1 Thess 4:17)—were misinterpreted by some Thessalonians as meaning that the second coming of the Lord was imminent; this made quite a few people restless, causing them to lose their common sense (cf. 2 Thess 2:2). However, Paul never meant to say that the Parousia was going to happen soon or that he himself would live to see the day.[1]

St Paul wrote the second letter, in fact, to make it clear that the second coming was not imminent (cf. 2 Thess 2:2); in that letter he tells them about some of the events which will signal it—rebellion, or apostasy and the appearing of the "man of lawlessness" (cf. 2 Thess 2:3).

At last the long-awaited moment will arrive, that of the coming of the Lord in glory in all his power and majesty. This will see "the righteous judgment of God" (2 Thess 1:5), when vengeance will be inflicted "upon those who do not know God and upon those who do not obey the gospel of our Lord Jesus. They shall suffer the punishment of eternal destruction and exclusion from the presence of the Lord and from the glory of his might" (2 Thess 1:8-9). At that point also, those who have suffered for their fidelity to the teaching of Christ will be "made worthy of the kingdom of God" (2 Thess 1:5) and will be with the Lord for ever more (cf. 1 Thess 4:17).

1.  Cf. Pontifical Biblical Commission, *Reply* concerning the Second Coming, 18 June 1915 (*EB*, 434).

# First Epistle to the Thessalonians

ENGLISH AND LATIN VERSIONS, WITH NOTES

# 1

<sup>1</sup>Paul, Silvanus, and Timothy,
    To the church of the Thessalonians in God the Father and
    the Lord Jesus Christ:
    Grace to you and peace.

2 Thess 1:1-2
Acts 15:22; 16:1

---

<sup>1</sup>Paulus et Silvanus et Timotheus ecclesiae Thessalonicensium in Deo Patre et Domino Iesu Christo: gratia vobis et pax. <sup>2</sup>Gratias agimus Deo semper pro omnibus vobis, memoriam facientes in orationibus nostris, sine intermissione

---

**1.** The heading is in keeping with the style of the period: it identifies the writer and the addressees and contains a greeting.

The names of Silvanus and Timothy, co-workers of St Paul, appears alongside his own. The heading is affectionate in tone but it is not the kind of opening typical of a simple family letter. This is an official letter, which is why two witnesses vouch for its content (in line with legal requirements: cf. Deut 17:6).

As in certain other letters (cf. 2 Thess, Phil, Philem), St Paul does not describe himself as an Apostle; the mention of his name is enough to convey his authority. Silvanus is the same person as Silas whom Acts describes as a "prophet" and one of the "leading men among the brethren" in Jerusalem (cf. Acts 15:22, 32); here the Latin transcription of his name is used. He had worked alongside St Paul in the evangelization of Thessalonica, so he would have been well known to the believers in that city (cf. Acts 17:4). Timothy was son of a Gentile father and a Jewish mother (his mother was a Christian convert); St Paul gave him instruction in the faith when he passed through Lystra during his second missionary journey, and ever since then he had always been a faithful helper of the Apostle. When St Paul was writing this letter, Timothy had just arrived in Corinth from Thessalonica with good reports of the spiritual health of that church (cf. 1 Thess 3:6).

The letter is addressed to "the church of the Thessalonians". The Greek word *ekklesia*, meaning "assembly, gathering of the people", was used from the apostolic age onwards to describe the Church, the new people of God. St Thomas Aquinas used this verse for his definition of the Church as "the assembly of the faithful brought together in God the Father and in the Lord Jesus Christ, through faith in the Trinity and in the divinity and humanity of Christ" (*Commentary on 1 Thess, ad loc.*). "All those, who in faith look towards Jesus, the author of salvation and the principle of unity and peace, God has gathered together and established as the Church, that it may be for each and everyone the visible sacrament of this saving unity" (Vatican II, *Lumen gentium*, 9).

"Grace to you and peace": a favourite greeting of St Paul's, expressing the wish that they will attain the fulness of heavenly good things. See the note on Rom 1:7.

# PART ONE

# THANKSGIVING

2 Thess 1:3
1 Thess 2:13
1 Cor 13:13
Col 1:4-5
Rev 2:2

2 Thess 2:12

### Thanksgiving for the Thessalonians' fidelity

²We give thanks to God always for you all, constantly mentioning you in our prayers, ³remembering before our God and Father your work of faith and labour of love and steadfastness of hope in our Lord Jesus Christ. ⁴For we

---

³memores operis fidei vestrae et laboris caritatis et sustinentiae spei Domini nostri Iesu Christi ante Deum et Patrem nostrum, ⁴scientes, fratres, dilecti a

**3.** The spiritual life of the Christian is based on the practice of the theological virtues, for "faith encourages men to do good, charity to bear pain and effort, and hope to resist patiently" (Severian of Gabala, *Commentary on 1 Thess, ad loc.*).

Faith needs to be reflected in one's conduct, for "faith apart from works is dead" (Jas 2:26). As St John Chrysostom teaches, "belief and faith are proved by works—not by simply saying that one believes, but by real actions, which are kept up, and by a heart burning with love" (*Hom. on 1 Thess, ad loc.*).

The service of others for God's sake is a proof of charity. A person who practises this virtue always rises to the occasion and does not try to dodge sacrifice or effort.

Hope is a virtue which "enables one to endure adversity" (St Thomas, *Commentary on 1 Thess, ad loc.*). St Paul encourages us to rejoice in hope and be patient in tribulation (cf. Rom 12:12), for hope fills the soul with joy and gives it the strength to bear every difficulty for love of God.

**4.** All men are "beloved by God" and, as St Thomas points out, this is the case "not just in the ordinary sense of having received natural existence from him, but particularly because he has called them to eternal good things" (*Commentary on 1 Thess, ad loc.*). Man's last end is happiness, and happiness cannot be found (other than in a relative sense) in wealth, honours, health or sensual satisfaction; it can only be found in knowing and loving God. By raising man to the supernatural order, God gave him a supernatural goal or end, which consists in "seeing God himself, triune and one, as he is, clearly" (Council of Florence, *Laetentur coeli*).

Deprived as he was of sanctifying grace on account of original sin and his personal sins, man was unable to attain any end exceeding his natural powers. But God loved us so much that he deigned to enable us "to share in the inheritance of the saints in light. He has delivered us from the dominion of darkness and transferred us to the kingdom of his beloved Son" (Col 1:12-13). Therefore, those who have been given the preaching of the Gospel and the fruits of Redemption through Baptism and the other sacraments are the object of a

know, brethren beloved by God, that he has chosen you;
<sup>5</sup>for our gospel came to you not only in word, but also in
power and in the Holy Spirit and with full conviction. You
know what kind of men we proved to be among you for

Acts 1:8
1 Cor 2:4

Deo, electionem vestram, <sup>5</sup>quia evangelium nostrum non fuit ad vos in sermone tantum, sed et in virtute et in Spiritu Sancto et in plenitudine multa, sicut scitis quales fuerimus vobis propter vos. <sup>6</sup>Et vos imitatores nostri facti estis et Domini,

special divine "choice". This "choice" or election is not the same as "salvation"; it is an initiative on God's part prior to the attainment of salvation. To be saved one must second this action of God by responding freely to grace.

**5.** St Paul reminds them that what he preached was the "gospel" foretold by the prophets (cf. Is 40:9; 52:7; 60:6; 61:1) and fulfilled by the Incarnation of the Word and by his work of salvation. The Apostle was pressed into service by the Holy Spirit to forward his work of sanctification. The Thessalonians were not won over by mere human words but by the "power" of God, who made those words effective. The term "power" refers not only to miraculous actions but also to the Holy Spirit moving the souls of those who heard Paul's preaching.

It is true that this activity, like all actions of God outside himself, is something done by all three Persons of the Blessed Trinity; but in the language of Scripture and of the Church it is customary "to attribute to the Father those works of the Divinity in which power excels; to attribute to the Son, those in which wisdom excels; and to the Holy Spirit, those in which love excels" (Leo XIII, *Divinum illud munus*, 5).

In the early years of the Church the proclamation of the Gospel was often marked by special graces of the Holy Spirit, such as prophecy, miracles, or the gift of tongues (cf. Acts 2:8). This profusion of gifts made it clear that the messianic era had begun (cf. Acts 2:16), for it meant the fulfilment of the ancient prophecies: "I will pour out my spirit on all flesh; your sons and your daughters shall prophesy, your old men shall dream dreams, and your young men shall see visions. Even upon the menservants and maidservants in those days, I will pour out my spirit" (Joel 3:1-3).

"In power and in the Holy Spirit": in line with the divine plan of salvation, the time of the Old Testament, which prepared the way for the coming of the Messiah, has reached its end, and a new era has begun, the Christian era, the key feature of which is the activity of the Spirit of God: "It must be said that the Holy Spirit is the principal agent of evangelization: it is he who impels each individual to proclaim the Gospel, and it is he who in the depths of consciences causes the word of salvation to be accepted and understood" (Paul VI, *Evangelii nuntiandi*, 75).

**6.** St Paul rejoices at the effect God has had on the Thessalonians. It is true that Christ is *the* model to be imitated, but the Apostle's own example played

2 Thess 3:7
1 Cor 11:1

1 Thess 4:10

Rom 1:8

1 Cor 12:2
Jn 17:3

your sake. ⁶And you became imitators of us and of the Lord, for you received the word in much affliction, with joy inspired by the Holy Spirit; ⁷so that you became an example to all the believers in Macedonia and in Achaia. ⁸For not only has the word of the Lord sounded forth from you in Macedonia and Achaia, but your faith in God has gone forth everywhere, so that we need not say anything. ⁹For they

excipientes verbum in tribulatione multa cum gaudio Spiritus Sancti, ⁷ita ut facti sitis forma omnibus credentibus in Macedonia et in Achaia. ⁸A vobis enim diffamatus est sermo Domini non solum in Macedonia et in Achaia, sed in omni loco fides vestra, quae est ad Deum, profecta est, ita ut non sit nobis necesse quidquam loqui; ⁹ipsi enim de nobis annuntiant qualem introitum habuerimus

its part in leading them to Christ (cf. 1 Cor 11:1). "To follow Christ: that is the secret. We must accompany him so closely that we come to live with him, as the first Twelve did; so closely, that we become identified with him. Soon we will be able to say, provided we have not put obstacles in the way of grace, that we have put on, have clothed ourselves with, our Lord Jesus Christ (cf. Rom 13:14). Our Lord is then reflected in our behaviour, as in a mirror. If the mirror is as it ought to be, it will capture our Saviour's most lovable face without distorting it or making a caricature of it; and then other people will have an opportunity of admiring him and following him" (J. Escrivá, *Friends of God*, 299).

"Joy", which is one of the fruits of the Holy Spirit (cf. Gal 5:22-23), is linked to unconditional acceptance of the word of God, and helps a person to overcome any obstacle he or she may meet on his way (cf. Acts 5:41). "One can be joyful despite lashes and blows, when these are accepted in the cause of Christ", St John Chrysostom comments. "A feature of the joy of the Holy Spirit is that it causes an uncontainable happiness to grow even out of affliction and sorrow [...]. In the natural course of events afflictions do not produce joy: joy is the privilege of those who accept sufferings for Jesus Christ's sake; it is one of the good things bestowed by the Holy Spirit" (*Hom. on 1 Thess, ad loc.*).

**7-8.** Thessalonica was an important centre of trade and a hub of communications for all Greece. The Christians in the city included a number of important people and even some women of the aristocracy (cf. Acts 17:4). The social standing of the converts and the prestige of the city partly explain the rapid spread of Christian teaching throughout the region.

What the Apostle says here only goes to show that when the Christian life is given full rein it spreads far and wide. This should give us every encouragement "always to act in public in accordance with our holy faith" (J. Escrivá, *Furrow*, 46).

**9.** We can see how happy the Apostle is to learn that the work of evangelization has borne fruit of conversion to God—which is the whole purpose of

themselves report concerning us what a welcome we had among you, and how you turned to God from idols, to serve a living and true God, [10]and to wait for his Son from heaven, whom he raised from the dead, Jesus who delivers us from the wrath to come.

1 Thess 4:16-17
Rom 5:9

---

ad vos, et quomodo conversi estis ad Deum a simulacris, servire Deo vivo et vero [10]et exspectare Filium eius de caelis, quem suscitavit ex mortuis, Iesum, qui eripit nos ab ira ventura.

---

Gospel preaching. "For the Church, evangelization means bringing the Good News into all the strata of humanity, and through its influence transforming humanity from within and making it new" (Paul VI, *Evangelii nuntiandi*, 18).

It is moving to see the way good news spread among the early Christian communities. Obviously anecdotes about the apostolate would go from church to church; this gave them an occasion to praise God while at the same time providing encouragement to stay true to Christ and to spread the Gospel.

**10.** The Christian message has this feature which differentiates it from Judaism—hope in Christ and expectation of Christ. Two central points of Christian teaching emerge from this verse: Jesus Christ is the Son of God, who rose from the dead, and he will come again to judge all. St John Chrysostom observes that "in a single text St Paul brings together a number of different mysteries concerning Jesus Christ—his glorious resurrection, his victorious ascension, his future coming, the judgment, the reward promised to the righteous, and the punishment reserved for evildoers" (*Hom. on 1 Thess, ad loc.*).

This verse probably contains a form of words used in oral preaching, and perhaps a profession of faith belonging to early Church liturgy.

"To wait for his Son (to come) from heaven": that Jesus Christ will come again is a truth of faith professed in the Creed: "He will come again in glory to judge the living and the dead." Christ will be the Judge of all mankind. Everyone will be personally judged by God twice: "The first judgment takes place when each one of us departs this life; for then he is instantly placed before the judgment-seat of God, where all that he has ever done or spoken or thought during life shall be subjected to the most rigid scrutiny. This is called the particular judgment. The second occurs when on the same day and in the same place all men shall stand together before the tribunal of their Judge, that in the presence and hearing of all human beings of all times each may know his final doom and sentence [. . .]. This is called the general judgment" (*St Pius V Catechism*, I, 8, 3).

The "wrath to come" is a metaphor referring to the just punishment of sinners. Our Lord Jesus Christ will exempt from it those who have consistently tried to live in the state of grace and fellowship with God. St Teresa of Avila warns that "it will be a great thing at the hour of death to know that we are going to be judged by him whom we have loved above all things. We can approach

**First Gospel preaching in Thessalonica**

1 Thess 1:9
Acts 16:20-24
Acts 17:1-5

¹For you yourselves know, brethren, that our visit to you was not in vain; ²but though we had already suffered and been shamefully treated at Philippi, as you know, we had courage in our God to declare to you the gospel of God in

---

¹Nam ipsi scitis, fratres, introitum nostrum ad vos quia non inanis fuit, ²sed ante passi et contumeliis affecti, sicut scitis, in Philippis, fiduciam habuimus in Deo

---

this trial with confidence. It will not be like going into a strange land but into our own land, for it is the land that belongs to him whom we love so much and who loves us" (*Way of Perfection*, 70, 3).

**1-2.** As we know from the Acts of the Apostles, St Paul and his companions arrived in Thessalonica after the persecution unleashed in Philippi (cf. Acts 16:19-40). Soon after that, jealousy led Jews in Thessalonica to provoke unrest and they had to leave that city too (cf. Acts 17:5-10). Opposition should never prevent a person from doing his duty to spread the word of God. "Whenever God opens a door for the word in order to declare the mystery of Christ, then the living God, and he whom he has sent for the salvation of all, Jesus Christ, are confidently and perseveringly proclaimed to all men. And this is in order that non-Christians, whose heart is being opened by the Holy Spirit, might, by believing, freely turn to the Lord" (Vatican II, *Ad gentes*, 13).

Laziness or cowardice can provide all kinds of excuses. Therefore, it "would be useful if every Christian and every evangelizer were to pray about the following thought: men can gain salvation also in other ways, by God's mercy, even though we do not preach the Gospel to them; but as for us, can we gain salvation if through negligence or fear or shame—what St Paul called 'being ashamed of the gospel' (Rom 1:16)—or as a result of false ideas we fail to preach it? For that would be to betray the call of God, who wishes the seed to bear fruit through the voice of the ministers of the Gospel; and it will depend on us whether this grows into trees and produces its full fruit. Let us therefore preserve our fervour of spirit. Let us preserve the delightful and comforting joy of evangelizing, even when it is in tears that we must sow" (Paul VI, *Evangelii nuntiandi*, 80).

Love of God and faithfulness to our calling should lead us "not to be afraid of the word of God in the midst of tribulation [. . .]; if someone has firm hope of attaining what he is promised, he will not yield, so as thereby to gain his reward" (St Thomas, *Commentary on 1 Thess, ad loc.*).

**3-6.** Those who teach the Gospel should always do so with the right intention, for God "tests our hearts". "Let us remember how near he is to us

the face of great opposition. 3For our appeal does not spring from error or uncleanness, nor is it made with guile; 4but just as we have been approved by God to be entrusted with the gospel, so we speak, not to please men, but to please God who tests our hearts. 5For we never used either words of flattery, as you know, or a cloak for greed, as God is witness; 6nor did we seek glory from men, whether from you or from others, though we might have made demands as apostles of Christ. 7But we were gentle[a] among you, like

2 Cor 2:17
1 Tim 1:11
Jer 1:10
Gal 1:10
2 Pet 2:3
Jn 5:41-44
1 Cor 3:2

nostro loqui ad vos evangelium Dei in multa sollicitudine. 3Exhortatio enim nostra non ex errore neque ex immunditia neque in dolo, 4sed sicut probati sumus a Deo, ut crederetur nobis evangelium, ita loquimur non quasi hominibus placentes, sed Deo, qui probat corda nostra. 5Neque enim aliquando fuimus in sermone adulationis, sicut scitis, neque sub praetextu avaritiae, Deus testis, 6nec quaerentes ab hominibus gloriam, neque a vobis neque ab aliis, 7cum possemus oneri esse ut Christi apostoli, sed facti sumus parvuli in medio vestrum,

and that not a single one of our thoughts or plans can ever be hidden from him" (St Clement of Rome, *Letter to the Corinthians*, 1, 21).

Instruction of others in the faith "is sincere when it is given in keeping with the tenor and purpose that Christ had when he taught" (*Commentary on 1 Thess, ad loc.*). St Paul castigates as "uncleanness" any betrayal of Christ's teaching: this is rather like the Old Testament's view of infidelity to Yahweh as adultery (cf. Is 1:21-26; Hos 1-3). When the Apostle says his preaching does not spring from uncleanness, he means that he does not do violence to or alter the content of the Christian message. As Paul VI puts it, "the preacher of the Gospel will be a person who even at the price of personal renunciation and suffering always seeks the truth that he must transmit to others. He never betrays or hides truth out of a desire to please men, in order to astonish or to shock, nor for the sake of originality or a desire to make an impression. He does not refuse truth. He does not obscure revealed truth by being too idle to search for it, or for the sake of his own comfort, or out of fear. He does not neglect to study it. He serves it generously, without making it serve him" (*Evangelii nuntiandi*, 78).

The Apostle makes the point that at no time did he try to deceive anyone or act for personal gain—unlike the spreaders of false doctrine then to be found all over the Roman empire (cf. Acts 17:18-21). The Second Vatican Council evokes this when it says that "from the very beginnings of the Church the disciples of Christ strove to convert men to confess Christ as Lord, not however by applying coercion or with the use of techniques unworthy of the Gospel but, above all, by the power of the word of God" (*Dignitatis humanae*, 11).

**7-9.** St Paul could have "made demands" in a double sense—by using the full force of his apostolic authority, and by exercising his right to financial

[a]Other ancient authorities read *babes*

2 Cor 12:15  a nurse taking care of her children. **8**So, being affectionately desirous of you, we were ready to share with you not only the gospel of God but also our own selves, because you had become very dear to us.

1 Cor 4:12
2 Thess 3:8
**9**For you remember our labour and toil, brethren; we worked night and day, that we might not burden any of you, while we preached to you the gospel of God. **10**You are

---

tamquam si nutrix foveat filios suos, **8**ita desiderantes vos, cupide volebamus tradere vobis non solum evangelium Dei, sed etiam animas nostras, quoniam carissimi nobis facti estis. **9**Memores enim estis, fratres, laboris nostri et fatigationis; nocte et die operantes, ne quem vestrum gravaremus, praedicavimus in vobis evangelium Dei. **10**Vos testes estis et Deus, quam sancte et

---

support from the community (cf. 1 Cor 9:14); but he did neither one thing (vv. 7-8) nor the other (v. 9).

On the contrary, he passed on the Gospel message and worked with the disinterested love and dedication of a nursing mother. St John Chrysostom, putting himself in St Paul's place, comments as follows: "It is true that I preached the Gospel to you in obedience to a commandment from God; but I love you with so great a love that I would have been ready to die for you. That is the perfect model of sincere, genuine love. A Christian who loves his neighbour should be inspired by these sentiments. He should not wait to be asked to give up his life for his brother; rather, he should offer it himself" (*Hom. on 1 Thess, ad loc.*).

"The work of evangelization presupposes in the evangelizer an ever increasing love for those whom he is evangelizing [. . .]. What is this love? It is much more than that of a teacher; it is the love of a father; and again, it is the love of a mother. It is this love that the Lord expects from every preacher of the Gospel, from every builder of the Church. A sign of love will be the concern to give the truth and to bring people into unity [. . .]. Yet another sign of love will be the effort to transmit to Christians not doubts and uncertainties born of an erudition poorly assimilated but certainties that are solid because they are anchored in the Word of God. The faithful need these certainties for their Christian life; they have a right to them, as children of God" (Paul VI, *Evangelii nuntiandi*, 79).

The Apostle's hardworking life strengthened his moral authority when he had to warn people against the temptation of idleness (cf. 1 Thess 4:11); it also was a very good example for the early generations of Christians.

**10-12.** "Each one of you": St Paul did not confine his preaching to the synagogue or other public places, or to liturgical assemblies of Christians. He took an interest in people as individuals, giving advice and consolation in a friendly, confidential way and telling them how they should conduct themselves in the presence of God. Christians should copy him in their own

witnesses, and God also, how holy and righteous and
blameless was our behaviour to you believers; [11]for you
know how, like a father with his children, we exhorted each
one of you and encouraged you and charged you [12]to lead
a life worthy of God, who calls you into his own kingdom
and glory.

Acts 20:31
1 Cor 4:15

Eph 4:1
Phil 1:27
1 Pet 5:10

### Their patience

[13]And we also thank God constantly for this, that when

1 Thess 1:2
Gal 1:11

---

iuste et sine querela vobis, qui credidistis, fuimus [11]sicut scitis, qualiter
unumquemque vestrum, tamquam pater filios suos, [12]deprecantes vos et con-
solantes testificati sumus, ut ambularetis digne Deo, qui vocat vos in suum
regnum et gloriam. [13]Ideo et nos gratias agimus Deo sine intermissione,

---

apostolate: "Those well-timed words, whispered in the ear of your wavering
friend; the helpful conversation you managed to start at the right moment; the
ready professional advice that improves his university work; the discreet
indiscretion by which you open up unexpected horizons for his zeal. This all
forms part of the 'apostolate of friendship'" (J. Escrivá, *The Way*, 973).

Those who have received the gift of faith naturally try to tell others about
their discovery. "When you come across something useful, you try to bring
other people," St Gregory comments. "So, you should want other people to join
you on the way of the Lord. If you are going to the forum or the baths and you
meet someone who has nothing to do, you invite him to go along with you.
Apply this earthly custom to the spiritual sphere and as you make your way to
God do not go alone" (*In Evangelia homiliae*, 6, 6). As can be seen clearly from
the lives of the first Christians, apostolate was not the preserve of pastors; all
believers had an apostolic role. And so the Second Vatican Council pointed out
that one kind of personal apostolate very suited to our times is "the witness of
a whole lay life issuing from faith, hope and charity [. . .]. Then, by the
apostolate of the word, which in certain circumstances is absolutely necessary,
the laity proclaim Christ, explain and spread his teachings, each one according
to his conditions and competence, and profess those teachings with fidelity"
(*Apostolicam actuositatem*, 16).

"Into his own kingdom and glory": "glory" is a divine attribute which
becomes manifest in the "Kingdom" of God; the Church is the as-yet-incom-
plete form on earth of that Kingdom, which will not become visible in its final
form until the Parousia at the end of time. God calls everyone to join the Church
so as to be able to enjoy the glory of the Kingdom of God in due course.

**13.** Initially divine Revelation was passed on to others orally. "It [Gospel
preaching] was done by the Apostles, who handed on (by the spoken word of
their preaching, by the example they gave, by the institutions they established)
what they themselves received—whether from the lips of Christ, from his way

Gal 1:22
Acts 2:23

you received the word of God which you heard from us, you accepted it not as the word of men but as what it really is, the word of God, which is at work in you believers. [14]For you, brethren, became imitators of the churches of God in Christ Jesus which are in Judea; for you suffered the same things from your own countrymen as they did from the

---

quoniam cum accepissetis a nobis verbum auditus Dei, accepistis non ut verbum hominum sed, sicut est vere, verbum Dei, quod et operatur in vobis, qui creditis. [14]Vos enim imitatores facti estis, fratres, ecclesiarum Dei, quae sunt in Iudaea in Christo Iesu, quia eadem passi estis et vos a contribulibus vestris, sicut et

---

of life and his works, or whether as something learned from the Holy Spirit" (Vatican II, *Dei Verbum*, 7). Thus, "the apostles, in handing on what they themselves had received warn the faithful to maintain the traditions which they had learned either by word of mouth or by letter (cf. 2 Thess 2:15); and they warn them to fight hard for the faith that had been handed on to them once and for all (cf. Jude 3). What was handed on by the apostles comprises everything that serves to make the people of God live their lives in holiness and increase their faith. In this way the Church, in her doctrine, life and worship, perpetuates and transmits to every generation all that she herself is, all that she believes" (*Dei Verbum*, 8).

Preaching is truly the "word of God" not only because it faithfully passes Revelation on but also because God himself speaks through those who proclaim the Gospel (cf. 2 Cor 5:20). This explains why "the word of God is living and active" (Heb 4:12), and "such is the force and power of the Word of God that it can serve the Church as her support and vigour, and the children of the Church as strength for their faith, food for the soul, and a pure and lasting fount of spiritual life" (*Dei Verbum*, 21).

**14.** Our Lord himself warned us that "If the world hates you, know that it has hated me before it hated you [. . .]. Remember the word that I said to you, 'A servant is not greater than his master.' If they persecuted me, they will persecute you" (Jn 15:18, 20). When preaching of the Gospel spells out what God's law requires people often react against it because they cannot, or do not want to, understand it. However, opposition should not inhibit those who have to spread the Gospel: "Therefore, count yourselves blessed. Consider that you have performed a mighty deed, if one of you suffers for God" (*Shepherd of Hermas*, 9th parable, 28, 6).

The Christian does not seek the applause of men; he simply wants to do God's will, "for it is quite foolish to try to please people whom we know do not please the Lord", St Gregory says. "[. . .] Thus, being despised by evildoers is a mark of approval, because when we begin to displease those who displease God it is a sign that we are to some degree righteous" (*In Ezechielem homiliae*, 1, 9, 12).

Jews, [15]who killed both the Lord Jesus and the prophets, and drove us out, and displease God and oppose all men [16]by hindering us from speaking to the Gentiles that they may be saved—so as always to fill up the measure of their sins. But God's wrath has come upon them at last![b]

Acts 2:23; 7:52<br>Gen 15:16<br>Mt 23:32f<br>Rom 1:18

### Paul's anxiety

[17]But since we were bereft of you, brethren, for a short time, in person not in heart, we endeavoured the more eagerly and with great desire to see you face to face; [18]because we wanted to come to you—I, Paul, again and

Rom 1:11<br>Col 2:5

---

ipsi a Iudaeis, [15]qui et Dominum occiderunt Iesum et prophetas et nos persecuti sunt et Deo non placent et omnibus hominibus adversantur, [16]prohibentes nos gentibus loqui, ut salvae fiant, ut impleant peccata sua semper. Pervenit autem ira Dei super illos usque in finem. [17]Nos autem, fratres, desolati a vobis ad

**15-16.** St Paul was a Jew and one who loved his people dearly. He is not condemning the Jewish people but rather the opposition of *some* Jews to the Gospel. Perhaps they thought they were doing right in objecting to Jesus Christ being presented as God. However, for an action to be morally good it is not enough for it to be inspired by a good intention; one must also take steps to seek the truth. "It is in accordance with their dignity that all men, because they are persons, that is, beings endowed with reason and free will and therefore bearing personal responsibility, are both impelled by their nature and bound by a moral obligation to seek the truth [. . .]. They are also bound to adhere to the truth once they come to know it, and to direct their whole lives in accordance with the demands of truth" (Vatican II, *Dignitatis humanae*, 2).

The words "God's wrath has come upon them at last" should not be taken to mean that he has definitively rejected Israel (cf. Rom 11:25). This statement may have a prophetic element in it, referring to the punishment God would inflict some twenty years later with the terrible destruction of the temple of Jerusalem (A.D. 70).

**17.** "Bereft": a more literal translation would be "orphaned". In Greek the term can refer both to children left without parents and to parents cut off from their children. St Paul, who just a little earlier compared his love and concern for the Thessalonians to a mother's care for her children (vv. 7-8), is using the term in the second sense.

**18.** On the difficulties which prevented his return to Thessalonica see "Introduction to the Epistles to the Thessalonians", pp. 22f above. In the last analysis, it was Satan who put obstacles in St Paul's way.

[b]Or *completely*, or *for ever*

Phil 2:16; 4:1
2 Cor 8:24 again—but Satan hindered us. ¹⁹For what is our hope or joy or crown of boasting before our Lord Jesus at his coming? Is it not you? ²⁰For you are our glory and joy.

---

tempus horae, facie non corde, abundantius festinavimus faciem vestram videre cum multo desiderio. ¹⁸Propter quod voluimus venire ad vos, ego quidem Paulus et semel et iterum, et impedivit nos Satanas. ¹⁹Quae est enim nostra spes aut gaudium aut corona gloriae—nonne et vos—ante Dominum nostrum Iesum in adventu eius? ²⁰Vos enim estis gloria nostra et gaudium.

---

Satan and the other angels who rebelled against God (cf. Fourth Council of the Lateran, chap. 1), whom we call demons, are forever trying to lead men astray and hinder the spread of Christ's teaching. Satan "attacked our first parents in Paradise; he assailed the prophets; he beset the Apostles in order, as the Lord says in the Gospel, that he might sift them as wheat (Lk 22:31). Nor was he abashed even by the presence of Christ the Lord himself" (*St Pius V Catechism*, IV, 15, 6).

**19-20.** This is the Apostle's first reference to the "coming" (in Greek, *parousia*) of Christ, which is one of the main themes of the epistle. *Parousia*, in the secular use of the term at the time, referred to the formal entry of a ruler into a city with all his entourage. In the New Testament the word usually refers to the coming of Christ in glory, with all his power and majesty, to judge mankind. In this text St Paul is referring to that definitive and solemn coming at the end of time. From other New Testament passages we know that everyone will undergo a "particular judgment" immediately after death (cf., e.g., Lk 16:19-31 and note; Lk 23:43 and note).

One of the things which will most make St Paul rejoice on the day of our Lord's coming will be the holiness of those whom he taught by word and example to lead lives consistent with their faith. "When the pupil is obedient, it speaks well of his teacher; his good behaviour is to his teacher's credit; a good result points to work well done. And so it is that the effort the pupil makes to do things well provides his teacher with laurels when Christ comes in judgment" (St Thomas, *Commentary on 1 Thess, ad loc.*).

# 3

### Timothy's mission to Thessalonica

¹Therefore when we could bear it no longer, we were willing to be left behind at Athens alone, ²and we sent Timothy, our brother and God's servant in the gospel of Christ, to establish you in your faith and to exhort you, ³that no one be moved by these afflictions. You yourselves know that this is to be our lot. ⁴For when we were with you, we told you beforehand that we were to suffer affliction; just

Acts 17:14f
Acts 16:1-3
1 Cor 3:9

1 Thess 1:6
2 Thess 1:4

Acts 14:22
2 Tim 3:12

---

¹Propter quod non sustinentes amplius, placuit nobis, ut relinqueremur Athenis soli, ²et misimus Timotheum, fratrem nostrum et cooperatorem Dei in evangelio Christi, ad confirmandos vos et exhortandos pro fide vestra, ³ut nemo turbetur in tribulationibus istis. Ipsi enim scitis quod in hoc positi sumus; ⁴nam

---

**2.** Timothy is God's "servant" or "cooperator". Like Timothy, Christians are called to cooperate with God in spreading faith and love in the world. That is no easy task, for man's life on earth is "a hard service" (Job 7:1); obedience and self-giving are needed if victory is to be achieved. "Think of those who enlist under the banners of our commanders", St Clement of Rome says. "Think of the discipline and promptness and obedience they render their officers. Not all of them are marshals, generals, colonels, captains and so on down the ranks; nevertheless, each at his own level executes the orders of the commander and the senior officers. For the great cannot exist without the small, nor the small without the great" (*Letter to the Corinthians*, 1, 37).

**3-4.** The cross should have a permanent place in the life of a disciple of Christ, so it is not surprising that he encounters difficulties. From the very start of his missionary work St Paul taught that "through many tribulations we must enter the kingdom of God" (Acts 14:22), and we find the same idea in his last letter: "all who desire to live a godly life in Christ Jesus will be persecuted" (2 Tim 3:12). Monsignor Escrivá says in this connexion: "Do not forget that being with Jesus means we shall most certainly come upon his Cross. When we abandon ourselves into God's hands, he frequently permits us to taste sorrow, loneliness, opposition, slander, defamation, ridicule, coming both from within and without. This is because he wants to mould us to his own image and likeness. He even tolerates that we be called lunatics and be taken for fools […]. That is the way Jesus fashions the souls of those he loves, while at the same time never failing to give them inner calm and joy" (*Friends of God*, 301).

**5.** The "tempter" is Satan, the devil (cf. Mt 4:3), who tempts men, not to test their virtue and find them faithful, but to lead them astray and cause them to fall into evil ways.

as it has come to pass, and as you know. ⁵For this reason, when I could bear it no longer, I sent that I might know your faith, for fear that somehow the tempter had tempted you and that our labour would be in vain.

**Paul rejoices over the good reports brought by Timothy**

Acts 18:5 ⁶But now that Timothy has come to us from you, and has brought us the good news of your faith and love and reported that you always remember us kindly and long to

2 Thess 1:4 see us, as we long to see you—⁷ for this reason, brethren, in all our distress and affliction we have been comforted about you through your faith; ⁸for now we live, if you stand

---

et cum apud vos essemus, praedicebamus vobis passuros nos tribulationes, sicut et factum est et scitis. ⁵Propterea et ego amplius non sustinens, misi ad cognoscendam fidem vestram, ne forte tentaverit vos is qui tentat, et inanis fiat labor noster. ⁶Nunc autem veniente Timotheo ad nos a vobis et annuntiante nobis fidem et caritatem vestram et quia memoriam nostri habetis bonam semper, desiderantes nos videre, sicut nos quoque vos, ⁷ideo consolati sumus, fratres, propter vos in omni necessitate et tribulatione nostra per vestram fidem, ⁸quoniam nunc vivimus si vos statis in Domino. ⁹Quam enim gratiarum

---

The devil can propose sin to us, but he has no power to make anyone commit sin; therefore, he usually acts in an indirect way, through our passions. "When tempting us", St Thomas explains, "he acts very cunningly. Like a skilful general laying siege to a fortress, the demon looks for the weak points of the person he wants to overcome, and goes for his weakest flank. He tempts man to those sins to which (after subduing the flesh) he is most inclined: for example, anger, pride and the other spiritual sins" (*On the Lord's Prayer*).

The Christian, therefore, needs to be on the watch—"Watch and pray that you may not enter into temptation" (Mt 26:41)—and humbly to ask God for help: "And lead us not into temptation, but deliver us from evil" (Mt 6:13). "Christ the Lord has commanded us to offer this petition so that we may commend ourselves daily to God, and implore his paternal care and assistance, being assured that, if we be deserted by the divine protection, we shall soon fall into the snares of our most crafty enemy" (*St Pius V Catechism*, IV, 15, 2).

**6-8.** St Paul discreetly allows the Thessalonians to see how zealous he is for their souls: far from being indifferent to their state of spiritual health, he sees it as a matter of life or death. Concern for the solid faith of those entrusted to him is his very life. Timothy has reported that the Thessalonians were "standing fast in the Lord" and that makes him very happy.

**9.** The fact that the Thessalonians are steadfast in the faith in spite of persecution is not due only to their own merits; the credit must go mainly to the grace of God; and so St Paul thanks the Lord for the help he has given them.

fast in the Lord. [9]For what thanksgiving can we render to
God for you, for all the joy which we feel for your sake
before our God, [10]praying earnestly night and day that we
may see you face to face and supply what is lacking in your
faith?

### He prays for the Thessalonians

[11]Now may our God and Father himself, and our Lord

---

actionem possumus Deo retribuere pro vobis in omni gaudio, quo gaudemus
propter vos ante Deum nostrum, [10]nocte et die abundantius orantes ut videamus
faciem vestram et compleamus ea, quae desunt fidei vestrae? [11]Ipse autem Deus

---

"For all the joy we feel . . . before our God": that is, in the presence of God.
Prayer provides the outlet the Christian needs for expressing his feelings and
desires; it is an intimate conversation with God which he can have at any time:
"While we carry out as perfectly as we can (with all our mistakes and limitations) the tasks allotted to us by our situation and duties, our soul longs to
escape. It is drawn towards God like iron drawn by a magnet. One begins to
love Jesus, in a more effective way, with the sweet and gentle surprise of his
encounter" (J. Escrivá, *Friends of God*, 296).

**10.** St Paul's first stay in Thessalonica was a very short one, because unrest
caused by Jews forced him to leave in a hurry (cf. Acts 17:5-10). That meant
that he was unable to give any advanced religious instruction to the believers—
which is why he wants to see them again.

He does not confine himself to wishing he could see them; he uses his
supernatural resources (including prayer) to obtain what he wants, for prayer
should precede and accompany preaching. Otherwise there is no reason to
expect apostolic work to bear fruit. Although faith is born of preaching (cf.
Rom 10:17), preaching alone cannot produce faith; St Thomas teaches that it
is necessary for grace to act on the heart of the listener (cf. *Commentary on
Rom*, 10, 2).

**11.** Earlier St Paul referred to the obstacles Satan put in the way of his return
to Thessalonica (cf. 2:18). That is why he now prays the Lord to "direct his
way"—prayer being the best resource he has.

"May our God and Father himself, and our Lord Jesus, direct [singular verb]
our way": it is interesting to note that the verb is singular even though it has
two subjects. It would be wrong to dismiss this as insignificant, for it hints at
the mystery of the three Persons in the one God.

**12-13.** Love is a supernatural virtue which inclines us to love God (for his
own sake) above all things, and our neighbour as ourselves for the love of God.
Given that charity is a virtue which God infuses into the soul, it is something
we must not only practise but also ask God to increase in us.

2 Thess 1:3
1 Thess 5:15
Gal 6:10
1 Thess 2:19
2 Thess 1:7-10
1 Thess 5:23
Jesus, direct our way to you; [12]and may the Lord make you increase and abound in love to one another and to all men, as we do to you, [13]so that he may establish your hearts unblamable in holiness before our God and Father, at the coming of our Lord Jesus with all his saints.

## PART TWO

## A CALL TO VIRTUE

## 4

### He calls for holiness and purity

2 Thess 3:6 [1]Finally, brethren, we beseech and exhort you in the Lord Jesus, that as you learned from us how you ought to live

---

et Pater noster et Dominus noster Iesus dirigat viam nostram ad vos; [12]vos autem Dominus abundare et superabundare faciat caritate in invicem et in omnes, quemadmodum et nos in vos, [13]ad confirmanda corda vestra sine querela in sanctitate ante Deum et Patrem nostrum, in adventu Domini nostri Iesu cum omnibus sanctis eius. Amen.
[1]De cetero ergo, fratres, rogamus vos et obsecramus in Domino Iesu, ut—

Supernatural love, or charity, embraces everyone without exception. "Loving one person and showing indifference to others", St John Chrysostom observes, "is characteristic of purely human affection; but St Paul is telling us that our love should not be restricted in any way" (*Hom. on 1 Thess, ad loc.*). When a person practises this virtue in an uninhibited way, his holiness gains in strength: he becomes irreproachable "before our Lord and Father"; "in this does the true merit of virtue really consist—and not in simply being blameless before men [. . .]. Yes, I shall say it again: it is charity, it is love, which makes us blameless" (*ibid.*).

"With all his saints": referring to believers who died in the grace of God.

**1.** St Paul encourages the Thessalonians "in the Lord Jesus" to follow his advice: he does not make this plea in his own name or using his personal influence but in the name of the Lord Jesus. Those who have positions of authority in the Church should be obeyed, above all, for supernatural reasons (that is what God desires) and not for any personal qualities they happen to have or simply because they are "superiors". It is this outlook which causes St Ignatius Loyola to say that "laying aside all private judgment, we ought to keep our minds prepared and ready to obey in all things the true Spouse of Christ our Lord, which is our Holy Mother, the hierarchical Church" (*Spiritual Exercises*, 353).

and to please God, just as you are doing, you do so more and more. ²For you know what instructions we gave you through the Lord Jesus. ³For this is the will of God, your

---

quemadmodum accepistis a nobis quomodo vos oporteat ambulare et placere Deo, sicut et ambulatis—ut abundetis magis. ²Scitis enim, quae praecepta dederimus vobis per Dominum Iesum. ³Haec est enim voluntas Dei, sancti-

---

The Thessalonians already knew the commandments, but knowing them is not enough; they must be put into practice. St John Chrysostom comments: "Good land does something more than give back the grain put into it; and therefore the soul should not limit itself to doing what is laid down, but should go further [. . .]. Two things make for virtue—avoiding evil and doing good. Fleeing from evil is not the be-all of virtue; it is the beginning of the path that leads to virtue. One needs, in addition, to have an ardent desire to be good and to do good" (*Hom. on 1 Thess, ad loc.*).

**3.** What the Apostle says here reflects our Lord's teaching in the Sermon on the Mount: "You, therefore, must be perfect, as your heavenly Father is perfect" (Mt 5:48). The call to holiness is a universal one: it is not addressed only to a few, but to everyone: "Christ, the Son of God, who with the Father and the Spirit is hailed as 'alone holy', loved the Church as his Bride, giving himself up for her so as to sanctify her (cf. Eph 5:25-26); he joined her to himself as his body and endowed her with the gift of the Holy Spirit for the glory of God. Therefore all in the Church, whether they belong to the hierarchy or are cared for by it, are called to holiness, according to the Apostle's saying: 'For this is the will of God, your sanctification' (1 Thess 4:3; cf. Eph 1:4)" (Vatican II, *Lumen gentium*, 39).

In the Old Testament holiness is the highest attribute of God. He is holy, and he asks men to be holy, pointing out that the model and cause of man's holiness is the holiness of God: "You shall be holy; for I the Lord your God am holy" (Lev 19:3).

The universal call to holiness was the core of the teaching of the founder of Opus Dei; it was a message he preached constantly from 1928 up to his death in 1975: "We are deeply moved, and our hearts profoundly shaken, when we listen attentively to that cry of St Paul: 'This is the will of God, your sanctification' [. . .]. He calls each and every one to holiness; he asks each and every one to love him—young and old, single and married, healthy and sick, learned and unlearned, no matter where they work, or where they are" (*Friends of God*, 294).

"Christ's invitation to holiness, which he addresses to all men without exception, puts each one of us under an obligation to cultivate our interior life and to struggle daily to practise the Christian virtues; and not just in any old way, nor in a way which is above average or even excellent. No; we must strive to the point of heroism, in the strictest and most exacting sense of the word" (*ibid.*, 3).

1 Cor 6:13-15
Acts 15:20

Jer 10:25
Ps 79:6

Ps 94:2

2 Thess 2:13

Lk 10:16
Ezek 36:27
Ezek 37:14

sanctification: that you abstain from immorality; [4]that each one of you know how to control his own body in holiness and honour, [5]not in the passion of lust like heathen who do not know God; [6]that no man transgress, and wrong his brother in this matter,[c] because the Lord is an avenger in all these things, as we solemnly forewarned you. [7]For God has not called us for uncleanness, but in holiness. [8]Therefore whoever disregards this, disregards not man but God, who gives his Holy Spirit to you.

ficatio vestra, [4]ut abstineatis a fornicatione, ut sciat unusquisque vestrum suum vas possidere in sanctificatione et honore, [5]non in passione desiderii, sicut et gentes, quae ignorant Deum, [6]ut ne quis supergrediatur neque circumveniat in negotio fratrem suum, quoniam vindex est Dominus de his omnibus, sicut et praediximus vobis et testificati sumus. [7]Non enim vocavit nos Deus in immunditiam sed in sanctificationem. [8]Itaque, qui spernit, non hominem spernit sed

**4-8.** Man "is obliged to regard his body as good and to hold it in honour since God has created it and will raise it up on the last day [. . .]. His very dignity therefore requires that he should glorify God in his body (cf. 1 Cor 6:13-20) and not allow it to serve the evil inclinations of his heart" (Vatican II, *Gaudium et spes*, 14).

"Immorality" (v. 3): the word used would be translated as "fornication", were the style classical Greek; however, by St Paul's time the word had come to refer to any kind of sexual practice outside marriage or not in accordance with the aims of marriage. The word translated as "body" literally means "vessel" and it can refer either to one's body or to one's own wife. If "wife" is meant, then the passage should be taken as an exhortation to married fidelity and to proper use of marriage. Whichever meaning is correct, the sacred text is saying that God calls us to exercise self-control in holiness and honour; that means that one's body and its functions should be used in the way God means them to be used. The Lord of life has entrusted to men and women the mission to preserve life and to transmit it in a manner in keeping with human dignity. "Man's sexuality and the faculty of reproduction wondrously surpass the endowments of lower forms of life; therefore the acts proper to married life are to be ordered according to authentic human dignity and must be honoured with the greatest reverence" (*Gaudium et spes*, 51).

"Therefore," Monsignor Escrivá comments, "when I remind you now that Christians must keep perfect chastity, I am referring to everyone—to the unmarried, who must practise complete continence; and to those who are married who practise chastity by fulfilling the duties of their state in life. If one has the spirit of God, chastity is not a troublesome and humiliating burden, but a joyful affirmation. Will-power, dominion, self-mastery do not come from the flesh or from instinct. They come from the will, especially if it is united to the

[c]Or *defraud his brother in business*

**Charity and good use of time**

⁹But concerning love of the brethren you have no need
to have any one write to you, for you yourselves have been
taught by God to love one another; ¹⁰and indeed you do love
all the brethren throughout Macedonia. But we exhort you,

Jn 13:34
Jn 6:45

1 Thess 1:7-8

---

Deum, qui etiam dat Spiritum suum Sanctum in vos. ⁹De caritate autem
fraternitatis non necesse habetis, ut vobis scribam; ipsi enim vos a Deo edocti
estis, ut diligatis invicem; ¹⁰etenim facitis illud in omnes fratres in universa

---

Will of God. In order to be chaste (and not merely continent or decent) we must
subject our passions to reason, but for a noble motive, namely, the promptings
of Love" (*Friends of God*, 177).

In addition to giving reasons for practising the virtue of chastity, the Apostle
warns that God will punish those who commit sins against this virtue. "These
crimes we are commenting on", says St John Chrysostom, "will in no way be
overlooked. The enjoyment they give us is quite outweighed by the pain and
suffering their punishment earns" (*Hom. on 1 Thess, ad loc.*).

**9-10.** "The greatest commandment of the law is to love God with one's
whole heart and one's neighbour as oneself (cf. Mt 22:37-40). Christ has made
this love of neighbour his personal commandment and has enriched it with a
new meaning when he willed himself, along with his brothers, to be the object
of this charity, saying, 'When you did it to one of the least of these my brethren,
you did it to me' (Mt 25:40). In assuming human nature he has united to himself
all mankind in a supernatural solidarity which makes of it one single family.
He has made charity the distinguishing mark of his disciples, in the words: 'By
this all men will know that you are my disciples, if you have love for one
another' (Jn 13:35). In the early days the Church linked the 'agape' to the
eucharistic supper, and by so doing showed itself as one body around Christ
united by the bond of charity. So too, in all ages, love is its characteristic mark"
(Vatican II, *Apostolicam actuositatem*, 8). Love for the other members of the
Church is fraternal love, a love which brothers and sisters should have for one
another, for the Church is one large family. The Thessalonians practised this
love not only among themselves but also with the other believers living in
Macedonia; fraternal charity is absolutely necessary for the unity of Christians.

"No tongue can tell the heights to which love uplifts us", St Clement of Rome
teaches. "Love unites us to God; love casts a veil over innumerable sins; there
are no limits to love's endurance, no end to its patience. There is nothing base,
nothing proud, about love [. . .]. It was in love that all God's chosen ones were
made perfect. Without love nothing is pleasing to God" (*Letter to the Corinthians*, 1, 49).

**11-12.** Everyone has certain obligations connected with his position in life
which he should conscientiously fulfil. They include, particularly, duties to do
with work and family, and they provide us with an opportunity for conversation

brethren, to do so more and more, [11]to aspire to live quietly, to mind your own affairs, and to work with your hands, as we charged you; [12]so that you may command the respect of outsiders, and be dependent on nobody.

### The second coming of the Lord

[13]But we would not have you ignorant, brethren, con-

---

Macedonia. Rogamus autem vos, fratres, ut abundetis magis [11]et operam detis, ut quieti sitis et ut vestrum negotium agatis et operemini manibus vestris, sicut praecipimus vobis, [12]ut honeste ambuletis ad eos, qui foris sunt, et nullius aliquid desideretis. [13]Nolumus autem vos ignorare, fratres, de dormientibus, ut

---

with God. St John Chrysostom teaches, for example: "A woman working in the kitchen or doing some sewing can always raise her thoughts to heaven and fervently invoke the Lord. If someone is on the way to market or is travelling alone, he can easily pray attentively. Someone else who is in his wine-cellar, engaged in stitching wine skins, is free enough to raise his heart to the Master" (*Fifth homily on Anna*, 4, 6).

Work is something of immense human and supernatural value, for it is a means readily at hand for personal sanctification and cooperation with others. It would be unworthy of a Christian to live an idle life and expect to be supported by the charity of others. St Paul counsels everyone who can to look after his family and "be dependent on nobody". And so we find the following in one of the very earliest Christian documents: "If someone wants to settle down among you, and is a skilled worker, let him find employment and earn his bread. If he knows no trade, use your discretion to make sure that he does not live in idleness on the strength of being a Christian. If he does not want to work, he is only trying to exploit Christ. Be on your guard against people of that sort" (*Didache*, 12). So, a person cannot be regarded as a good Christian if he does not try to work well, for "our professional vocation is an essential and inseparable part of our condition as Christians. Our Lord wants you to be holy in the place where you are, in the job you have chosen" (J. Escrivá, *Friends of God*, 60).

In addition to promoting personal sanctification and cooperation with others, work gives the Christian a share in Christ's work of Redemption. "Sweat and toil, which work necessarily involves in the present condition of the human race, present the Christian and everyone who is called to follow Christ with the possibility of sharing lovingly in the work that Christ came to do (cf. Jn 17:4). This work of salvation came about through suffering and death on a Cross. By enduring the toil of work in union with Christ crucified for us, man in a way collaborates with the Son of God for the redemption of humanity. He shows himself a true disciple of Christ by carrying the cross in his turn every day (cf. Lk 9:23) in the activity that he is called upon to perform" (John Paul II, *Laborem exercens*, 27).

**13.** "Those who are asleep": this expression, already to be found in some

cerning those who are asleep, that you may not grieve as others do who have no hope. [14]For since we believe that Jesus died and rose again, even so, through Jesus, God will

non contristemini sicut et ceteri, qui spem non habent. [14]Si enim credimus quod

pagan writings, was often used by the early Christians to refer to those who died in the faith of Christ. In Christian writings it makes much more sense, given Christian belief in the resurrection of Jesus and in the resurrection of the body. It is not just a euphemism: it underlines the fact that death is not the end. "Why does it say that they are asleep", St Augustine asks, "if not because they will be raised when their day comes?" (*Sermon* 93, 6). Hence Monsignor Escrivá's advice: "When facing death, be calm. I do not want you to have the cold stoicism of the pagan, but the fervour of a child of God who knows that life is changed, not taken away. To die is to live!" (*Furrow*, 876).

Even though we have this hope, it is perfectly understandable for us to feel sad when people we love die. This sadness, provided it is kept under control, is a sign of affection and piety, but "to be excessively downcast by the death of friends is to act like someone who does not have the spirit of Christian hope. A person who does not believe in the resurrection and who sees death as total annihilation has every reason to weep and lament and cry over those friends and relations who have passed away into nothingness. But you are Christians, you believe in the resurrection, you live and die in hope: why should you mourn the dead excessively?" (Chrysostom, *Hom. on 1 Thess, ad loc.*).

**14.** "It is appointed for men to die once" (Heb 9:27). However, for a person who has faith, death does not just mean the end of his days on earth. Our Lord Jesus Christ died and rose again, and his resurrection is a pledge of our resurrection: death "in Christ" is the climax of a life in union with him, and it is the gateway to heaven. And so St Paul tells Timothy, "If we have died with him, we shall also live with him; if we endure, we shall also reign with him" (2 Tim 2:11-12).

The resurrection the Christian will experience is not only similar to our Lord's; his resurrection is in fact the cause of ours. St Thomas Aquinas explains this as follows: "Christ is the model of our resurrection, because he took flesh and he rose in the flesh. However, he is not only our model; he is also the efficient cause (of our resurrection) because anything done by the human nature of Christ was done not only by the power of his human nature but also by the power of the godhead united to that nature. And so, just as his touch cured the leper by virtue of its being the instrument of his godhead, so the resurrection of Christ is the cause of our resurrection" (*Commentary on 1 Thess, ad loc.*). Although this passage of the letter does not say so explicitly, it is implied that we will rise with our bodies, just as Jesus rose with his.

**15-17.** The religious instruction of the Thessalonians was cut short because St Paul had to leave the city in a hurry. One of the doubts remaining in their

1 Cor 15:51

1 Cor 15:23
2 Thess 1:7

Mk 24:30f

bring with him those who have fallen asleep. [15]For this we declare to you by the word of the Lord, that we who are alive, who are left until the coming of the Lord, shall not precede those who have fallen asleep. [16]For the Lord himself will descend from heaven with a cry of command, with

---

Iesus mortuus est et resurrexit, ita et Deus eos, qui dormierunt, per Iesum adducet cum eo. [15]Hoc enim vobis dicimus in verbo Domini, quia nos, qui vivimus, qui relinquimur in adventum Domini, non praeveniemus eos, qui dormierunt; [16]quoniam ipse Dominus in iussu, in voce archangeli et in tuba Dei

---

minds can be expressed as follows: Will the dead be under any disadvantage *vis-à-vis* those who are still alive when the Parousia of the Lord happens? The Apostle replies in two stages: first he says that we will have no advantage of any kind over them (vv. 15-18); then he makes it clear that we do not know when that event will come about (5:1-2).

In his reply he does not explicitly speak about the general resurrection; he refers only to those who die "in Christ". He distinguishes two groups as regards the situation people find themselves in at our Lord's second coming—1) those who are alive: these will be "caught up", that is, changed (cf. 1 Cor 15:51; 2 Cor 5:2-4) by the power of God and will change from being corruptible and mortal to being incorruptible and immortal; 2) those who have already died: these will rise again.

St Paul's reply is adapted to the tenor of the question; so, when he writes, "we who are alive, who are left" he does not mean that the Parousia will happen soon or that he will live to see the day (cf. Pontifical Biblical Commission, *Reply* concerning the Parousia, 18 June 1915). He uses the first person plural because at the time of writing both he and his readers were alive. However, his words were misinterpreted by some of the Thessalonians, and that was the reason he wrote the second epistle a few months later (in which he puts things more clearly: "Now concerning the coming of our Lord Jesus Christ and our assembling to meet him, we beg you, brethren, not to be quickly shaken in mind or excited [. . .], to the effect that the day of the Lord has come" (2 Thess 2:1-2). However, even in the first letter there are enough indications that St Paul was not saying the Parousia was imminent, for he implies that he does not know when it will happen (cf. 5:1-2).

To describe the signs which will mark the Lord's coming, St Paul uses imagery typical of apocalyptic writing—the voice of the archangel, the sound of the trumpet, the clouds of heaven. These signs are to be found in the Old Testament theophanies or great manifestations of Yahweh (cf. Ex 19:16); on the day of the Parousia, too, they will reveal God's absolute dominion over the forces of nature, as also his sublimity and majesty.

When the Lord Jesus comes in all his glory, those who had died in the Lord (who already were enjoying the vision of God in heaven) and those who have been changed will go to meet the Lord "in the air", for both will now have

the archangel's call, and with the sound of the trumpet of
God. And the dead in Christ will rise first; [17]then we who
are alive, who are left, shall be caught up together with them
in the clouds to meet the Lord in the air; and so we shall
always be with the Lord. [18]Therefore comfort one another
with these words.

Jn 12:26
Jn 17:24

# 5

[1]But as to the times and the seasons, brethren, you have no

Mt 24:36
Acts 1:7

descendet de caelo, et mortui, qui in Christo sunt, resurgent primi; [17]deinde nos,
qui vivimus, qui relinquimur, simul rapiemur cum illis in nubibus obviam
Domino in aera, et sic semper cum Domino erimus. [18]Itaque consolamini
invicem in verbis istis.

[1]De temporibus autem et momentis, fratres, non indigetis, ut scribatur vobis;

glorified bodies (cf. 1 Cor 15:43) endowed with the gift of "agility", "by which
the body will be freed from the heaviness that now presses it down, and will
take on a capability of moving with the utmost ease and swiftness, wherever
the soul pleases" (*St Pius V Catechism*, I, 12, 13).

After the general judgment, which will take place that day, the righteous will
be "always with the Lord." That is in fact the reward of the blessed—to enjoy
forever, in body and soul, the sight of God, thereby attaining a happiness which
more than makes up for whatever they have had to do to obtain it, for "the
sufferings of this present life are not worth comparing with the glory that is to
be revealed to us" (Rom 8:18). "If at any time you feel uneasy at the thought
of our sister death because you see yourself to be such a poor creature, take
heart. Think of this: Heaven awaits us; what will it be like when all the infinite
beauty and greatness and happiness and Love of God are poured into the poor
clay vessel that the human being is, to satisfy it eternally with the freshness of
an ever-new joy?" (J. Escrivá, *Furrow*, 891).

**1-3.** "The day of the Lord" is an expression used a number of times in Sacred
Scripture to refer to that point at which God will intervene decisively and
irreversibly. The prophets speak of the "day of Yahweh" sometimes fearfully
(cf. Amos 5:18-20), sometimes hopefully (cf. Is 6:13). In his eschatological
sermon (cf. Mt 24; Mk 13; Lk 21), Jesus foretold the destruction of Jerusalem
in a style very reminiscent of that used by the prophets (cf. Amos 8:9ff) when
speaking of the "day of Yahweh". The destruction of the city brings to an end
the Jewish era in the history of salvation and prefigures the second coming of
Christ as Judge of all. In St Paul's letters, as in other New Testament writings,
the "day of the Lord" is the day of the general judgment when Christ will appear
in the fulness of glory as Judge (cf. 1 Cor 1:8; 2 Cor 1:14). The Apostle brings

Mt 24:43
2 Pet 3:10
Rev 3:3; 16:15
Jer 6:14
Mt 24:8, 39

Jn 8:12
Rom 13:12
Eph 5:8
1 Pet 1:13;
4:7; 5:8

need to have anything written to you. ²For you yourselves know well that the day of the Lord will come like a thief in the night. ³When people say, "There is peace and security," then sudden destruction will come upon them as travail comes upon a woman with child, and there will be no escape. ⁴But you are not in darkness, brethren, for that day to surprise you like a thief. ⁵For you are all sons of light and sons of the day; we are not of the night or of darkness. ⁶So then let us not sleep, as others do, but let us keep awake and be sober. ⁷For those who sleep sleep at night, and those who

---

²ipsi enim diligenter scitis quia dies Domini sicut fur in nocte ita veniet. ³Cum enim dixerint: "Pax et securitas", tunc repentinus eis superveniet interitus, sicut dolor in utero habenti, et non effugient. ⁴Vos autem, fratres, non estis in tenebris, ut vos dies ille tamquam fur comprehendat; ⁵omnes enim vos filii lucis estis et filii diei. Non sumus noctis neque tenebrarum; ⁶Igitur non dormiamus sicut ceteri, sed vigilemus et sobrii simus. ⁷Qui enim dormiunt, nocte dormiunt;

---

in some examples used by our Lord in his preaching about the fall of Jerusalem and the end of the world (the "thief in the night": cf. Mt 24:43; the pains of childbirth: cf. Mt 24:19) to warn people that that day will come unexpectedly, and to exhort them to be always ready.

The Christian, therefore, should always be on the watch, for he never knows for sure when the last day of his life will be. The second coming of the Lord will take people by surprise; it will catch them doing good or doing evil. So, it would be rash to postpone repentance to some time in the future.

**4-6.** A thief works by night because he thinks that darkness will find the householder unprepared. Our Lord also used this metaphor when he said that if the father of the family had known when the thief would come, he would have kept a look-out (cf. Mt 24:43)—in other words, we need to be always alert, in the state of grace, surrounded by light. So, "if we walk in the light, as he is in the light, we have fellowship with one another, and the blood of Jesus his Son cleanses us from all sin" (1 Jn 1:7).

On the same subject the Church teaches that our souls are "illumined by the light of faith" (*St Pius V Catechism*, II, 2, 4).

We should therefore live a transparent life, with the divine light shining clearly through it; if we do, the "day of the Lord" (which can also be applied to the day each person dies) will not find us unprepared, even if it comes suddenly. "A true Christian is always ready to appear before God. Because, if he is fighting to live as a man of Christ, he is ready at every moment to fulfil his duty" (J. Escrivá, *Furrow*, 875).

**7-8.** "The drunkenness St Paul is speaking of here", St John Chrysostom says, "is not only that which comes from wine; it is mainly the kind that results

get drunk are drunk at night. [8]But, since we belong to the day, let us be sober, and put on the breastplate of faith and love, and for a helmet the hope of salvation. [9]For God has not destined us for wrath, but to obtain salvation through our Lord Jesus Christ, [10]who died for us so that whether we

Eph 6:14-17
Is 59:17
2 Thess 2:14
1 Thess 4:14
Rom 14:8

et, qui ebrii sunt, nocte inebriantur. [8]Nos autem, qui diei sumus, sobrii simus, *induti loricam* fidei et caritatis et *galeam* spem *salutis*; [9]quoniam non posuit nos Deus in iram sed in acquisitionem salutis per Dominum nostrum Iesum Christum, [10]qui mortuus est pro nobis, ut sive vigilemus sive dormiamus, simul

from sin. Wealth, ambition, covetousness and all the passions connected with them are the cause of spiritual drunkenness. However, why is sleep described as a sin? Because the slave of sin feels enervated, unable to engage in works of virtue. Enveloped as he is by illusions and the heady delights of evildoing, his actions are unreal; there is nothing solid in them; all he is doing is chasing things that do not exist" (*Hom. on 1 Thess, ad loc.*).

The Apostle's words refer to military armour of the period. Taken as a whole, the text depicts the struggle Christian life entails. The Christian's weapons are the three theological virtues—faith, love and hope—which help him live a sober, upright and pure life, the life of a sincere, straightforward person who has nothing to hide or be ashamed of. No one can live that sort of life without making an effort and being hard on himself, as our Lord teaches (cf. Mt 11:12); in the battle to live like this there is no room for compromise (cf. Job 7:1). Elsewhere the Apostle advises Timothy to act like "a good soldier of Christ Jesus" (2 Tim 2:3). In this daily battle we need to use the armour God gave us in the sacrament of Baptism—the breastplate of faith and love, and the helmet of hope (cf. also Eph 6:11-17).

**9-10.** "Wrath" refers to the condemnation earned by those who die in sin; and "salvation", in the New Testament, means being protected from danger and able to live free from anxiety. Being saved from wrath means obtaining eternal salvation.

Salvation comes to us "through our Lord Jesus Christ". The name Jesus ("God saves") conveys this mission which Christ attributed to himself (cf. Mt 1:21): "The Son of man came to seek and to save the lost" (Lk 19:10). Christ is the Saviour: "there is salvation in no one else, for there is no other name under heaven given among men by which we must be saved" (Acts 4:12). He will give us forgiveness of sins (cf. Acts 5:31); that was why he "died for us". "Through suffering" (Heb 2:10) he fulfilled the mission entrusted to him. By dying in obedience to the Father "he became the source of eternal salvation" (Heb 5:9). "Therefore he had to be made like his brethren in every respect, so that he might become a merciful and faithful high priest in the service of God, to make expiation for the sins of the people. For because he himself has suffered

53

Jude 20
Rom 14:19
wake or sleep we might live with him. [11]Therefore encourage one another and build one another up, just as you are doing.

**Various counsels**

1 Cor 16:16, 18
1 Tim 5:17
[12]But we beseech you, brethren, to respect those who labour among you and are over you in the Lord and admonish you, [13]and to esteem them very highly in love because of their work. Be at peace among yourselves.[c2]

---

cum illo vivamus. [11]Propter quod consolamini invicem et aedificate alterutrum, sicut et facitis. [12]Rogamus autem vos, fratres, ut noveritis eos, qui laborant inter vos et praesunt vobis in Domino et monent vos, [13]ut habeatis illos superabundanter in caritate propter opus illorum. Pacem habete inter vos. [14]Hortamur

and been tempted, he is able to help those who are tempted" (Heb 2:17-18). So it is that Jesus intercedes for all believers until the end of time (cf. Heb 7:25).

When he receives the sacrament of Baptism, the Christian becomes identified with Christ, the eternal high priest, in a special way: the "character" or mark conferred by the sacrament indicates that he is destined to live with Christ. As he makes his pilgrim way through this life he is able to enjoy, through grace, a foretaste of that divine life which he will enjoy permanently and much more fully in heaven.

Verse 10 contains another of St Paul's plays on words. The word "sleep" here (unlike vv. 6-7) means "die", and "being awake" means "being alive". For a Christian, death is a step which enables him to "live with Christ" forever, in eternal beatitude.

**12-13.** Those who form the hierarchy of the Church have a Christ-given mission to govern and instruct and give spiritual attention to the faithful. The positions they hold are not honours; they are positions of ministry or service. As St Augustine explains, "those who rule serve those whom they seem to rule. The reason for this is that they do not command out of a desire to be in authority, but because their ministry is to look after others; it is love, not pride, which leads them to look after others" (*The City of God*, 19, 14).

St John Chrysostom also exhorts Christians to show love and reverence to the pastors of the Church: "Love them the way a son loves his father! Through them you receive the mark of supernatural and divine rebirth; they open up for you the gates of heaven, and through them you receive all good things [. . .]. A person who loves Jesus Christ loves his pastor, whoever he may be, for by his hands he is given the sacred mysteries" (*Hom. on 1 Thess, ad loc.*).

**14.** There needs to be a certain order in our love of others; first we should

---

[c2]Or *with them*

¹⁴And we exhort you, brethren, admonish the idle, encourage the faint-hearted, help the weak, be patient with
them all. ¹⁵See that none of you repays evil for evil, but

autem vos, fratres: corripite inquietos, consolamini pusillanimes, suscipite infirmos, longanimes estote ad omnes. ¹⁵Videte, ne quis malum pro malo alicui

love those who hold positions of authority in the Church (cf. vv. 12-13); second come all our brethren in the faith, whom we should help to be holy, "for if we have a duty to draw pagans away from their idols and give them instruction in the faith," St Clement of Rome says, "how much more must we strive to ensure that no soul is lost who already has knowledge of God! Let us therefore help one another, striving to lead to virtue those who are weak, so that we may all be saved and may all help one another to be converted and corrected" (*Letter to the Corinthians*, 2, 17).

The first Christians gave each other this help by fraternal correction, in line with our Lord's teaching (cf. Mt 18:15ff). When someone noticed a defect in another, he was good enough to draw his attention to the matter so that he could take steps to correct it. Speaking of this practice, St Clement of Rome points out that correction should be gratefully received: "Let us accept correction, dearly beloved; it is something no one should resent. Mutual admonition is something very good and most beneficial, for it leads us to conform to the will of God" (*Letter to the Corinthians*, 1, 56).

"The idle": literally, those who break ranks. St Paul is applying a Greek military term to the Christian life. People who act in this way need to be corrected, whereas the weak and fainthearted need encouragement and should be dealt with very patiently.

**15.** In the Law of Christ there is no room for revenge, not even to redress the balance. The old "eye for an eye, tooth for a tooth" has been overtaken by the law of charity (cf. Mt 5:38-39). Wrongdoing and ignorance are never solved by vindictiveness or by committing further injustice. St Paul's teaching to the Romans is worth recalling: "Do not be overcome by evil, but overcome evil with good" (Rom 12:21).

The forgiving attitude of the Christian and serene defence of one's rights will help bring those who act unjustly closer to God. In the early years of the second century St Ignatius of Antioch gave the following advice: "Give them a chance to learn from you, or at all events from the way you act. Meet their animosity with mildness, their abuse with your prayers, their misconduct with your firmness in the faith. If they grow violent, be gentle instead of paying them back in their own coin. Let us show by our forebearance that we are their brothers; as far as imitation is concerned, the only one we should try to imitate is the Lord" (*Letter to the Ephesians*, 10, 1-3).

**16.** Being at peace with God and with others fills one with joy and serenity, so much so that even great suffering and sorrow, if borne with faith, cannot

Phil 3:1; 4:4
Rom 12:12
Eph 5:20 always seek to do good to one another and to all. [16]Rejoice always, [17]pray constantly, [18]give thanks in all circum-

reddat, sed semper, quod bonum est, sectamini et in invicem et in omnes. [16]Semper gaudete, [17]sine intermissione orate, [18]in omnibus gratias agite; haec

take away one's joy. "Being children of God, how can we be sad? Sadness is the end product of selfishness. If we truly want to live for God, we will never lack cheerfulness, even when we discover our errors and wretchedness. Cheerfulness finds its way into our life of prayer, so much so that we cannot help singing for joy. For we are in love, and singing is a thing that lovers do" (J. Escrivá, *Friends of God*, 92).

When someone allows sadness to overwhelm him, even his prayers to God are of no avail because he is failing to accept God's will. An anonymous second-century Christian writer, in a famous document, says: "Why does the prayer of the melancholy man not reach up to the altar of God? [. . .] Because supplication when mixed with melancholy is prevented from ascending pure to the altar. Just as wine mixed with vinegar has no longer the same flavour, so the Holy Spirit mixed with melancholy has not the same power of supplication. Cleanse yourself, therefore, of this evil melancholy, and you will live for God. So, too, will they live for God who cast away melancholy and clothe themselves entirely in joy" (*The Shepherd of Hermas*, 10th commandment, 3).

**17.** Our Lord impressed on his Apostles the need for prayer at all times, and underlined this by his own life of prayer (cf. Lk 18:1). "The Apostle", St Jerome says, "tells us to pray always. For holy people, even sleep is a prayer. However, we should have certain times of prayer spread out over the day so that, even if we are involved in some task, the timetable we have given ourselves will remind us that duty calls" (*Letter*, 22, 37).

"A Christian life should be one of constant prayer, trying to live in the presence of God from morning to night and from night to morning. A Christian can never be a lonely person, since he lives in continual contact with God, who is both near us and in heaven [. . .]. In the middle of his daily work, when he has to overcome his selfishness, when he enjoys the cheerful friendship of other people, a Christian should rediscover God" (J. Escrivá, *Christ is passing by*, 116).

**18.** This verse completes the triptych which shows the Christian how to live in line with "the will of God"—joy (v. 16), prayer (v. 17) and thanksgiving.

"There is no one", St Bernard says, "who, if he just thinks about it a little, cannot find very good reasons to express his gratitude to God" (*Sermon on the sixth Sunday after Pentecost*, 2, 1). In addition to life itself and all the natural gifts we have received, there are the fruits of the Redemption wrought by Christ, and even "the natural order of things requires that he who has received a favour should, by repaying it, turn to his benefactor in gratitude" (*Summa theologiae*, II-II, q. 106, a. 3). It follows that gratefulness should be a permanent attitude

stances; for this is the will of God in Christ Jesus for you.
[19]Do not quench the Spirit, [20]do not despise prophesying,
[21]but test everything; hold fast what is good, [22]abstain from
every form of evil.

---

enim voluntas Dei est in Christo Iesu erga vos. [19]Spiritum nolite exstinguere,
[20]prophetias nolite spernere; [21]omnia autem probate, quod bonum est tenete,
[22]ab omni specie mala abstinete vos. [23]Ipse autem Deus pacis sanctificet vos

---

of the children of God, whether they find themselves in pleasant or disagreeable
circumstances, for they know that "in everything God works for good with those
who love him" (Rom 8:28). "If things go well, let us rejoice, blessing God who
makes them prosper. And if they go badly? Let us rejoice, blessing God who
allows us to share in the sweetness of his Cross" (J. Escrivá, *The Way*, 658).

**19-22.** No one should smother the graces and charisms the Holy Spirit
grants as he wishes (cf. 1 Cor 13 and 14); and the gift of prophecy (v. 20) should
be held in special regard. The "prophets" referred to in the New Testament were
Christians to whom God gave special graces to encourage, console, correct or
instruct others. They did not constitute a special class or group, as was the case
in the Old Testament. Some of them may at times have abused their gifts and
tried to impose their counsel on others, but that does not mean that those who
had this gift were not to be held in high regard, for thanks to this charism they
were a great asset to the Church.

"It is only through the sacraments and the ministrations of the Church that
the Holy Spirit makes holy the people of God, leads them and enriches them
with his virtues. Allotting his gifts according as he wills it (cf. 1 Cor 12:11), he
also distributes special graces among the faithful of every rank. By these gifts
he makes them fit and ready to undertake various tasks and offices for the
renewal and building up of the Church, as it is written, 'to each is given the
manifestation of the Spirit for the common good' (1 Cor 12:7). Whether these
charisms be very remarkable or more simple and widely diffused, they are to
be received with thanksgiving and consolation since they are fitting and useful
for the needs of the Church. Extraordinary gifts are not to be rashly desired,
nor is it from them that the fruits of apostolic labours are to be presumptuously
expected. Those who have charge over the Church should judge the genuine-
ness and proper use of these gifts, though their office is not indeed to extinguish
the Spirit, but to test all things and hold fast to what is good (cf. 1 Thess 5:12
and 19-21)" (*Vatican II, Lumen gentium*, 12).

**21.** This verse refers directly to charisms and the discernment of charisms;
but it can be taken as advice to reflect prudently before taking any decision, so
as always to do the right thing.

**23.** "Spirit and soul and body": three aspects which go to make up a
well-integrated human person. Spirit and soul are in fact two forms of the same

**Closing prayer and farewell**

²³May the God of peace himself sanctify you wholly; and may your spirit and soul and body be kept sound and blameless at the coming of our Lord Jesus Christ. ²⁴He who calls you is faithful, and he will do it.

---

per omnia, et integer spiritus vester et anima et corpus sine querela in adventu Domini nostri Iesu Christi servetur. ²⁴Fidelis est, qui vocat vos, qui etiam faciet.

---

principle. Here soul refers to the principle of sensitive life, whereas "spirit" is the source of man's higher life; his intellectual life derives from his spirit, and this intellectual life, once enlightened by faith, is open to the action of the Holy Spirit (cf. Rom 1:9).

In this verse God is being invoked to "sanctify" believers, to preserve the purity of the human person at all levels (spirit, soul and body). Given that even after Baptism man has an inclination towards sin and often does offend the Lord (even if not gravely), he needs to practise penance in order to stay unsullied. Moreover, the "sanctification" which God brings about in man affects his entire being. In the last analysis, Christian holiness is the fulness of the order established by God at the Creation and re-established after man's sin. And so the Apostle invokes God as "the God of peace", for peace is, according to theological definition, "tranquillity in order". Sanctity gives all man's faculties, physical as well as spiritual, their perfection and wholeness, thereby rounding off and perfecting the natural order, without superseding it.

Sanctification is the joint work of God and man. God's action begins at Baptism and develops thereafter (cf. 3:13); but for a person to attain lasting sanctity he needs to make a constant effort to second God's action. "Conversion is the task of a moment; sanctification is the work of a lifetime. The divine seed of charity, which God has sown in our souls, desires to grow, to express itself in deeds, to yield results which continually coincide with what God wants. Therefore, we must be ready to begin again, to find again—in new situations— the light and the stimulus of our first conversion" (J. Escrivá, *Christ is passing by*, 58).

**24.** "He who calls you": the Greek text conveys the idea of continuous action. The calling which God addresses to a person is not an isolated event occurring at a single point in his life; it is a permanent attitude of God, who is continually calling us to be holy. Therefore, vocation is not something which can be lost; but man's response can cease. Faithfulness is an attitude of God: he always keeps his promises and never ceases in his salvific purpose: "He who began a good work in you will bring it to completion" (Phil 1:6); so holiness depends on divine grace (which is always available) and on man's response. Final perseverance is a grace but it will not be denied to anyone who strives to do good. "Buoyed up by this hope," St Clement of Rome comments, "let us

[25]Brethren, pray for us.
[26]Greet all the brethren with a holy kiss.
[27]I adjure you by the Lord that this letter be read to all the brethren.
[28]The grace of our Lord Jesus Christ be with you.

Rom 15:30
2 Thess 3:1

1 Cor 16:20

Col 4:16

Rom 16:20

---

[25]Fratres, orate etiam pro nobis. [26]Salutate fratres omnes in osculo sancto. [27]Adiuro vos per Dominum, ut legatur epistula omnibus fratribus. [28]Gratia Domini nostri Iesu Christi vobiscum.

---

bind our souls to him who is true to his word and righteous in his judgments. He who has forbidden us to use any deception can much less be a deceiver himself" (*Letter to the Corinthians*, 1, 27).

# Second Epistle to the Thessalonians

ENGLISH AND LATIN VERSIONS, WITH NOTES

# 1

Greeting

¹Paul, Silvanus, and Timothy,                    1 Thess 1:1
To the church of the Thessalonians in God our Father
and the Lord Jesus Christ:
²Grace to you and peace from God the Father and the       Rom 1:7
Lord Jesus Christ.

---

¹Paulus et Silvanus et Timotheus ecclesiae Thessalonicensium in Deo Patre
nostro et Domino Iesu Christo: ²gratia vobis et pax a Deo Patre nostro et

**1-2.** This heading is similar to that of the first letter. Two slight differences
bear comment. The first is the adjective "our" applied to God the Father. This
underlines the divine filiation of Christians. Only the second person, the Word,
is the Son of God by nature; human beings are children of God by adoption,
thanks to the Son's deigning to make us sharers in the divine filiation which is
his in all its fulness; in theology this is expressed in the well-known proposition
that we are "filii in Filio," sons in the Son. "The Son of God, his only son by
nature," St Augustine says, "deigned to become Son of man, so that we who
are sons of man by nature might become sons of God by grace" (*The City of
God*, 21, 15). And St Irenaeus explains that "if the Word became flesh, and if
the Son of God became Son of man, he did this so that man, by entering into
communion with the Word and receiving the privilege of adoption, might
become a son of God" (*Against Heresies*, 2, 19).

The Second Vatican Council gives the same teaching when it says that "the
followers of Christ, called by God not in virtue of their works but by his design
and grace, and justified in the Lord Jesus, have been made sons of God in the
baptism of faith and partakers of the divine nature, and so are truly sanctified"
(*Lumen gentium*, 40). The full import of what Christian life means becomes
clear if one keeps in mind "this expressible and simple fact—that he is our
Father and we are his children" (J. Escrivá, *Friends of God*, 144).

The second difference in the heading (as compared with the first letter) is
that it specifically says that grace comes "from God the Father and [from] the
Lord Jesus Christ". Peace is inseparable from grace and has its source in God.
That is why the Second Vatican Council emphasizes that "peace on earth, which
flows from love of one's neighbour, symbolizes and derives from the peace of
Christ which proceeds from God the Father" (*Gaudium et spes*, 78).

See the note on 1 Thess 1:1-2.

**3-4.** As in other letters, the Apostle expresses his deep gratitude to the Lord
(cf. Phil 4:6; Col 3:15-17; 1 Tim 2:1; etc.). By doing so he is imitating Jesus
himself, who at the start of prayer used to praise the Father and give him thanks
(cf. Mt 11:25; 15:36; 26:27 and par.; Jn 11:41; etc.). In its supreme act of

# PART ONE

# GOD IS JUST

**Thanksgiving**

2 Thess 2:13
1 Thess 1:2
1 Cor 1:4
1 Thess 2:14,
19; 3:3, 7
2 Cor 8:23f

³We are bound to give thanks to God always for you, brethren, as is fitting, because your faith is growing abundantly, and the love of every one of you·for one another is increasing. ⁴Therefore we ourselves boast of you in the churches of God for your steadfastness and faith in all your persecutions and in the afflictions which you are enduring.

---

Domino Iesu Christo. ³Gratias agere debemus Deo semper pro vobis, fratres, sicut dignum est, quoniam supercrescit fides vestra, et abundat caritas uniuscuiusque omnium vestrum in invicem, ⁴ita ut et nos ipsi in vobis gloriemur in ecclesiis Dei pro patientia vestra et fide in omnibus persecutionibus vestris et

---

worship, the Mass, the Church exclaims at the start of the Preface: "We do well always and everywhere to give you thanks."

In addition to showing the nobility of our feelings, gratefulness also puts us in the way of further gifts, because the Lord is particularly well disposed to a humble and grateful heart. As St Bernard teaches, "someone who humbly recognizes himself as obliged for gifts and who is grateful for them, is bound to receive many more. For if he shows that he is faithful in little things, he has a right to be entrusted with many; whereas on the contrary, someone who does not appreciate the favours he has been given renders himself unworthy of being given additional favours" (*Sermons on Psalm 90*, 4).

That is why the Christian feels the need to express his gratitude to God: "Thank you, my Jesus, for your choosing to become perfect Man, with a most loving and lovable heart; a heart which loves unto death; a heart which suffers; which is filled with joy and sorrow; which delights in the things of men and shows us the way to heaven; which subjects itself heroically to duty and acts with mercy; which watches over the poor and the rich, which cares for sinners and the just. . . . Thank you, my Jesus. Give us hearts to measure up to Yours!" (J. Escrivá, *Furrow*, 813).

"Your faith is growing": faith needs to grow, it needs to be alive. It grows when it is joined to love. The Thessalonians were active in their practice of faith and love, and this meant that their morale was good despite persecution and affliction. "Observe how the love and mutual solidarity of the believers is a great help in resisting evils and bearing affliction," St John Chrysostom says. "That deep fraternity was a great source of consolation. It is only a weak faith and an imperfect charity that afflictions cause to waver; but a solid, robust faith is in fact strengthened by affliction. A weak, languid soul derives no benefit from suffering, whereas a generous soul finds in suffering a source of new energy" (*Hom. on 2 Thess*, ad loc.).

⁵This is evidence of the righteous judgment of God, that
you may be made worthy of the kingdom of God, for which
you are suffering—⁶since indeed God deems it just to repay
with affliction those who afflict you, ⁷and to grant rest with
us to you who are afflicted, when the Lord Jesus is revealed
from heaven with his mighty angels in flaming fire, ⁸in-
flicting vengeance upon those who do not know God and
upon those who do not obey the gospel of our Lord Jesus.
⁹They shall suffer the punishment of eternal destruction and

1 Thess 2:12
Acts 14:22
Rom 12:19
Rev 18:6
Phil 1:28

1 Thess 3:13
Mt 25:31

Is 66:4, 15
Jer 10:25

Is 2:10, 19, 21

tribulationibus, quas sustinetis, ⁵indicium iusti iudicii Dei, ut digni habeamini
regno Dei, pro quo et patimini, ⁶siquidem iustum est apud Deum retribuere
tribulationem his, qui vos tribulant, ⁷et vobis, qui tribulamini, requiem nobis-
cum in revelatione Domini Iesu de caelo cum angelis virtutis eius, ⁸*in igne
flammae, dantis vindictam his, qui non noverunt Deum* et qui non oboediunt
evangelio Domini nostri Iesu, ⁹qui poenas dabunt interitu aeterno *a facie*

**5.** Fidelity to God, even in a situation which is adverse and difficult, is a
guarantee of future reward. Our Lord sometimes allows us to experience
suffering for the sake of the Gospel; he thereby tests our love and makes us
worthy of the enduring Kingdom which awaits us in the life to come.

In a particularly authoritative way, Paul VI taught that "the Kingdom of God
begun here below in the Church of Christ is not of this world whose form is
passing, and [. . .] its proper growth cannot be confounded with the progress of
civilization, of science or of human technology, but [. . .] consists in an ever
more profound knowledge of the unfathomable riches of Christ, an ever
stronger hope in eternal blessings, an ever more ardent response to the Love of
God, and an ever more generous bestowal of grace and holiness among men"
(*Creed of the People of God*, 27).

Suffering, like faith, should be accepted as a mark of God's special love: "it
has been granted to you that . . . you should not only believe in him but also
suffer for his sake" (Phil 1:29). Making the same point John Paul II reminds us
that "in bringing about the Redemption through suffering, Christ *has* also *raised
human suffering to the level of the Redemption.* Thus each man, in his suffering,
can also become a sharer in the redemptive suffering of Christ" (*Salvifici
doloris*, 19).

**9-10.** The Apostle is very explicit about the fact that God will judge each
of us according to his works; "he will come again, this time in glory, to judge
the living and the dead: each according to his merits—those who have respond-
ed to the Love and Pity of God going to eternal life, those who have refused
them to the end going to the fire that is not extinguished" (*Creed of the People
of God*, 12). The fact that there is a hell—fear of going there—should not be
the main motive for fidelity to God; however, this punishment could be ours if
we offend God.

exclusion from the presence of the Lord and from the glory of his might, [10]when he comes on that day to be glorified in his saints, and to be marvelled at in all who have believed, because our testimony to you was believed.

### Prayer for perseverance

Phil 2:13

[11]To this end we always pray for you, that our God may make you worthy of his call, and may fulfil every good

---

*Domini et a gloria virtutis eius,* [10]cum venerit glorificari in sanctis suis et admirabilis fieri in omnibus, qui crediderunt, quia creditum est testimonium nostrum super vos in die illo. [11]Ad quod etiam oramus semper pro vobis, ut

---

In contrast to the position of the damned, eternal glory awaits the righteous. The Apostle also speaks of this elsewhere (cf. Rom 6:22; Gal 6:8). St Paul combines his proclamation of the second coming of Christ with a reminder of our Lord's promise: "And when I go and prepare a place for you, I will come again and will take you to myself, that where I am you may be also" (Jn 14:3).

Jesus also told us that those who prove faithful will receive a great reward: "Rejoice in that day ..., for behold, your reward is great in heaven" (Lk 6:23). "In heaven a great Love awaits you, with no betrayals and no deceptions. The fulness of love, the fulness of beauty and greatness and knowledge ...! And it will never cloy: it will fill you, yet you will always want more" (J. Escrivá, *The Forge,* 995).

"That day": the day of the general judgment. See the note on 1 Thess 5:1-3.

**11.** St Paul takes up the thread of the prayer he began in v. 4, asking God to keep the believers true to their calling. He himself is a very good example of how teachers of Christian doctrine should approach their work; he does not confine himself to expounding the truths of faith: the first step he takes is to pray for his work to be fruitful. St Augustine observes that anyone who wants to teach the word of God "tries as far as possible to make his words understandable, pleasing and persuasive. But he should be convinced that if he is to obtain a good result it will be due more to the piety of his prayers than to his gifts of speech. And so, praying for those he is to address, he should be more a supplicant than a speaker. When the time comes for him to speak, before actually doing so he should raise his parched soul to God that he may utter only what he has himself eaten and drunk" (*Christian Instruction,* 4, 15).

The Apostle asks God to make the Thessalonians "worthy of his call", that their efforts should have the support of divine grace, for no supernatural action can be planned, begun or brought to a conclusion without the grace of God (cf. Boniface II, *Per filium nostrum, Dz-Sch,* 399). Hence the liturgical prayer: "Lord, be the beginning and end of all that we do and say. Prompt our actions with your grace, and complete them with your all-powerful help" (*Liturgy of the Hours,* morning prayer, Monday Week 1).

resolve and work of faith by his power, [12]so that the name of our Lord Jesus may be glorified in you, and you in him, according to the grace of our God and the Lord Jesus Christ.

Is 66:5; 24:15
Jn 17:10
2 Thess 2:14

# 2

### The coming of the Lord

[1]Now concerning the coming of our Lord Jesus Christ and our assembling to meet him, we beg you, brethren, [2]not to

1 Thess 4:13-17
2 Thess 3:17

dignetur vos vocatione sua Deus noster et impleat omnem voluntatem bonitatis et opus fidei in virtute, [12]ut glorificetur nomen Domini nostri Iesu Christi in vobis, et vos in illo, secundum gratiam Dei nostri et Domini Iesu Christi.

[1]Rogamus autem vos, fratres, circa adventum Domini nostri Iesu Christi et nostram congregationem in ipsum, [2]ut non cito moveamini a sensu neque

**12.** The Greek formula here translated as "according to the grace of our God and the Lord Jesus Christ" could also be interpreted as "according to the grace of our God and Lord Jesus Christ"—in which case we would have here a confession of christological faith which would be of enormous value on account of its antiquity. It would be an acknowledgment of Christ being both God (*Theos*) and Lord (*Kyrios*), that is, *Iesus Christus, Dominus et Deus noster*. However, the expression "our God" often appears in Pauline writings (cf., in this very chapter, vv. 2 and 11); he also frequently uses the formula "Lord Jesus Christ". This suggests that there is a distinction between "our God" and "the Lord Jesus Christ" (or even "our Lord Jesus Christ"); hence the preferred translation.

**1-2.** The main theme of the letter is given here—the timing of the second coming of the Lord. Some people had been unsettling the minds of the Thessalonians by saying that the Parousia was about to happen.

The phrase "by spirit" is a reference to people claiming to have a charismatic gift of prophecy from the Holy Spirit who were spreading their own ideas as if they came from God. Others preferred to pass off what they had to say as coming from St Paul (orally or in writing).

Those who try to mislead the people of God by teachings contrary to Christian faith often use methods of the same sort. By twisting the meaning of Sacred Scripture (cf. Mt 4:6) they not infrequently promote wrong teaching as if it were a revelation from the Holy Spirit. The Second Vatican Council has reminded us how to identify subjective interpretation of that kind: "The task of giving an authentic interpretation, whether in its written form or in the form of Tradition, has been entrusted to the living teaching office of the Church alone. Its authority is exercised in the name of Jesus Christ" (*Dei Verbum*, 10).

1 Tim 4:1
Jn 17:12
1 Jn 2:18
Rev 13:1-8

Dan 11:36
Ezek 28:2

be quickly shaken in mind or excited, either by spirit or by word, or by letter purporting to be from us, to the effect that the day of the Lord has come. [3]Let no one deceive you in any way; for that day will not come, unless the rebellion comes first, and the man of lawlessness[a] is revealed, the son of perdition, [4]who opposes and exalts himself against every

---

terreamini, neque per spiritum neque per verbum neque per epistulam tamquam per nos, quasi instet dies Domini. [3]Ne quis vos seducat ullo modo; quoniam nisi venerit discessio primum, et revelatus fuerit homo iniquitatis, filius perditionis, [4]qui adversatur et extollitur supra omne, quod dicitur Deus aut quod

Even in our own day there are sects and impressionable people who put a lot of effort into working out when the second coming will take place, sometimes making specific predictions which the passage of time disproves. They are missing the main point, which is that we should be always on the watch, always ready joyfully to meet the Lord.

"To the effect that the day of the Lord has come": this is literally what the Greek says—or "as if the day of the Lord is here", in the sense of "about to come any minute now". The New Vulgate [and the Navarre Spanish: trs.] translate it as "as if the day of the Lord were imminent", which is faithful to the tenor of the text and reads more clearly.

**3-4.** Our Lord's second coming is not imminent, for two things must happen first—the "rebellion" and the advent of the "man of lawlessness". It is extremely difficult to make any definite predictions as to the nature of these events because the Apostle says very little about them—and nothing to indicate *when* they may occur.

The "rebellion" or apostasy seems to suggest that a massive flight from God, affecting a substantial part of the world's population, will signal that time is coming to an end. When speaking about the fall of Jerusalem and the destruction of the temple (events prefiguring what would happen at the end of the world) Jesus himself predicted (cf. Mt 24:11-13) that this would happen. He said that most people's love would grow cold (cf. Mt 24:12), to such an extent that they would lose all knowledge of God; when their rebellion had run its course, the End would come and the general judgment would take place.

"The man of lawlessness": it is not clear whether this refers to a particular individual, someone uniquely evil, or whether it is a literary device indicating a multitude of people given over to sin and actively hostile to Christ's work in the world. It is more likely to refer to all the forces of evil taken together as a tool used by Satan to pursue his ends. "Man of lawlessness" and "son of perdition" are Semitic expressions indicating that these people have a particularly close connexion with sin and with eternal perdition.

The "man of lawlessness" is a declared enemy of God who is systematically

[a]Other ancient authorities read *sin*

so-called god or object of worship, so that he takes his seat in the temple of God, proclaiming himself to be God. 5Do you not remember that when I was still with you I told you this? 6And you know what is restraining him now so that he may be revealed in his time. 7For the mystery of lawlessness is already at work; only he who now restrains it

colitur, ita ut in templo Dei sedeat, ostendens se quia sit Deus. 5Non retinetis quod, cum adhuc essem apud vos, haec dicebam vobis? 6Et nunc quid detineat scitis, ut ipse reveletur in suo tempore. 7Nam mysterium iam operatur ini-

hostile to everything to do with the service of God. The Apostle stresses that he is so brazen that "he takes his seat in the temple of God", that is, insists on divine honours. He will go to great lengths to induce people to rebel against God before the end of the world, just as false prophets tried to lead people astray prior to the fall of Jerusalem (cf. Mt 24:4-5, 11, 23-24).

The description of this adversary of God is very like that of the "antichrist" whom St John speaks of (cf. 1 Jn 2:18 and note on same).

5. In the midst of these teachings about the signs of the Parousia comes this informal remark serving to remind us that the Apostle's ministry was by no means confined to writing: this present letter and the other texts in the New Testament were preceded by oral instruction or catechesis (cf. note on 1 Thess 2:13). "I told you this": the Greek verb is in the imperfect indicative, suggesting extensive oral preaching over a period of time.

After initial evangelization St Paul continues to attend to the Christian instruction of the believers. St John Chrysostom says that this makes him a good model for those responsible for the pastoral care of souls: "When a labourer casts the seed into the ground his work does not end there; he has to cover the seed because otherwise the birds will take it. The same is true of the pastors of the Church. If they do not keep on preaching, thereby supporting what they taught the first time round, do they not run the risk of having preached in vain? The devil will waste no time in spoiling the first sowing, the sun will dry it up, the rain will wash it away, the thorns will smother it; our cold indifference can lead to its disruption and ruin. So, then, it is not enough for the farmer to sow the seed and go back home; he has to spend time looking after it" (*Hom. on 2 Thess, ad loc.*).

6-7. Although it is not altogether clear what St Paul means here (commentators ancient and modern have offered all kinds of interpretations), the general thrust of his remarks seems clear enough: he is exhorting people to persevere in doing good, because that is the best way to avoid doing evil (evil being the "mystery of lawlessness"). However, it is difficult to say precisely what this mystery of lawlessness consists in or who is restraining it.

Some commentators think that the mystery of lawlessness is the activity of

will do so until he is out of the way. ⁸And then the lawless one will be revealed, and the Lord Jesus will slay him with the breath of his mouth and destroy him by his appearing and his coming. ⁹The coming of the lawless one by the

---

quitatis; tantum qui tenet nunc, donec de medio fiat. ⁸Et tunc revelabitur ille *iniquus*, quem Dominus Iesus *interficiet spiritu oris sui* et destruet illustratione adventus sui, ⁹eum, cuius est adventus secundum operationem Satanae in omni

---

the man of lawlessness (cf. v. 2), which is being restrained by the rigid laws enforced by the Roman Empire. Others suggest that St Michael is the one who is holding lawlessness back; they base this view on certain scriptural texts (Dan 12:1; Rev 12:7-9; 20:1-3, 7) which show him combating Satan, restraining him or letting him free, depending on what God wanted. Finally, others think that the curb on the man of lawlessness is the active presence of Christians in the world, who through word and example bring Christ's teaching and grace to many. If Christians let their zeal grow cold (this interpretation says), then the curb on evil will cease to apply and the rebellion will ensue.

Another interpretation which currently has a following takes the "mystery of lawlessness" in a very general sense and says that what is being restrained and is still to be revealed is not the activity of the man of lawlessness but the second coming of Christ; what is preventing the Parousia happening is the fact that rebellion has not yet become rife, and the man of lawlessness has not yet appeared. Basically what the Apostle is saying is that the Parousia is not imminent because certain significant events have to happen before it does.

**8-12.** Even though the man of lawlessness will seem to have gained control, that will not be the case: when Jesus reveals himself in all his might and majesty at the Parousia, he will destroy him.

In the meantime, Satan is striving to sow confusion to bring about man's damnation. Each individual has to choose between "love of the truth" offered by Christ and the "pretended signs and wonders" of the lawless one. Countering the devil's deceptions, the text stresses that saving truth is to be found in Christ and should be readily accepted. In this connexion St John of Avila says, "If you realize how much the truth we believe in can help us serve God and attain salvation, you will see also that it is gravely wrong not to love this truth and obey its teaching" (*Audi, filia*, 48).

Everyone, therefore, has a grave duty to try to discover the truth and to follow it. As Leo XIII teaches, "he who, through malice, resists the truth and turns away from it, sins most gravely against the Holy Spirit, because he is the very Spirit of Truth. In our day, this sin has become so frequent that those most evil times, foretold by St Paul, would seem to have arrived. Men, then, blinded by the just judgment of God, will hold falsehood as truth, and will believe in the 'prince of the world', who is a liar and the father of lies, as being the teacher of truth" (*Divinum illud munus*, 14).

activity of Satan will be with all power and with pretended
signs and wonders, [10]and with all wicked deception for
those who are to perish, because they refused to love the
truth and so be saved. [11]Therefore God sends upon them a
strong delusion, to make them believe what is false, [12]so
that all may be condemned who did not believe the truth
but had pleasure in unrighteousness.

Jn 8:44
2 Tim 4:4
Rom 1:25
Is 6:10

Rom 1:32
Jn 3:19

### The need for steadfastness

[13]But we are bound to give thanks to God always for you,
brethren beloved by the Lord, because God chose you from
the beginning[b] to be saved, through sanctification by the
Spirit[c] and belief in the truth. [14]To this he called you through

1 Thess 1:4; 5:9

1 Thess 4:7

virtute et signis et prodigiis mendacibus [10]et in omni seductione iniquitatis his,
qui pereunt, eo quod caritatem veritatis non receperunt, ut salvi fierent. [11]Et
ideo mittit illis Deus operationem erroris, ut credant mendacio, [12]ut iudicentur
omnes, qui non crediderunt veritati, sed consenserunt iniquitati. [13]Nos autem
debemus gratias agere Deo semper pro vobis, fratres, dilecti a Domino, quod
elegerit vos Deus primitias in salutem, in sanctificatione Spiritus et fide
veritatis: [14]ad quod et vocavit vos per evangelium nostrum in acquisitionem

God sends "a strong delusion" upon those who act rebelliously. Quite often
this type of expression is used in the Bible attributing to God things which he
simply *permits*. God wants everyone to be saved and never encourages anyone
to do evil; however, out of respect for man's freedom, he does allow people
who persist in evildoing to damn themselves. See the note on Rom 1:24-32.

**13-14.** Although there may be some people who refuse to accept the truth,
the Apostle feels moved to thank God for his readers' "sanctification by the
Spirit" and their "belief in the truth". This will bring them to salvation. The
brethren too should thank God for choosing them, for their election shows that
they are "beloved by the Lord". (On the meaning of the expression "beloved
by God", see the note on 1 Thess 1:4.)

The mention of the three divine Persons reminds us that salvation is the joint
work of the Blessed Trinity: *God the Father* chooses the person to obtain the
glory of our Lord *Jesus Christ* through the sanctifying action of the *Spirit*. Man,
who is submerged in sin and unable to free himself by his own efforts, is offered,
by the entire Trinity, the means to attain faith, salvation and sanctification:
"There was no power great enough to raise us and free us from such a
catastrophic and eternal death. But God, the Creator of the human race, who is
infinitely merciful, did this through his only-begotten Son. By his kindness,
man was not only restored to the position and nobility whence he had fallen,

[b]Other ancient authorities read *as the first converts*
[c]Or *of spirit*

2 Thess 3:6
1 Cor 11:2

our gospel, so that you may obtain the glory of our Lord Jesus Christ. [15]So then, brethren, stand firm and hold to the traditions which you were taught by us, either by word of mouth or by letter.

gloriae Domini nostri Iesu Christi. [15]Itaque, fratres, state et tenete traditiones, quas didicistis sive per sermonem sive per epistulam nostram. [16]Ipse autem

but was adorned with even richer gifts. No one can express the greatness of this work of divine grace in the souls of men. Because of it, men, both in Sacred Scripture and in the writings of the Fathers of the Church, are described as being reborn, new creatures, sharers in the divine nature, sons of God, deified" (*Divinum illud munus*, 9).

For the fifth time in these two short letters to the Thessalonians we find the verb "to give thanks" (cf. 1 Thess 1:2; 2:13; 5:18; 2 Thess 1:3 and 2:13). It is good to realize that in these two earliest New Testament texts there is evidence of frequent, spontaneous thanks to God for his fatherly kindness. It is not a matter of a minion thanking his master for benefits received; rather it is an expression of filial, heartfelt, joyful gratitude (cf. Jn 11:41).

"From the beginning": as the RSV note says, "other ancient authorities read *as the first converts*", that is, as the first fruits—probably a reference to the fact that the church at Thessalonica was one of the first churches founded by St Paul in Europe.

**15.** To avoid being led astray by unsound or unreliable teaching the thing to do is to hold fast to the faith one received and to apostolic tradition.

"Traditions": this term (cf. also 2 Thess 3:6) seems to refer to the Christian teaching St Paul himself received and which he preached to them. Elsewhere the Apostle uses a term with a more specific meaning, the *paratheke* ("deposit") of teachings concerning the Christian faith (cf. 1 Tim 6:20 and 2 Tim 1:14 and notes on same). He makes the point a number of times (cf. 1 Cor 11:23; 15:1-3) that he was not preaching his personal opinions but rather passing on truths given him as revealed doctrine. That is why he cannot allow his message to be tampered with.

"It is obvious", St Thomas Aquinas observes, "that many things which are not written down in the Church were taught by the Apostles and therefore should be followed" (*Commentary on 2 Thess, ad loc.*). Thus, the truth revealed by God is passed on through Sacred Scripture and Sacred Tradition. The Second Vatican Council teaches that both "are bound closely together, and communicate one with the other. For both of them, flowing out from the same divine well-spring, come together in some fashion to form one thing, and move towards the same goal [. . .]. Tradition transmits in its entirety the Word of God which has been entrusted to the apostles by Christ the Lord and the Holy Spirit. It transmits it to the successors of the apostles so that, enlightened by the Spirit of truth, they may faithfully preserve, expound and spread it abroad by their preaching. Thus it comes about that the Church does not draw her certainty

<sup>16</sup>Now may our Lord Jesus Christ himself, and God our 1 Thess 3:11-13<br>Rom 5:2 Father, who loved us and gave us eternal comfort and good hope through grace, <sup>17</sup>comfort your hearts and establish them in every good work and word.

---

Dominus noster Iesus Christus et Deus Pater noster, qui dilexit nos et dedit consolationem aeternam et spem bonam in gratia, <sup>17</sup>consoletur corda vestra et confirmet in omni opere et sermone bono.

---

about all revealed truths from the Sacred Scriptures alone. Hence, both Scripture and Tradition must be accepted and honoured with equal feelings of devotion and reverence" (*Dei Verbum*, 9).

**16-17.** God chose believers without any merit on their part; that choice marks the first stage in their path to salvation; the journey to the goal of salvation involves cooperation between God's grace and man's freedom. Man needs the help of that "good hope" which comes from recognizing that he is a son of God. "In my case, and I wish the same to happen to you", Monsignor Escrivá writes, "the certainty I derive from feeling—from knowing—that I am a son of God fills me with real hope which, being a supernatural virtue, adapts to our nature when it is infused in us, and so is also a very human virtue [. . .]. This conviction spurs me on to grasp that only those things that bear the imprint of God can display the indelible sign of eternity and have lasting value. Therefore, far from separating me from the things of this earth, hope draws me closer to these realities in a new way, a Christian way, which seeks to discover in everything the relation between our fallen nature and God, our Creator and Redeemer" (*Friends of God*, 208).

By inspiring us with hope, God fills our hearts with consolation and at the same time encourages us to put our faith into practice in daily life—"in every good work and word."

# 3

## PART TWO

## A CALL TO VIRTUE

**Paul asks for prayers**

Col 4:3
1 Thess 5:25

Rom 15:21
Rom 10:16

[1]Finally, brethren, pray for us, that the word of the Lord may speed on and triumph, as it did among you, [2]and that we may be delivered from wicked and evil men; for not all

---

[1]De cetero, fratres, orate pro nobis, ut sermo Domini currat et glorificetur sicut et apud vos, [2]et ut liberemur ab importunis et malis hominibus; non enim omnium est fides. [3]Fidelis autem Dominus est, qui confirmabit vos et custodiet

---

**1.** The whole Church, not just the Apostles, is given the task of spreading the message of Jesus. All believers can and should play an active part in this, at least by way of prayer. The Apostle's request for prayers also shows that he realizes that the supernatural work entrusted to him is beyond him and yet he does not shirk the work of apostolate. St John Chrysostom comments on St Paul's approach: "The Apostle [. . .] now encourages them to offer prayers to God for him, but he does not ask them to pray God to free him from dangers he ought to face up to (for they are an unavoidable consequence of his ministry); rather, he asks them to pray 'that the word of the Lord may speed on and triumph'" (*Hom. on 2 Thess, ad loc.*).

The "speed and triumph" is evocative of the Games, which had such a following in Greece: the winner of a race was given a victory wreath. The victory, the triumph, of the word of the Lord is its proclamation reaching everyone and being accepted by everyone.

**2.** "Not all have faith": literally, "faith is not something that belongs to all", that is, not everyone has believed the Apostle's preaching though he has excluded no one from it. The "wicked and evil men" may be a reference to certain Jews hostile to Christianity who had persecuted Paul in Macedonia and were now putting obstacles in his way at Corinth.

It must be remembered that faith is a supernatural virtue, a gift from God, and cannot be obtained by man's unaided effort: "Even though the assent of faith is by no means a blind impulse, still, no one can assent to the gospel preaching as he must in order to be saved without the enlightenment and inspiration of the Holy Spirit, who gives all men their joy in assenting to and believing the truth" (Vatican I, *Dei Filius*, chap. 3).

God "desires all men to be saved and to come to the knowledge of the truth" (1 Tim 2:4) and so to all men he gives his grace and offers the gift of faith; however, they are free to reject or accept the light he offers them.

74

have faith. ³But the Lord is faithful; he will strengthen you
and guard you from evil.ᵈ ⁴And we have confidence in the
Lord about you, that you are doing and will do the things
which we command. ⁵May the Lord direct your hearts to
the love of God and to the steadfastness of Christ.

1 Thess 5:24<br>1 Cor 10:13<br><br>2 Cor 7:16<br>1 Thess 4:2, 10

**Avoiding idleness. Earning one's living**

⁶Now we command you, brethren, in the name of our

Rom 16:17<br>1 Thess 5:14<br>1 Thess 4:1

a malo. ⁴Confidimus autem de vobis in Domino, quoniam, quae praecipimus,
et facitis et facietis. ⁵Dominus autem dirigat corda vestra in caritatem Dei et
patientiam Christi. ⁶Praecipimus autem vobis, fratres, in nomine Domini nostri

**3.** "But the Lord is faithful": and therefore, unlike those who are unfaithful
(v. 2), we should put our trust in God: "Do not doubt it", Chrysostom comments,
"God is faithful. He has promised salvation, he will save you. But, as he said,
he will do so on one condition—that we love him, that we listen to his word
and his Law. He will not save us unless we cooperate" (*Hom. on 2 Thess, ad
loc.*).

"He will strengthen you and guard you from evil": These words may be
meant to echo the prayer contained in the Our Father (cf. Mt 6:13; cf. Mt 5:37).

**4-5.** The Apostle is confident that the Thessalonians will stay true to Christ,
and he asks God to give them the endurance they need in the midst of their
difficulties. "The steadfastness of Christ" may be a reference to the example
Christ gave during his passion by enduring unto death on the cross, out of love
for the Father and for us; believers should love God in that kind of way (cf. Heb
12:1). However, "the steadfastness of Christ" can also be interpreted as referring to the need for Christians to be patient as they wait for the second coming
of Christ (cf. 1 Thess 1:3).

Love and steadfastness are two Christian virtues which make us resemble
God: "Therefore be imitators of God, as beloved children. And walk in love,
as Christ loved us and gave himself up for us, a fragrant offering and sacrifice
to God" (Eph 5:1-2). So, love and endurance are interconnected and com-
plement each other: "Jesus came to the Cross after having prepared himself for
thirty-three years, all his life! If they really want to imitate him, his disciples
have to turn their lives into a co-redemption of Love, by means of active and
passive self-denial" (J. Escrivá, *Furrow*, 255).

**6.** St Paul wants to prevent the misconduct of some Christians spreading to
others; and at the same time he wants to help the transgressors to turn
back—which they may do if they are made to feel isolated. Excessive tolerance
of irregular behaviour does nothing to encourage reform and only helps the
spread of permissiveness.

ᵈOr *the evil one*

1 Thess 2:9

Mt 10:10
Phil 3:17

1 Thess 4:11

Lord Jesus Christ, that you keep away from any brother who is living in idleness and not in accord with the tradition that you received from us. [7]For you yourselves know how you ought to imitate us; we were not idle when we were with you, [8]we did not eat any one's bread without paying, but with toil and labour we worked night and day, that we might not burden any of you. [9]It was not because we have not that right, but to give you in our conduct an example to imitate. [10]For even when we were with you, we gave you this command: If any one will not work, let him not eat. [11]For we hear that some of you are living in idleness, mere

Iesu Christi, ut subtrahatis vos ab omni fratre ambulante inordinate et non secundum traditionem, quam acceperunt a nobis. [7]Ipsi enim scitis quemadmodum oporteat imitari nos, quoniam non inordinati fuimus inter vos, [8]neque gratis panem manducavimus ab aliquo sed in labore et fatigatione, nocte et die operantes, ne quem vestrum gravaremus; [9]non quasi non habuerimus potestatem, sed ut nosmetipsos formam daremus vobis ad imitandum nos. [10]Nam et cum essemus apud vos, hoc praecipiebamus vobis: Si quis non vult operari, nec manducet. [11]Audimus enim inter vos quosdam ambulare inordinate, nihil

That was the Apostle's usual policy: "I wrote to you in my letter not to associate with immoral men; not at all meaning the immoral of this world, or the greedy and robbers, or idolaters, since then you would need to go out of the world. But rather I wrote to you not to associate with any one who bears the name of brother if he is guilty of immorality or greed, or is an idolater, reviler, drunkard, or robber" (1 Cor 5:10-11).

**7-12.** Some of the Thessalonians, wrongly thinking that the Parousia was about to happen, had given up working and were living in idleness, minding everyone's business but their own. So the Apostle reminds them all that when he was among them he worked to keep himself and was a burden on no one.

The Second Vatican Council underlines the value of work when it exhorts "Christians, as citizens of both cities, to perform their duties faithfully in the spirit of the Gospel." Far from neglecting earthly responsibilities, they should, the Council goes on, realize that by their faith they "are bound all the more to fulfil these responsibilities according to the vocation of each one (cf. 2 Thess 3:6-13; Eph 4:28)" (*Gaudium et spes*, 43).

"For the love of God, for the love of souls, and to live up to our Christian vocation, we must give good example. So as not to give scandal, or to provoke even the faintest suspicion that the children of God are soft and useless, so as not to disedify . . . , you must strive to show an example of balanced justice, to behave properly as responsible people. The farmer who ploughs his field while constantly raising his heart to God, just as much as the carpenter, the blacksmith, the office worker, the academic—all Christians in fact—have to be an

busybodies, not doing any work. [12]Now such persons we
command and exhort in the Lord Jesus Christ to do their
work in quietness and to earn their own living. [13]Brethren,
do not be weary in well-doing.
[14]If any one refuses to obey what we say in this letter,
note that man, and have nothing to do with him, that he may
be ashamed. [15]Do not look on him as an enemy, but warn
him as a brother.

Gen 3:19

Gal 6:9

1 Cor 5:9, 11
2 Thess 3:6

1 Thess 5:14

---

operantes sed curiose agentes; [12]his autem, qui eiusmodi sunt, praecipimus et
obsecramus in Domino Iesu Christo, ut cum quiete operantes suum panem
manducent. [13]Vos autem, fratres, nolite deficere benefacientes. [14]Quod si quis
non oboedit verbo nostro per epistulam, hunc notate, non commisceamini cum
illo, ut confundatur; [15]et nolite quasi inimicum existimare, sed corripite ut

---

example for their colleagues at work, and to be humble about it. Therefore,
everyone, in his job, in whatever place he has in society, must feel obliged to
make his work God's work, sowing everywhere the peace and joy of the Lord"
(J. Escrivá, *Friends of God*, 70).

**13.** Our Lord told us that "he who endures to the end will be saved" (Mt
10:22). He also said that "No one who puts his hand to the plough and looks
back is fit for the kingdom of God" (Lk 9:62). He was obviously very conscious
of man's fickleness and inconstancy. We need to be persistent and dogged, and
to keep on trying to do things well right up to the end, for only he who is faithful
right up to death will be given the crown of life (cf. Rev 2:10).
John Paul II warns us that "fidelity always has to undergo the real test, that
of endurance [. . .]. It is easy to live consistent (with one's beliefs) for a day or
a few days [. . .]. But only a consistency which lasts right through life deserves
the name 'fidelity'" (*Address in Mexico City Cathedral*, 26 January 1979).

**14-15.** St Paul is outspoken: a person in authority in the Church has the
Christ-given mission (cf. 2 Thess 3:6) to try to see that no one harms others by
bad example. Disobedience should be pointed out and reprimanded; if that is
done, people are less likely to be confused or led astray. A person's persistent
misconduct should lead one to avoid him until he mends his ways; otherwise,
one could scandalize others. However, that does not mean that one should not
do everything possible to persuade the wrongdoer to turn over a new leaf.
When the Church, as is sometimes the case, imposes canonical sanctions on
a person, it does so out of charity—charity towards others (keeping them away
from danger) and charity towards the guilty party (because sanctions are
designed to help him repent, rather than as a punishment). Any correction
should be essentially fraternal.

**Prayer and farewell wishes**

1 Thess 5:23
Jn 14:27
Rom 15:33
2 Thess 2:2
1 Cor 16:21
Gal 6:11
Rom 16:20
1 Thess 5:28

[16]Now may the Lord of peace himself give you peace at all times in all ways. The Lord be with you all.
[17]I, Paul, write this greeting with my own hand. This is the mark in every letter of mine; it is the way I write. [18]The grace of our Lord Jesus Christ be with you all.

---

fratrem. [16]Ipse autem Dominus pacis det vobis pacem sempiternam in omni modo. Dominus cum omnibus vobis. [17]Salutatio mea manu Pauli, quod est signum in omni epistula, ita scribo. [18]Gratia Domini nostri Iesu Christi cum omnibus vobis.

---

**16.** "The Lord of peace", or "the God of peace", is a title found in a number of St Paul's letters (cf. Rom 15:33; 2 Cor 13:11; Phil 4:9; 1 Thess 5:23), because Redemption, by wiping out sin, establishes people's friendship with God and with one another. The wish expressed by the Apostle here echoes the greeting Christians normally used with one another, a greeting our Lord himself recommended: "Whatever house you enter, first say, 'Peace be to this house'" (Lk 10:5). The Jews used and continue to use the same greeting—*Shalom* (= peace). When a Christian greets someone in this way it should be a sincere expression of his love of God and love of others and not just mere polite well-wishing, hoping people will "enjoy themselves".

Referring to empty, selfish peace of that sort, our Lord said that he had come to bring not peace but a sword (cf. Mt 10:34). He also warned us that the peace he gives us is not peace of the type the world gives (cf. Jn 14:27), but a peace which comes from the Holy Spirit (cf. Gal 5:22) and which "passes all understanding" (Phil 4:7). "It is useless to call for exterior calm if there is no calm in men's consciences, in the centre of their souls" (J. Escrivá, *Christ is passing by*, 73).

We should therefore always be "eager to maintain the unity of the Spirit in the bond of peace" (Eph 4:3). If we are, we will be builders of peace and will receive the reward Christ promised when he proclaimed, "Blessed are the peacemakers, for they shall be called sons of God" (Mt 5:9). In this connexion John Paul II has said, "Peace is work we have to do; it calls for commitment and solidarity with one another. But it is also (inseparably and above all) something in God's gift: we need to pray for it" (*Address*, 8 December 1978).

**17.** In ancient times letters were usually dictated to an amanuensis or secretary, and therefore St Paul followed that custom (cf. Rom 16:22). Often the sender would add a few words at the end in his own handwriting, out of good manners and to vouch for the document; the Apostle sometimes did so (cf. 1 Cor 16:21; Gal 6:11; Col 4:18).

# Introduction to the Pastoral Epistles

The two Epistles to Timothy and the Epistle to Titus are usually described as the "Pastoral Epistles". This name, which began to be used in the early eighteenth century, has to do with their content and the original addressees: they were sent to two of the Apostle's co-workers in charge of local churches (Timothy at Ephesus and Titus at Crete). Their whole thrust is pastoral because they largely consist of rules and advice on the best way to govern those communities and prevent their being led astray by false teachers. They also contain directives on how churches should be organized and on the role of sacred ministers. The three letters are all written in the same simple, friendly style and are very much concerned with the formation of people who have a pastoral mission.

## CANONICITY AND AUTHENTICITY

The Church has never been in any doubt about the fact that these three letters are inspired. The Council of Trent included them in its list or canon of sacred books written under the inspiration of the Holy Spirit.

From the very beginning Christian tradition has regarded them as letters written by St Paul; this is confirmed by very early testimonies: it is probable that 2 Peter 3:15 is a quotation from 1 Timothy 1:16; and by the start of the second century the three letters were known to and quoted by St Clement of Rome, St Polycarp and St Ignatius of Antioch. The Muratorian Fragment (c. A.D. 180) explicitly mentions them, as do St Irenaeus and Tertullian. The Church historian Eusebius includes them among the writings "accepted by all" (*homologoumena*).

In the nineteenth century some liberal Protestants argued against Pauline authorship; others were ready to accept that the letters contain many parts written by St Paul and later edited together with a lot of touching up. Early in the present century the Pontifical Biblical Commission pronounced that there were insufficient grounds for saying that St Paul was not the author.[1]

Today, although there are some scholars who doubt the letters' Pauline authenticity, many others meet the objections they raise. The main objections have to do with: 1) the fact that the language and style is different from the rest of the Pauline corpus; 2) the different kind of content—practical or moral as distinct from theological; 3) the Church organization reflected in the letters,

1. *Reply*, 12 June 1913; cf. *EB*, 412-415.

and the errors they refer to, suggest the second rather than the first century; and even 4) the difficulty of working out when the Apostle could have written them. However, when the question is studied carefully there are not really all that many differences in terminology or doctrine, and there are many more ways in which these and the other letters coincide. Also, one needs to bear in mind the circumstances in which these letters were written: given that St Paul was older when he wrote them, it is easy to explain why the style is less vigorous than that of the Great Epistles; and, since he was writing in a Hellenist environment, he naturally brings in new terms. Also, one needs to remember that as elsewhere the Apostle may have used an amanuensis or secretary who took the Apostle's ideas and wrote the letter in his own words. As far as the content is concerned, the purpose of the Pastoral Epistles is to give Timothy and Titus advice on how to manage the churches entrusted to their care, so one would expect him to give more attention to specific details and to take as read the major themes explored in other letters.

The errors tackled in these letters are not organized heretical movements but simply heterodox tendencies influenced by Gnosticism or certain rabbinical schools, interlaced with "myths and endless genealogies" (1 Tim 1:4; cf. 4:7; Tit 3:9), or hidebound by legalism (cf. Tit 3:9; 1 Tim 1:7-11). As far as the organizational structure of the Church is concerned, it does not yet have the form reflected later on in the letters of St Ignatius of Antioch (second century); in the Pastoral Epistles the terms "bishop" and "elder" (priest) do not yet refer to ministers with distinct functions.

As regards dating, the most likely dates are the year 65 for 1 Timothy and Titus and the year 67 for 2 Timothy. It would appear that once St Paul was released from his first Roman imprisonment (cf. Acts 28:30-31), he made a number of journeys. He may have gone to Spain and he also returned to the Middle East. He passed through Ephesus, leaving Timothy in charge of that community, and visited Crete and put Titus in charge there. Then he made his way to Macedonia, from where he sent each of these disciples a letter giving them guidelines for their ministry; this would have been near the end of the year 65. Soon after that he was arrested again and taken to Rome; this second imprisonment ended with his martyrdom, which definitely occurred in the year 67. The Second Letter to Timothy must have been written shortly before his death.

Finally, it should be pointed out that the teaching contained in these letters is closely connected with that in the rest of the Pauline corpus. Even if they were not written by St Paul, that would not affect the permanent value of their content, for the fact that they are inspired is not in doubt. Pauline authorship does add to their interest because it shows that the hierarchy of Church ministers had begun to take shape in the lifetime of the Apostle.

DOCTRINE

The basic idea in the Pastoral Epistles and therefore the one most in evidence is that of salvation: God is referrred to as the "Saviour" (1 Tim 1:1; 2:3; 4:10; Tit 1:3; 2:10; 3:4), who in his infinite love "desires all men to be saved and to come to the knowledge of the truth" (1 Tim 2:4). This divine plan was revealed and put into effect by Jesus Christ, the only Mediator (1 Tim 2:5), who "came into the world to save sinners" (1 Tim 1:15; cf. 1 Tim 2:5-6); the Church extends and applies the saving action of Christ, constituting as it does the people redeemed from iniquity and purified by sacrifice (cf. Tit 2:14); Christians attain their personal salvation through a life rich in good deeds (cf. Tit 3:14) which are an expression of their love of God. In other words, the Pastoral Letters have to do with Jesus Christ, the Church and everyday Christian living.

1. *Jesus Christ* Although St Paul is not giving a formal exposition of Christology, the letters do contain some very memorable expressions (many of them taken from liturgical hymns) which show his profound understanding of Jesus and his salvific work.

Linking up with other Pauline writings where "the mystery" refers to God's plan of salvation put into effect by Christ (cf. Rom 16:25; Col 1:26; Eph 1:9; 3:3-5), these letters make mention of the "mystery of the faith" and the "mystery of our religion" (1 Tim 3:9, 16) when speaking of our Saviour. Paul stresses that there is only "one mediator between God and men, the man Christ Jesus, who gave himself as a ransom for all" (1 Tim 2:5-6); here and elsewhere Christ's human nature and incarnation are underlined (cf. 2 Tim 1:10; Tit 2:11; 3:4); but his divinity is also explicitly acknowledged, for he is described as "our great God and Saviour" (Tit 2:13; cf. 1 Tim 1:2, 12; 6:3, 14; 2 Tim 1:2, 8). Christ, therefore, being God and man, unites all men to God.

Christ's entire life is one of mediation, for he "gave himself for us to redeem us from all iniquity and to purify (us)" (Tit 2:14). In the hymn to the mystery of our religion (1 Tim 3:15-16), redemption is described as the great work of reconciling men to God (cf. notes on 1 Tim 3:15 and 3:16). Furthermore, the salvation which Jesus extends to us does not cease with his ascension into heaven; it continues to be effective in the Church; it is on-going, right up to the end of time when Christ comes in glory. It is important to note that this second coming is described as his "appearing" (manifestation, epiphany: cf. 1 Tim 6:14; 2 Tim 4:1, 8; Tit 2:13), a term which is also applied to the Incarnation (cf. 2 Tim 1:10; Tit 2:11; 3:4). Jesus Christ, therefore, by obtaining salvation for us, is the most sublime expression of the Father's love, and he is this from the moment he appears in the world as man to his final coming when his divinity will shine forth in all its splendour. "Following the Pauline teaching, we can affirm that this same *mystery of God's infinite loving kindness towards us* is capable of penetrating to the hidden roots of our iniquity, in order to evoke in the soul a movement of conversion, in order to redeem it and set it on course towards reconciliation."[2]

2. John Paul II, *Reconciliatio et paenitentia*, 20.

**2. The Church**   Because these letters are addressed in the first instance to people in charge of Christian communities, they naturally contain much about the Church and its structure, although clearly they do not constitute a treatise on ecclesiology.

Linking up with the central idea in the letters (God desires all men to be saved), the Apostle teaches that the Church has been entrusted with the task of carrying out this divine plan. Jesus has established the New Covenant in his blood, making the Church "a people of his own" (Tit 2:14), that is, "a people belonging to him, a people consecrated to him".[3] The Church is the "household of God" (1 Tim 3:15), which means that God acts in and through the Church like a Father in and through his family. The Church, then, is not just a human society in which those who hold office can act as they see fit; it belongs to God and therefore its ministers have duties which they are under an obligation to perform: "I am writing these instructions so that you may know how one ought to behave in the household of God, which is the church of the living God, the pillar and bulwark of the truth" (1 Tim 3:15).

The expression "the pillar and the bulwark of the truth" describes one of the most important characteristics and functions of the Church. It is like a solid building, something strong and stable and enduring; hence St Jerome's teaching: "I am going to tell you a simple, clear conviction of my soul: one must stay within the Church which, founded on the Apostles, has endured down to our own day."[4] The solidity of the Church also points to the fact that it holds *the truth*; this distinguishes it from deceitful teachers, who promote ungodliness and upset the faith of some (cf. 2 Tim 2:17-19). Because the Church is the supporting pillar of the truth, it cannot err in its exposition of revealed truth and, moreover, the "Tradition that comes from the Apostles makes progress in the Church, with the help of the Holy Spirit. There is a growth in insight into the realities and words that are being passed on. This comes about in various ways. It comes through the contemplation and study of believers who ponder these things in their hearts (cf. Lk 2:19 and 51). It comes from the intimate sense of spiritual realities which they experience. And it comes from the preaching of those who have received, along with their right of succession in the episcopate, the sure charism of truth. Thus, as the centuries go by, the Church is always advancing towards the plenitude of divine truth, until eventually the words of God are fulfilled in her."[5]

The Church's ministers, then, have as an essential mission the preaching of the word of God, the instruction of the people. St Paul tells Timothy to give priority to the ministry of the word; he must strive to "convince, rebuke and exhort" (2 Tim 4:2), devote himself to teaching, work hard at evangelization (2 Tim 4:5) and, in liturgical assemblies, attend to the reading of the sacred books, to preaching and teaching (1 Tim 4:13). Candidates for the episcopacy-priesthood must be competent teachers (1 Tim 3:2; 2 Tim 2:24); they must be

3. Cf. St Thomas Aquinas, *Commentary on Tit, ad loc.*
4. *Contra Luciferianos*, 28.
5. Vatican II, *Dei Verbum*, 8.

82

faithful men if they are to pass on intact the doctrine they themselves have received (2 Tim 2:2). Deceitful teachers twist and distort the truth; the ministers of the Church must communicate "sound" doctrine; this adjective, normally applied to physical health and nourishment which promotes good health, is applied to doctrine (Tit 1:9; 2 Tim 4:3), to words (1 Tim 6:3; Tit 2:8; 2 Tim 1:13) and to people "sound in the faith" (Tit 1:13; 2:2).

The Pastoral Epistles contain many warnings against the spread of false doctrine (cf. 1 Tim 1:3-11; 4:1-7; 6:1-11, 20-21; 2 Tim 2:14-21; 3:1-9; 4:3-4; Tit 1:9-16; 3:10-11) and repeatedly stress the need to conserve and pass on intact "what has been entrusted", the deposit of truth (1 Tim 6:20; 2 Tim 1:14): Revelation is like a treasure given to the Church to guard and administer.

The solemn duty of ministers to preach is based on the fact that God wants to lead all men to salvation: salvation, which God promised in remote times and which has come about with the advent of Christ, is extended to all mankind through the preaching of the word entrusted to the Apostles (cf. Tit 1:1-3).

What we can learn from these epistles about *the structure of the Church* is very important because it has to do with the start of "apostolic succession": St Paul authoritatively lists the functions of Timothy and Titus as leaders of the Christian communities of Ephesus and Crete and gives the guidelines to be followed by those who will take over hierarchical responsibilities.

Timothy and Titus, long-standing helpers of St Paul and people he had charged with specific tasks—such as the collection in Corinth (cf. 2 Cor 8:6) or occasional missions in Thessalonica (cf. 1 Thess 3:2) and Corinth (cf. 1 Cor 4:17; 6:10)—now have a more definite and fixed role: they are to take charge of teaching and preaching (cf. 1 Tim 4:13, 2 Tim 2:15; 4:1-5), of the government of the community (cf. 1 Tim 5:19), of Church discipline (cf. 1 Tim 5:1-16; Tit 2:1-10; 3:1-2) and of liturgical matters (cf. 1 Tim 2:1-12). In other words, they have the triple office of teaching, ruling and sanctifying. Moreover, because their mission has to have continuity (and must go on after the Apostle's death: cf. 2 Tim 4:1-8), it is their duty to choose successors—deacons, priests and bishops (cf. 1 Tim 3:1-13; 5:17-22; Tit 1:5-9).

Deacons (1 Tim 3:8-12) are helpers of the bishop and carry out their ministry in subordination to him; they must be of exemplary moral conduct, both publicly and in the intimacy of their own family life (1 Tim 3:8, 9, 12). Before taking up their appointments they should be seen to be suitable (1 Tim 3:10). Their functions are not specified, so it would seem that they could be given a wide range of tasks, as circumstances required. However, they never have the office of presiding or ruling, for they are not required to have the specific qualifications of the bishop, such as that of representing the community before pagans. We do know that the seven disciples picked in Jerusalem (cf. Acts 6:1-7) took part in the administration of resources (Acts 6:2) and in preaching and administration of the sacraments—particularly Stephen and Philip; but there is no evidence that they acted as leaders of any community.

Bishops and elders (priests) are referred to in these letters but the terminology is still ambiguous: the two terms may be used with reference to the same individual(s). When St Paul reminds Titus that he left him in Crete to "appoint elders in every town" (Tit 1:5), he immediately goes on to say that "a bishop ... must be blameless" (Tit 1:7); also when telling Timothy (1 Tim 3:1-13) about the responsibilities of ministers, he moves directly from the bishop to deacons (vv. 8-13), without saying anything about priests; and in 1 Timothy 5:17-19, he speaks about priests and makes no mention of the bishop. However, there are some indications that the term "bishop" applied only to one of the elders or priests, one who had a presiding role, for the bishop is always mentioned in the singular whereas priests (as also deacons) always appear in the plural. It can be said, therefore, that when these letters were written the term "bishop" seems to have a more precise meaning than elsewhere in the New Testament (cf. Acts 20:21; Phil 1:1), but there is as yet no clear distinction between bishop and priest such as is to be found at the start of the second century in the letters of St Ignatius of Antioch,[6] who differentiates them in the manner which has obtained right down to our own time.

To the bishop, and in conjunction with him to the priests, are assigned as proper functions those of teaching, presiding and giving example of good Christian living. As teacher, the bishop should preach and zealously guard the deposit of revealed truth (cf. 1 Tim 6:20-21), refuting error and silencing those who spread it (1 Tim 1:3-5; Tit 1:11); his teaching should be drawn from inspired writings (2 Tim 3:14-15) and the tradition of the Church (2 Tim 1:13-14). The bishop is in charge of the various groups of Christians (the elderly, the young, women, widows, slaves): 1 Tim 5:1-16; Tit 2:1-10; 3:1-2); when the need arises he has authority to act as a judge and must do so without fear or favour (1 Tim 5:19-21). He is responsible for the liturgy and the organization of prayers, intercessions etc. (1 Tim 2:1-12; 4:13); it is for him to decide on which candidates to confer priestly ordination by the laying on of hands (1 Tim 5:22). It is also his duty to ensure that morality is observed, and he himself must be a model of Christian life and holiness (1 Tim 4:12; Tit 2:7-8); the virtues proper to a bishop (cf. 1 Tim 3:1-7; 5:17-19; Tit 1:5-9) show that he has to make every effort to ensure that his life is beyond reproach.

3. *The Christian life* Because these are essentially pastoral letters, they have things to say about Christian living, particularly about the imitation of Christ (the Christian's only model) and the practice of piety.

By bringing about the Redemption, Christ has acquired "a people of his own who are zealous for good deeds" (Tit 2:14); the Christian is called to lead a good life, because Christ has set him free from all evildoing; Baptism and renewal in the Holy Spirit have justified us and destined us to eternal life (Tit 3:5-7). The basis of the Christian life, therefore, is the salvation won by Christ and the moral rules it implies.

God gives us grace which trains us "to renounce irreligion and worldly passions, and to live sober, upright and godly lives in this world" (Tit 2:12).

6. Cf. *Epist. ad Magnesios* 6, 1; *Epist. ad Trallianos* 7, 2; *Epist. ad Philadelphos* 7, 1.

The grace mentioned in this text can be understood in two ways, St Thomas says—as the supreme grace of the Incarnation which is the greatest proof God has given of his love for us (in this sense the Christian life is our response to God's love); or as the gift of Christ's teaching, for prior to his coming "the world was in ignorance and heresy, whereas he trains us in the same way as a man trains his child."[7]

A Christian, therefore, has to apply himself to good deeds because he believes in God (Tit 3:8), because he is conscious of having been redeemed by Christ (Tit 2:14) and because grace gives him the strength to be good.

The "good deeds" so often recommended in these letters are the practice of virtue, especially the virtues of faith (2 Tim 3:15; 1 Tim 1:5) and hope (1 Tim 4:10; Tit 2:13), and particularly works of charity (1 Tim 1:5; 2:15) such as hospitality (1 Tim 5:10) and helping the needy (Tit 3:4) and widows (1 Tim 5:3-16).

If we were to summarize the spirit which should imbue the entire ethical life of the Christian, we would have to do so in one word—*eusebeia, pietas* (godliness or the virtue of religion); this word, which is to be found in the New Testament only in the Second Letter of St Peter (2 Pet 1:3, 6; 3:11) and in the Pastoral Epistles (1 Tim 2:2; 3:16; 4:7, 8; 6:3, 5, 6; 2 Tim 3:5; Tit 1:1), is full of theological meaning. In its more general sense it betokens the intimate, familiar relationship that exists between God and man. It refers particularly to God offering man his love, as the Incarnation plainly shows; St Paul calls that event *"mysterion tes eusebias"*, *pietatis mysterium*, the mystery of our religion (1 Tim 3:16); this truly amazing union of God and human nature, God's manifestation in the flesh, is "great indeed". By the Incarnation God reveals both himself and the truths in which we should believe; and so St Paul exhorts us to know the truth which accords with godliness (Tit 1:1; cf. 2 Pet 1:3) and warns against the dangers of not keeping to "the teaching which accords with godliness" (1 Tim 6:3).

Applied to man, godliness means accepting God's loving initiative and living in accordance with the moral demands that stem from it. Hence the Apostle's exhortation to "train yourself in godliness" (1 Tim 4:7), putting much more effort into attaining the crown of eternal life than an athlete puts into winning perishable laurels (cf. 1 Tim 4:8); godliness is the best business a Christian can undertake (1 Tim 6:6). A person who lives a godly life, who actively wages the good warfare (1 Tim 1:18; 2 Tim 4:7), for such is God's will, must be ready to endure persecution (2 Tim 3:12); godliness is incompatible with a life of comfort; it calls for inner strength which gives serenity (1 Tim 2:2) and leads one to practise virtue (1 Tim 6:11; Tit 2:12). "The piety which is born of divine filiation is a profound attitude of the soul which eventually permeates one's entire existence. It is there in every thought, every desire, every affection. Have you not noticed in families how children, even without realizing it, imitate their parents? They imitate their gestures, their habits; much of their behaviour is the same as that of their parents. Well, the

7. *Commentary on Tit, ad loc.*

85

same kind of thing happens to a good son of God. One finds oneself acquiring—without knowing how, or by what means—a marvellous godliness, which enables us to focus events from the supernatural viewpoint of faith".[8]

8. J. Escrivá, *Friends of God*, 146.

# Introduction to the First Epistle to Timothy

There is a considerable amount of material in St Paul's letters about Timothy, whom the Apostle describes as working with him "as a son with a father" (Phil 2:22). Timothy was the son of a Gentile father and a devout Jewish Christian mother (Acts 16:1). On his way through Lystra during his second missionary journey, St Paul received excellent reports about this young Christian. He had him circumcised and then brought him along to help in the foundation of the churches at Philippi and Thessalonica (Acts 16:12). We know that he was in Beroea shortly after that (Act 17:14) and was later sent by the Apostle from Athens to Thessalonica (1 Thess 3:2). He appears again at the Apostle's side in Corinth (Acts 18:5), and he accompanied him on his third journey, visiting Ephesus (Acts 19:22) and Macedonia (1 Cor 4:17; 16:20; 2 Cor 1:1) and travelling through Asia Minor (Acts 20:4); during the Apostle's first imprisonment Timothy was with him (Col 1:1; Phil 1:1; 2:19); in the Letter to the Hebrews there is a reference to Timothy's "release", but the time and circumstances are not given (Heb 13:23). Finally, during his last journey to the Middle East St Paul put him in charge of the church at Ephesus.

One of the outstanding things about Timothy was his loyalty to St Paul, who put great reliance on him; when Timothy was still a young man we find the Apostle asking the Corinthians to treat him with respect (1 Cor 16:11) and he was still quite young when he was commissioned to preside over the church of Ephesus (1 Tim 4:12; 2 Tim 2:22). There is mention of his having a stomach complaint (1 Tim 5:23) but that does not necessarily mean his health was delicate.

THE CHURCH OF EPHESUS

From the Acts of the Apostles we know that St Paul was in Ephesus around the year 52, at the end of his second missionary journey (Acts 18:19-21), and that at the start of his third journey (around the years 54-57) he spent a further two years in that city (Acts 19:1, 8-10), preaching the Gospel to Jews and Gentiles alike. The Apostle did, however, encounter serious difficulties and eventually had to leave the city after the riot instigated by Demetrius the silversmith (Acts 19:23-40). However, the net result of his work was the establishment of a flourishing Christian community in Ephesus, an important city in Asia Minor.[1]

[1] Cf. "Introduction to the Epistle to the Ephesians" in *The Navarre Bible: Captivity Epistles*, pp. 21-28.

The information that can be drawn from the letter suggests that Ephesus had a fairly well established church but one which was experiencing the difficulties typical of the early stages. The pagan environment in which it lived, the doctrines being spread by certain heterodox teachers and some instances of loose living were threatening the stability of the young church. Like Titus in Crete, Timothy is told to make sure that the correct teaching is adhered to and to encourage the faithful to live good Christian lives. He must keep intact "what has been entrusted to you", the deposit of faith (1 Tim 6:20) and devote himself to instructing the faithful (1 Tim 6:16), convinced that the Church is the pillar and bulwark of truth (1 Tim 3:15); false doctrines are to be vigorously rejected and their promoters refuted (1 Tim 1:3). However, although Timothy has to be sure to exercise his authority, he must also in his personal life be a model for his flock (1 Tim 6:11) and put his trust in divine mercy, for "Christ Jesus came into the world to save sinners" (1 Tim 1:15). The practice of virtue (at which ministers must be exemplary) is the "good warfare, holding faith and a good conscience" (1 Tim 1:18-19).

Timothy is also charged with improving Church administration—making sure that deacons are men of the right calibre (1 Tim 3:10), and not being hasty in conferring holy orders (1 Tim 5:22). The letter specifies the virtues bishops, priests, deacons and widows should have (1 Tim 3:1-7; 3:8-13; 5:9-15). Timothy should impartially investigate any complaints against elders (1 Tim 5:17-25).

CONTENT

The letter deals with four subjects basically, not in any particular order. Firstly, Timothy's duty to defend the truth against false teaching promoting "myths and endless genealogies" (1:3-20). Secondly, the way worship should be regulated—public prayer, preaching, seemly behaviour at liturgical assemblies (2:1-15). Thirdly, the duties of those who hold Church office—and the qualities required in a bishop and in deacons. Finally, pastoral guidelines on how to deal with false teachers (3:1-16), how to act towards different groups of believers (5:1 - 6:2), and how to distinguish good from bad teachers (6:3-19).

# The First Epistle to Timothy

ENGLISH AND LATIN VERSIONS, WITH NOTES

# 1

**Greeting**

¹Paul, an apostle of Christ Jesus by command of God our Saviour and of Christ Jesus our hope, ²To Timothy, my true child in the faith: Grace, mercy, and peace from God the Father and Christ Jesus our Lord.

Col 1:27
Rom 1:1

Tit 1:4
2 Tim 1:2

¹Paulus apostolus Christi Iesu secundum praeceptum Dei salvatoris nostri et

---

**1-2.** The heading is the standard heading used in correspondence at the time—the names of the sender and addressee, and some words of greeting (cf. note on 1 Cor 1:1).

"Apostle of Christ Jesus by *command* of God": the word can be translated as "command", "order", "disposition"; whichever is used, the expression is stronger than that used in other letters—"by the *will* of God" (1 Cor 1:1; 2 Cor 1:1; Eph 1:1; etc.)—and it shows that St Paul holds authority from God (he wants to underline this because he has things to say in the letter about how the church at Ephesus should be organized).

"God our Saviour": in other letters the Apostle seldom uses this title, "Saviour", and when he does he applies it to Jesus (Eph 5:23; Phil 3:20). In the Pastoral Epistles it occurs often and is used of Jesus (cf. 2 Tim 1:10; Tit 3:6) and especially of God the Father (cf. 1 Tim 2:3; 4:10; Tit 2:10; 3:4). In the Greco-Roman world it was quite common to describe people as saviours; for example, we find the word (applied to emperors and pagan gods) in stone inscriptions. St Paul, however, uses it in a restrictive sense; reviving a very typical Old Testament teaching (cf. Deut 32:15; 1 Sam 10:19; etc.), he teaches that God is our only Saviour. Reflecting on this, St John Chrysostom comments: "We suffer many evils, but we harbour great hopes; we are exposed to dangers and snares, but we have a Saviour, who is not just man, but God. Strength will never fail our Saviour, for he is God; no matter how great the dangers, we will overcome them" (*Hom. on 1 Tim, ad loc.*).

"Timothy, my true son in the faith": when St Paul wrote to the Philippians he praised Timothy's proven worth: "you know how as a son with a father he has served with me in the gospel" (Phil 2:22). Now, in this letter to his co-worker, he highlights Timothy's fidelity to Christian truth, in contrast to the behaviour of self-appointed teachers who refuse to obey authority (cf. Heb 12:8).

"Grace, mercy and peace": a wish for "mercy" is added to the by now traditional wish for "grace and peace" (cf. note on Rom 1:7; perhaps this is meant to be an allusion to "the salvation accomplished by the Lord and his mercy" (John Paul II, *Dives in misericordiae*, 4), for in the language of the Bible asking for mercy is the same as asking for salvation: "Show us thy steadfast love [= mercy], O Lord, and grant us thy salvation" (Ps 85:7).

# PART ONE

# SOUND DOCTRINE

**False teachers to be admonished**

Acts 20:1

1 Tim 4:7
2 Tim 4:4
Tit 3:9

Rom 13:10

[3]As I urged you when I was going to Macedonia, remain at Ephesus that you may charge certain persons not to teach any different doctrine, [4]nor to occupy themselves with myths and endless genealogies which promote speculations rather than the divine training[a] that is in faith; [5]whereas the

---

Christi Iesu spei nostrae, [2]Timotheo, germano filio in fide: gratia, misericordia, pax a Deo Patre et Christo Iesu Domino nostro. [3]Sicut rogavi te, ut remaneres Ephesi, cum irem in Macedoniam, ut praeciperes quibusdam, ne aliter docerent [4]neque intenderent fabulis et genealogiis interminatis, quae quaestiones praestant magis quam dispensationem Dei, quae est in fide; [5]finis autem

---

**3-4.** "Remain at Ephesus": the original Greek verb refers not only to staying in the city physically but also to keeping at the task he has been given and resisting those who are preaching misinterpretations of the Christian message. The false teachers at Ephesus seem to have been converts of Jewish background who still had a very fixed Jewish mentality (which would explain why they wanted to be "teachers of the law": v. 7). The "myths" and "endless genealogies" they were so caught up in and which could confuse the believers must have been rather like the legends about the patriarchs and other biblical heroes, and their genealogies, popular in certain rabbinical schools. We know of some of these legends through the apocryphal books.

The Church has always tried to ensure that religious instruction covers the basics of the faith and does so simply and clearly: this saves time and avoids the confusion which can result from people being offered theories which are marginal to the faith, or speculation which is unsound. John Paul II refers to this passage from St Paul when he says that catechists "must refuse to trouble the minds of children and young people, at this stage of their catechesis, with outlandish theories, useless questions and unproductive discussions, things that St Paul often condemned in his pastoral letters" (*Catechesi tradendae*, 61).

"The divine training (*stewardship*, or *order*) that is faith": the Spanish version reads "the [salvific] plan of God in the faith" and the commentary says that it is not clear what the original means but that it basically has to do with God's plan for the salvation of mankind, a plan which we know about through faith.

**5.** "The aim of our charge is love": St Paul's instruction to Timothy to give good religious instruction to the believers and to keep erroneous teachings at bay is a commandment designed to promote supernatural love. St John

[a]Or *stewardship, or order*

92

aim of our charge is love that issues from a pure heart and a good conscience and sincere faith. <sup>6</sup>Certain persons by swerving from these have wandered away into vain discussion, <sup>7</sup>desiring to be teachers of the law, without understanding either what they are saying or the things about which they make assertions.

1 Tim 6:20

Tit 1:10

### The purpose of the Law

<sup>8</sup>Now we know that the law is good, if any one uses it

Rom 7:12, 16

---

praecepti est caritas de corde puro et conscientia bona et fide non ficta, <sup>6</sup>a quibus quidam aberrantes conversi sunt in vaniloquium, <sup>7</sup>volentes esse legis doctores, non intellegentes neque quae loquuntur neque de quibus affirmant. <sup>8</sup>Scimus

---

Chrysostom comments that "faith teaches the truth, and a faith that is pure gives birth to charity" (*Hom. on 1 Tim, ad loc.*); and St Thomas Aquinas explains that that is the case because "those who do not hold the true faith cannot love God, for a person who believes things about God which are untrue no longer loves God" (*Commentary on 1 Tim, ad loc.*); at best he would love the caricature of God he believed in.

"Love that issues from a pure heart": that is, love that is effective in a pure heart. Charity is a virtue which God infuses into the soul and it should be received with "a pure heart" (a heart purified from sins: cf. Heb 1:3), "a good conscience" (a conscience correctly educated in accordance with faith and morals), and "sincere faith" (literally, "an unhypocritical faith": that is, a faith backed up by behaviour which reflects the truths one professes).

**6-7.** "Have wandered away into vain discussion": people who project themselves as teachers but teach their own theories instead of the truths of faith do harm to the Church by spreading doubt and confusion.

The content of the faith as taught by the Apostles is not something of man's devising; it derives from God's Revelation to mankind. Therefore, if people prove unfaithful in transmitting this Revelation to others, they deserve the reproach which Jeremiah places on the lips of Yahweh: "for my people have committed two evils: they have forsaken me, the fountain of living waters, and hewed out cisterns for themselves, broken cisterns, that can hold no water" (Jer 2:13). People who leave to one side the authority of God the revealer and base their teaching on purely human reasoning will never manage to build anything worthwhile or lasting. St Paul points out the paradox in their whole approach: the dogmatism with which they speak is merely a way of disguising their own ignorance.

**8-10.** From the context it seems fairly clear that it is the Mosaic Law that is being referred to. The Law is good but it is inadequate because it tells one what is sinful but does not provide the wherewithal to conquer sin (cf. Rom

Rom 1:28-30 lawfully, ⁹understanding this, that the law is not laid down for the just but for the lawless and disobedient, for the ungodly and sinners, for the unholy and profane, for murderers of fathers and murderers of mothers, for manslayers, ¹⁰immoral persons, sodomites, kidnappers, liars, perjurers, and whatever else is contrary to sound doctrine, ¹¹in accor-

1 Thess 2:4
Tit 1:3

---

autem quia bona est lex, si quis ea legitime utatur, ⁹sciens hoc quia iusto lex non est posita, sed iniustis et non subiectis, impiis et peccatoribus, sceleratis et contaminatis, patricidis et matricidis, homicidis, ¹⁰fornicariis, masculorum concubitoribus, plagiariis, mendacibus, periuris, et si quis aliud sanae doctrinae adversatur, ¹¹secundum evangelium gloriae beati Dei, quod creditum est mihi.

---

4:13-16; 7:7-12; Gal 3:19-25 and notes). Those who have been baptized can count on the help of grace which enables them to do what God has laid down and even to enjoy doing it.

The "just" (v.9) are those who have been justified by Christ and therefore live by faith and not by mere observance of the Law (cf. Gal 3:11-12; Rom 1:17; 5:19; Col 2:20-22). When the Apostle says that "the law is not laid down for the just", he is referring to the fact that the very detailed prescriptions of the Mosaic Law do not apply to the Christian.

He then immediately moves on to list the vices of the false teachers. They cannot be regarded as "just", for they do not seem to have understood what justification by Christ means: they are still arguing about tiny details of Old Testament interpretation, forgetting that our Lord has brought Revelation to its fulness. And so the list ends by more or less saying that all sin is really "whatever . . . is contrary to sound doctrine".

The expressions "sound doctrine" and "sound teaching" are features of the Pastoral Epistles and occur fairly often (cf. 1 Tim 6:3; 2 Tim 1:13; 4:3; Tit 1:9; 1:13; 2:1-2).

In the Greek of St Paul's time, particularly in the language of philosophy, "sound" means more or less the same as "reasonable"; so, the reference to "sound" teaching is meant to convey the idea that faith and morals do not contradict sound human reasoning but rather help to guide it and bring it beyond what reason alone can attain. St Paul is probably also using the original meaning of the word in a metaphorical way: just as a healthy diet makes for a healthy body, so healthy doctrine (the genuine Christian message, expounded in its entirety and expounded clearly) is of great benefit to the soul.

**11.** In giving Timothy all these instructions (vv. 5-10), St Paul is exercising his apostolic authority. He is not giving his personal view (which is what the false teachers are doing) but the teaching of the "gospel", all the revealed truths taken together, which determine the content of the faith and with which he has been entrusted.

The phrase "the glorious gospel" or "the gospel of glory" is rich in meaning.

dance with the glorious gospel of the blessed God with which I have been entrusted.

**Paul recalls his own conversion**

<sup>12</sup>I thank him who has given me strength for this, Christ Jesus our Lord, because he judged me faithful by appointing me to his service, <sup>13</sup>though I formerly blasphemed

Acts 9:15
1 Cor 15:9f
Phil 4:13
Gal 1:13
Acts 8:3

<sup>12</sup>Gratiam habeo ei, qui me confortavit, Christo Iesu Domino nostro, quia fidelem me existimavit ponens in ministerio, <sup>13</sup>qui prius fui blasphemus et

For one thing, it points to the divine origin and supernatural character of the Christian message, which provides light for the mind and has power to sanctify and save. It also has an eschatological dimension, conveying the idea that the Gospel leads man to share in the eternal blessedness of God.

"The blessed God": this can also be translated as "the happy God". The term is used only here and in 1 Timothy 6:15. As with certain other words, St Paul may be using a term taken from emperor-worship rites: his readers would have been familiar with it and by applying it to God he would be making it clear that strictly speaking only God merits this title and it should not be applied to mere men (cf. note on 6:15-16).

**12-13.** This clearly autobiographical passage, which shows the Apostle's humility (cf., e.g., 1 Cor 15:9-10), is evidence of the letter's Pauline authorship: it is difficult to believe that a later disciple would have dared to call St Paul a "blasphemer", "persecutor" or "insulter" or made him describe himself as "the foremost of sinners".

St Paul's conversion is an example of a miracle of grace; only by the mercy of God could he have been changed and become the Apostle of the Gentiles and such a faithful minister of the Gospel. This change which grace worked in Paul can also help all who approach the Church to have great confidence in God's mercy and forgiveness; like a good father, God is always ready to receive the repentant sinner.

The sacred text shows quite clearly that the initiative lies with God when it comes to calling people to Church office. The call to the priesthood is a grace from God; it is God who makes the choice and then he gives the person he has chosen the strength to fulfil his office worthily. In this connexion Bishop Alvaro del Portillo has written: "Christian priesthood is not, then, in the line of ethical relationships among men nor on the level of a merely human attempt to approach God: it is a gift from God and it is irreversibly located on the vertical line of the search for man by his Creator and Sanctifier and on the sacramental line of the gratuitous opening up to man of God's intimate life. In other words, Christian priesthood is essentially (this is the only possible way it can be understood) an eminently sacred mission, both in its origin (Christ) and in its content (the divine mystery) and by the very manner in which it is conferred—a sacrament" (*On Priesthood*, pp. 59f).

and persecuted and insulted him; but I received mercy
Rom 5:20 because I had acted ignorantly in unbelief, ¹⁴and the grace
of our Lord overflowed for me with the faith and love that
Lk 15:2; 19:10 are in Christ Jesus. ¹⁵The saying is sure and worthy of full
acceptance, that Christ Jesus came into the world to save
1 Cor 15:9-10 sinners. And I am the foremost of sinners; ¹⁶but I received

---

persecutor et contumeliosus; sed misercordiam consecutus sum, quia ignorans
feci in incredulitate, ¹⁴superabundavit autem gratia Domini nostri cum fide et
dilectione, quae sunt in Christo Iesu. ¹⁵Fidelis sermo et omni acceptione dignus:
Christus Iesus venit in mundum peccatores salvos facere; quorum primus ego

---

**14.** "In Christ Jesus": this expression is being used with a special technical
meaning: it refers to the position of the new man who, after the "washing of
regeneration and renewal in the Holy Spirit" (Tit 3:5) which takes place at
Baptism, is now united to Christ, made a Christian. At Baptism the mercy of
God not only justifies the sinner but causes him to share profoundly in God's
own life by means of grace, faith and love. These three gifts are a sign that the
Christian has truly been built into the body of Christ (cf. 2 Tim 1:13).

**15.** "The saying is sure and worthy of full acceptance": or, more literally,
"Word of honour, which you can totally rely on". This form of words is used
a number of times in the Pastoral Epistles to focus attention on some important
doctrinal point (cf. 1 Tim 3:1; 4:9; 2 Tim 2:11; Tit 3:8).

The point being emphasised here is that "Christ Jesus came into the world
to save sinners". The Apostle has condensed into very few words God's plan
for the redemption of mankind, which he will go on to say more about later (cf.
1 Tim 2:3-7; Tit 2:11-14; 3:3-7). "The mercy of God is infinite," says St Francis
of Assisi, "and, according to the Gospel, even if our sins were infinite, his mercy
is yet greater than our sins. And the Apostle St Paul has said that Christ the
blessed came into the world to save sinners" (*The Little Flowers of St Francis*,
chap. 26).

This is in fact one of the basic truths of faith and appears in the Creed: "For
us men and for our salvation he came down from heaven". He came to save us
from the only evil, that which can separate us from God—sin.

By his victory over sin Christ gave men and women the honour of being
sons and daughters of God; this new character and status equips them to light
up the world around them with the brightness of their Christian lives (cf. Phil
2:15). They can have this effect on others if they really commit themselves to
have the same mind as "was in Christ Jesus" (Phil 2:5), for "it is impossible to
live according to the heart of Jesus Christ and not to know that we are sent, as
he was, 'to save all sinners' (1 Tim 1:15), with the clear realisation that we
ourselves need to trust in the mercy of God more and more every day. As a
result, we will foster in ourselves a vehement desire to be co-redeemers with
Christ, to save all souls with him" (J. Escrivá, *Christ is passing by*, 121).

mercy for this reason, that in me, as the foremost, Jesus Christ might display his perfect patience for an example to those who were to believe in him for eternal life. [17]To the king of ages, immortal, invisible, the only God, be honour and glory for ever and ever.[b] Amen.

Rom 16:27
Col 1:15

### Timothy's responsibilities

[18]This charge I commit to you, Timothy, my son, in

1 Tim 4:14
2 Tim 4:7

sum, [16]sed ideo misericordiam consecutus sum, ut in me primo ostenderet Christus Iesus omnem longanimitatem, ad informationem eorum, qui credituri sunt illi in vitam aeternam. [17]Regi autem saeculorum, incorruptibili, invisibili, soli Deo honor et gloria in saecula saeculorum. Amen. [18]Hoc praeceptum

**17.** This section (vv. 12-17) closes with a solemn doxology. Similar exclamatory passages in praise of God appear elsewhere in the Apostle's writings (Rom 2:36; 16:27; Phil 4:20; etc.). This was probably an early formula used in the liturgy of Ephesus and other Asia Minor churches. The fact that it ends with an "Amen" seems to confirm this. In contrast to the energetic attempts of the civil authorities at the time to foster emperor-worship, Christians proclaimed that God is lord of the universe and will reign forever.

It is true, of course, that because God's glory is infinite, it cannot be enhanced by man extolling God's attributes. However, once one knows the greatness of God, creator and ruler of the universe, and knows that all things are dependent on him, one has a duty to show God due honour both internally and externally. Actions of that kind are expressions of the virtue of religion, whose "actions are directly and immediately ordered to the honour of God" (*Summa theologiae*, II-II, q. 81, a. 6). "Of all the duties which man has to fulfil that, without doubt, is the chiefest and holiest which commands him to worship God with devotion and piety. This follows of necessity from the truth that we are ever in the power of God, are ever guided by his will and providence, and, having come forth from him, must return to him" (Leo XIII, *Libertas praestantissimum*, 25).

**18-19.** In the New Testament the word "prophecy" does not usually refer to the foretelling of some event but rather to the words of one who speaks "to men for their upbuilding and encouragement and consolation" (1 Cor 14:3). The "prophetic utterances" may refer to the good reports about Timothy which St Paul received when he was in Lystra and Iconium, reports which led him to make Timothy his helper (cf. Acts 16:1-3); or they may have to do with something said under the influence of the Spirit by some Christian who had the gift of prophecy (like the sign the church of Antioch was given to send Paul and Barnabas on their first apostolic journey: cf. Acts 13:1-3). It is also possible (bearing in mind 1 Timothy 4:14, where the gift of prophecy is linked to the laying on of hands by the elders) that St Paul is reminding Timothy of the time

[b]Greek *to the ages of ages*

accordance with the prophetic utterances which pointed to you, that inspired by them you may wage the good warfare, <sup>19</sup>holding faith and a good conscience. By rejecting conscience, certain persons have made shipwreck of their faith, <sup>20</sup>among them Hymenaeus and Alexander, whom I have delivered to Satan that they may learn not to blaspheme.

1 Tim 3:9

2 Tim 2:17
1 Cor 5:5

---

commendo tibi, fili Timothee, secundum praecedentes super te prophetias, ut milites in illis bonam militiam <sup>19</sup>habens fidem et bonam conscientiam, quam quidam repellentes circa fidem naufragaverunt; <sup>20</sup>ex quibus est Hymenaeus et Alexander, quos tradidi Satanae, ut discant non blasphemare.

---

he was ordained a priest. However, the most likely interpretation is that the "prophetic utterances" are simply words of exhortation the Apostle addressed to his helper before he (Paul) left and which he already repeated at the start of his letter (vv. 3-4)—a call to do all he can to protect the faith and sound consciences of the believers entrusted to his care.

The Apostle suggests to Timothy that he approach this pastoral mission as a general would a military operation. The word translated here as "warfare" means "military expedition" in classical Greek. Timothy's mission at the head of the church at Ephesus is not simply a question of fighting a single battle: he is engaged in a war and he has to continue to act as the believers' leader until final victory is obtained. St Paul likes using military metaphors to describe the Christian life (cf., e.g., 1 Cor 9:25; 2 Cor 10:3-6; Eph 6:10-17; 2 Tim 2:3); this practice has been continued in ascetical writing. "The entire tradition of the Church", Monsignor Escrivá points out, "has described Christians as *milites Christi*, soldiers of Christ, soldiers who bring peace to men's souls while continually fighting against their own bad inclinations [. . .]. Our spiritual combat in the presence of God and of all our brothers in the faith is a necessary result of being a Christian. So, if you do not fight, you are betraying Jesus Christ and the whole Church, his mystical body" (*Christ is passing by*, 74).

**19-20.** When conscience goes astray, it means shipwreck of the faith: "For he who says goodbye to the Christian life, devises for himself a faith which accords with his moral conduct", St John Chrysostom warns (*Hom. on 1 Tim, ad loc.*). Doctrinal confusion often originates in moral misconduct.

We do not know much about the two people St Paul refers to here. Hymenaeus may well be the same heretic he warns Timothy about in his second letter, who believed that the resurrection had already taken place (2 Tim 2:17). Alexander is a more common name—which makes him more difficult to identify; he may be the coppersmith whom Paul warns Timothy about (2 Tim 4:14-15); in the Acts there is mention of an Alexander in Ephesus (cf. Acts 19:33-34). These people must have been doing considerable harm to the Church because St Paul has excommunicated them (as he did someone else in Corinth: cf. 1 Cor 5:1-8). This excommunication has a pastoral, medicinal purpose (cf.

# 2

## PART TWO

## REGULATIONS ABOUT PRAYER

### God desires the salvation of all

Phil 4:6
1 Tim 4:6

¹First of all, then, I urge that supplications, prayers, inter-

¹Obsecro igitur primo omnium fieri obsecrationes, orationes, postulationes, gratiarum actiones pro omnibus hominibus, ²pro regibus et omnibus, qui in

Tit 3:10)—the good of believers and the reform of the heretics themselves "that they may learn not to blaspheme". Excommunication is an extreme step which the Church takes "only when he [the Ordinary] perceives that neither by fraternal correction or reproof, nor by any methods of pastoral care, can the scandal be sufficiently repaired, justice restored and the offender reformed" (*The Code of Canon Law*, can. 1341).

1. St Paul here establishes regulations for the public prayer of all the faithful; it is up to Timothy, as head of the church of Ephesus, to specify these in detail, and to preside over them. He refers to four types of prayer; however, since the first three are almost synonymous, he is probably just stressing the key importance of prayer in the Christian life. St Augustine uses this text to explain the various parts of the Mass: "We take as 'supplications' those prayers which are said in celebrating the Mysteries before beginning to bless (the bread and wine) that lie on the table of the Lord. We understand 'prayers' as meaning those prayers that are said when (the offering) is blessed, consecrated and broken for distribution, and almost the whole Church closes this prayer with the Lord's prayer [. . .]. 'Intercessions' are made when the blessing is being laid on the people [. . .]. When this rite is completed and all have received this great Sacrament, the whole ceremony is brought to an end by 'thanksgiving'—which is also the word which concludes this passage of the Apostle's" (*Letter* 149, 2, 16).

St Paul orders that prayers be said for all, not just for friends and benefactors and not just for Christians. The Church helps people keep this command by the Prayers of the Faithful or at Mass when "the people exercise their priestly function by praying for all mankind" and "pray for Holy Church, for those in authority, for those oppressed by various needs, for all mankind, and for the salvation of the entire world" (*General Instruction on the Roman Missal*, 45).

2. This desire to lead "a quiet and peaceful life" does not in any way imply a relaxation of the demands St Paul makes in other letters. He specifically says

99

Rom 13:1-7 cessions, and thanksgivings be made for all men, [2]for kings and all who are in high positions, that we may lead a quiet 1 Tim 1:1 and peaceable life, godly and respectful in every way. [3]This

sublimitate sunt, ut quietam et tranquillam vitam agamus in omni pietate et castitate. [3]Hoc bonum est et acceptum coram salvatore nostro Deo, [4]qui omnes

that prayers have to be said "for kings and all who are in high positions" because they are responsible for ensuring that civil law is in line with the natural law, and when it is citizens are able to practise religious and civil virtues (to be "godly and respectful"). Rulers have a heavy responsibility and therefore deserve to be prayed for regularly.

St Paul's instruction to pray for kings and others is particularly interesting if one bears in mind that when he was writing this letter, Nero was on the throne—the emperor who instigated a bloody persecution of Christians. St Clement of Rome, one of the first successors of St Peter at the see of Rome, has left us touching evidence of intercession for civil authority: "Make us to be obedient to your own almighty and glorious name and to all who have rule and governance over us on earth [. . .]. Grant unto them, O Lord, health and peace, harmony and security, that they may exercise without offence the dominion you have accorded them [. . .]. Vouchsafe so to direct their counsels as may be good and pleasing in your sight, that in peace and mildness they might put to godly use the authority you have given them, and so find mercy with you" (*Letter to the Corinthians*, 1, 60-61).

If one bears in mind the injustices and brutality of the world in which Christians lived when St Paul wrote this letter, the tone of his teaching shows that Christianity has nothing to do with fermenting political or social unrest. The message of Jesus seeks, rather, to change men's consciences so that they for their part can change society from within by working in an upright and noble way. The Church, through its ordinary magisterium, teaches that "the political and economic running of society is not a direct part of (the Church's) mission (cf. *Gaudium et spes*, 42). But the Lord Jesus has entrusted to her the word of truth which is capable of enlightening consciences. Divine love, which is her life, impels her to a true solidarity with everyone who suffers. If her members remain faithful to this mission, the Holy Spirit, the source of freedom, will dwell in them, and they will bring forth fruits of justice and peace in their families and in the places where they work and live" (SCDF, *Libertatis conscientia*, 61).

**3-4.** God's desire that all should be saved is a subject which appears frequently in the Pastoral Epistles (cf. 1 Tim 4:10; Tit 3:4), and so he is often given the title of "Saviour" (cf. note on 1 Tim 1:1-2). Here it is given special emphasis: pray for all men (v. 1), particularly those in high positions (v. 2), that all may be saved (v. 6).

Since God wants all men to be saved, no one is predestined to be damned (cf. Council of Trent, *De Iustificatione*). "He came on earth because *omnes homines vult salvos fieri*, he wants to redeem the whole world. While you are

100

is good, and it is acceptable in the sight of God our Saviour,
⁴who desires all men to be saved and to come to the
knowledge of the truth. ⁵For there is one God, and there is

---

homines vult salvos fieri et ad agnitionem veritatis venire. ⁵Unus enim Deus,

---

at your work, shoulder to shoulder with so many others, never forget that there is no soul that does not matter to Christ!" (J. Escrivá, *The Forge*, 865).

God desires man to be free as intensely as he desires his salvation; by making man free he has made it possible for man to cooperate in attaining his last end. "God, who created you without you," St Augustine reminds us, "will not save you without you" (*Sermon*, 169, 13).

In order to attain salvation, the Apostle lists as a requirement that one must "come to the knowledge of the truth". "The truth" is firstly Jesus (cf. Jn 14:6; 1 Jn 5:20); knowledge of the truth is the same as knowing the Christian message, the Gospel (cf. Gal 2:5, 14). The human mind needs to come into play if one is to be saved; for, although affections, emotions and good will are also involved, it would be wrong to give them so much importance that the content of the truths of faith is played down. As the original Greek word suggests, this "knowledge" is not just an intellectual grasp of truth: it is something which should have an impact on one's everyday life; knowledge of the faith involves practice of the faith.

"The Church's essential mission, following that of Christ, is a mission of evangelization and salvation. She draws her zeal from the divine love. Evangelization is the proclamation of salvation, which is a gift of God. Through the word of God and the Sacraments, man is freed in the first place from the power of sin and the power of the Evil One which oppress him; and he is brought into a communion of love with God. Following her Lord who 'came into the world to save sinners' (1 Tim 1:15), the Church desires the salvation of everyone. In this mission, the Church teaches the way which man must follow in this world in order to enter the Kingdom of God" (SCDF, *Libertatis conscientia*, 63).

**5.** Verses 5 and 6 compress a series of statements into the rhythmic format of a liturgical hymn, a kind of summarized confession of faith containing the truths one needs to believe in order to be saved (cf. v. 4).

"One mediator between God and men, the man Christ Jesus": the Apostle lays stress on Christ's humanity, not to deny his divinity (which he explicitly asserts elsewhere: cf. Tit 2:13) but because it is as man particularly that Christ is mediator; for if the function of a mediator is to join or put two sides in touch, in this particular case it is only as man that he is as it were "distant both from God by nature and from man by dignity of both grace and glory [. . .], and that he can unite men to God, communicating his precepts and gifts to them, and offering satisfaction and prayers to God for them" (*Summa theologiae*, III, q. 26, a. 2). Christ is the perfect and only mediator between God and men, because being true God and true man he has offered a sacrifice of infinite value (his life) to reconcile men to God.

Gal 1:4
Mt 20:28
Tit 2:14
2 Cor 5:15

2 Tim 1:11
Gal 2:7-8

one mediator between God and men, the man Christ Jesus, <sup>6</sup>who gave himself as a ransom for all, the testimony to which was borne at the proper time. <sup>7</sup>For this I was appointed a preacher and apostle (I am telling the truth, I am not lying), a teacher of the Gentiles in faith and truth.

**Men at prayer, women at prayer**

<sup>8</sup>I desire then that in every place the men should pray,

---

unus et mediator Dei et hominum, homo Christus Iesus, <sup>6</sup>qui dedit redemptionem semetipsum pro omnibus, testimonium temporibus suis; <sup>7</sup>in quod positus sum ego praedicator et apostolus—veritatem dico, non mentior—doctor gentium in fide et veritate. <sup>8</sup>Volo ergo viros orare in omni loco levantes puras

---

The fact that Jesus is the only mediator does not prevent those who have reached heaven from obtaining graces and helping to build up the Church's holiness (cf. *Lumen gentium*, 49). Angels and saints, particularly the Blessed Virgin, can be described as mediators by virtue of their union with Christ: "Mary's function as mother of men in no way obscures or diminishes this unique mediation of Christ, but rather shows its power. But the Blessed Virgin's salutary influence on men originates not in any inner necessity but in the disposition of God. It flows forth from the superabundance of the merits of Christ" (*Lumen gentium*, 60).

**6.** "Ransom": in the Old Testament God is said to ransom or redeem his people particularly when he sets them free from slavery in Egypt and makes them his own property (cf. Ex 6:6-7; 19:5-6; etc.). The liberation which God will bring about in the messianic times is also described as redemption (cf. Is 35:9) and implies, above all, liberation from sin: "he will redeem Israel from all his iniquities" (Ps. 130:8). The same idea occurs in this verse: Jesus "gave himself" in sacrifice to make expiation for our sins, to set us free from sin and restore to us our lost dignity. "Unceasingly contemplating the whole of Christ's mystery, the Church knows with all the certainty of faith that the Redemption that took place through the Cross has definitively restored his dignity to man and given back meaning to his life in the world, a meaning that was lost to a considerable extent because of sin" (John Paul II, *Redemptor hominis*, 10).

"At the proper time": God's plan for man's salvation is eternal, it did not start at a particular time; however, it unfolds gradually in God's good time (see the note on Eph 1:10).

**8.** The raising of the hands at prayer is a custom found among both Jews (cf. Ex 9:29; Is 1:15; etc.) and pagans; it was also adopted by the early Christians, as can be seen from murals in the Roman catacombs.

External stances adopted during prayer should reflect one's inner attitude: "we extend our arms", Tertullian explains, "in imitation of the Lord on the

lifting holy hands without anger or quarrelling; ⁹also that 1 Pet 3:3-5
women should adorn themselves modestly and sensibly in
seemly apparel, not with braided hair or gold or pearls or 1 Tim 5:10
costly attire ¹⁰but by good deeds, as befits women who Is 3:16-23
profess religion. ¹¹Let a woman learn in silence with all 1 Cor 14:34
submissiveness. ¹²I permit no woman to teach or to have Eph 5:22

---

manus sine ira et disceptatione; ⁹similiter et mulieres in habitu ornato cum
verecundia et sobrietate ornantes se, non in tortis crinibus et auro aut margaritis
vel veste pretiosa, ¹⁰sed, quod decet mulieres, profitentes pietatem per opera
bona. ¹¹Mulier in tranquillitate discat cum omni subiectione; ¹²docere autem

---

Cross; and praying we confess Christ" (*De oratione*, 14). St Thomas Aquinas,
referring to liturgical rites, comments that "what we do externally when we
pray helps to move us internally. Genuflexions and other gestures of that type
are not pleasing to God in themselves; they please him because they are signs
of respect whereby man humbles himself interiorly; similarly, the raising of the
hands signifies the lifting of the heart" (*Commentary on 1 Tim, ad loc.*).

Everyone should pray regularly (vv. 1-2) and be sure to have the right
dispositions; men need to make sure that they do not approach prayer with their
thoughts full of earthly ambition; and women need to be sure vanity does not
creep in. "Holy hands" refers to the need to pray with a calm conscience, free
from anger and spite. We already have our Lord's teaching that "if you are
offering your gift at the altar, and there remember that your brother has
something against you, leave your gift there before the altar and go; first be
reconciled to your brother, and then come and offer your gift" (Mt 5:23-24).

**9-10.** In his remarks about women the Apostle begins by stating explicitly
that what he has just said about men also applies to them. The fact that they are
put on the same level, as equals, is very remarkable, for in the liturgy of the
synagogue only men were allowed to lead the prayers. Women were kept in an
area apart and had no active role; in fact if there was not a quorum of men,
public prayer could not take place, even if there were many women present.

For their attendance at liturgical acts (and their general deportment) St Paul
offers suggestions about dress and grooming quite like what St Peter says in
his first letter (cf. 1 Pet 3:3-4). The essence of these guidelines will always
remain unchanged: women should try to dress with an elegance that reflects
the modesty appropriate to devout Christian women.

**11-14.** "I permit no woman to teach": in this chapter St Paul is giving
general regulations for liturgical assemblies; therefore, this prohibition is not
an absolute one: it refers only to public acts of worship. In order to make it clear
that he is not just giving a personal opinion, he sets the prohibition into the
context of the divine plan of Creation and the biblical account of the Fall; his
arguments are not sociological ones, not confined to a particular culture; they
are theological arguments.

Gen 2:7, 22
1 Cor 11:8f
Gen 3:6
2 Cor 11:3
1 Tim 5:14
authority over men; she is to keep silent. [13]For Adam was formed first, then Eve; [14]and Adam was not deceived, but the woman was deceived and became a transgressor. [15]Yet woman will be saved through bearing children,[c] if she continues[d] in faith and love and holiness, with modesty.

---

mulieri non permitto, neque dominari in virum, sed esse in tranquillitate. [13]Adam enim primus formatus est, deinde Eva; [14]et Adam non est seductus, mulier autem seducta in praevaricatione fuit. [15]Salvabitur autem per filiorum generationem, si permanserint in fide et dilectione et sanctificatione cum sobrietate.

---

There are no grounds for accusing St Paul of being anti-woman; no one of his time spoke as vigorously as he did about the basic equality of man and woman (cf. Gal 3:28), and certain women (Priscilla and Lydia, for example) played an important part in helping him to spread the Gospel. What he is saying is simply this: the essential equality of man and woman does not mean that they have identical roles in the Church (see the note on 1 Cor 14:33-35). Also, although women are forbidden to teach in a public, official setting (that is the role of the hierarchy) they can and should teach religion in the context of catechesis and family life.

**15.** "Woman will be saved through bearing children": it is possible that St Paul wants to stress that marriage is a holy calling (some heretics were arguing the contrary: cf. 1 Tim 4:3); but that does not mean that motherhood is the only way to salvation for women; elsewhere he speaks of the excellence of virginity (cf. 1 Cor 7:25-38).

What the Apostle says here should be interpreted in the light of conditions at the time. However, some present-day documents of the Magisterium point to aspects of it which have perennial value. Nowadays there is a tendency to undervalue motherhood, so we find Pope John Paul II teaching that "the true advancement of women requires that clear recognition be given to the value of their maternal and family role, by comparison with all other public roles and all other professions [. . .]. While it must be recognised that women have the same right as men to perform various public functions, society must be structured in such a way that wives and mothers are *not in practice compelled* to work outside the home, and that their families can live and prosper in a dignified way even when they themselves devote their full time to their own family" (*Familiaris consortio*, 23).

A woman who runs a home is rendering an essential service to both family and society: "This is a wonderful job which is very worthwhile. Through this profession—because it is a profession, in a true and noble sense—they are an influence for good, not only in their family, but also among their many friends

[c]Or *by the birth of the child*
[d]Greek *they continue*

PART THREE

CHURCH OFFICE

**Qualifications for bishops**

¹The saying is sure: If any one aspires to the office of

¹Fidelis sermo: si quis episcopatum appetit, bonum opus desiderat. ²Oportet

and acquaintances, among people with whom they come into contact in one way or another. Sometimes their impact is much greater than that of other professional people [. . .]. A mother has three, five, ten or more children in her care and she can make of them a true work of art, a marvel of education, of balance and understanding, a model of the Christian way of life. She can teach them to be happy and to make themselves really useful to those around them" (J. Escrivá, *Conversations*, 88 and 89).

**1.** "The office of bishop": as explained in the "Introduction to the Pastoral Epistles", above, when these epistles were written the titles and responsibilities of the various church offices had not yet become fixed. The "bishop" (in Greek *episcopos* = overseer) was a priest who was in charge of some particular community. As a minister of the Church, his role was one of teaching (cf. v. 2) and governance (cf. v.5); his task was a demanding one and called for self-sacrifice, because any office in a Christian community is essentially a form of service: "The holders of office, who are invested with a sacred power, are, in fact, dedicated to promoting the interests of their brethren, so that all who belong to the people of God, and are consequently endowed with true Christian dignity, may, through their free and well-ordered efforts towards a common goal, attain to salvation" (Vatican II, *Lumen gentium*, 18).

In spite of the regard in which those "bishops" were held by the faithful, there seems to have been a shortage of candidates for the office. Hence St Paul's stressing that it is a "noble task"—to encourage a generous response by those who feel the Lord's call. From the very beginning, both pastors of the Church and many other members of the faithful have striven to nurture the germs of vocation which God places in people's souls. "Beyond question, the society founded by Christ will never lack priests. But we must all be vigilant and do our part, remembering the word: 'The harvest is plentiful, but the labourers are few' (Lk 10:2). We must do all that we can to secure as many holy ministers of God as possible" (Pius XII, *Menti nostrae*, 36).

**2-7.** The quality and virtues required for a "bishop" are similar to those for "elders" given in Titus 1:5-9. In the Pastoral Epistles "bishop" and "elder" (or priest) mean almost the same thing. In listing qualifications St Paul is not giving

bishop, he desires a noble task. [2]Now a bishop must be above reproach, the husband of one wife, temperate, sen-

ergo episcopum irreprehensibilem esse, unius uxoris virum, sobrium, pru-

a complete list; he is simply saying that candidates for Church office should have qualities which make them suited to the work and should be morally irreproachable.

The Church, in its legislation, has always tried to see that suitable people are chosen as ministers. The Second Vatican Council lays it down that before the priesthood is conferred on anyone careful enquiry should be made "concerning his right intention and freedom of choice, his spiritual, moral and intellectual fitness etc." (*Optatam totius*, 6). In other words, a person needs qualifications in the form of human qualities and ability if he is to live up to the demands of Church office.

"This need for the secular priest to develop human virtues stems from the nature of his apostolic ministry which must be carried out in the everyday world and in direct contact with people who tend to be stern judges of a priest and who watch particularly his behaviour as a man. There is nothing new about all this—but it does seem useful now to emphasise it again. From St Paul to the most recent doctors of the Church (take the teaching of St Francis de Sales, for example) one finds this question dealt with. It is none other than that of the contact between nature and supernature to achieve both the death of that man which must die under the sign of the Cross, and the perfect development of all the nobility and virtue which exists in man, and its direction towards the service of God" (A. del Portillo, *On Priesthood*, p. 12).

**2.** "The husband of one wife": this is also a requirement of "elders" (cf. Tit 1:6) and "deacons" (1 Tim 3:12); it does not mean that the person is under an obligation to marry, but he must not have married more than once. From the context it clearly does not mean that candidates are forbidden to be polygamous (polygamy is forbidden to everyone); the condition that one be married only once ensures that candidates will be very respectable, exemplary people; in the culture of the time second marriages, except in special circumstances, were looked at askance, among Gentiles as well as Jews.

In the apostolic age celibacy was not a requirement for those who presided over the early Christian communities. However, it very soon became customary to require celibacy. "In Christian antiquity the Fathers and ecclesiastical writers testify to the spread through the East and the West of the voluntary practice of celibacy by sacred ministers because of its profound suitability for their total dedication to the service of Christ and his Church. The Church of the West, from the beginning of the fourth century, strengthened, spread, and approved this practice by means of various provincial councils and through the Supreme Pontiffs" (Paul VI, *Sacerdotalis caelibatus*, 35-36).

From then on all priests of the Latin rite were required to be celibate. Celibacy is appropriate to the priesthood for many reasons: "By preserving

sible, dignified, hospitable, an apt teacher, [3]no drunkard, not violent but gentle, not quarrelsome, and no lover of money. [4]He must manage his own household well, keeping his children submissive and respectful in every way; [5]for if a man does not know how to manage his own household, how can he care for God's church? [6]He must not be a recent convert, or he may be puffed up with conceit and fall into the condemnation of the devil; f [7]moreover he must be well thought of by outsiders, or he may fall into reproach and the snare of the devil.f

1 Tim 3:12

2 Cor 8:21

---

dentem, ornatum, hospitalem, doctorem, [3]non vinolentum, non percussorem, sed modestum, non litigiosum, non cupidum, [4]suae domui bene praepositum, filios habentem in subiectione cum omni castitate [5]—si quis autem domui suae praeesse nescit, quomodo ecclesiae Dei curam habebit?—, [6]non neophytum, ne in superbia elatus in iudicium incidat Diaboli. [7]Oportet autem illum et

---

virginity or celibacy for the sake of the kingdom of heaven priests are consecrated in a new and excellent way to Christ. They more readily cling to him with undivided heart and dedicate themselves more freely in him and through him to the service of God and of men. They are less encumbered in their service of his kingdom and of the task of heavenly regeneration. In this way they become better fitted for a broader acceptance of fatherhood in Christ" (Vatican II, *Presbyterorum ordinis*, 16).

**6.** "He must not be a recent convert": one of the functions of the "bishop" was to preside over the community; therefore, it would be imprudent to expose the office-holder to the danger of vanity and pride. As St Thomas says in his commentary, it is not wise to appoint young people and recent converts to positions of honour and responsibility, because they can easily begin to think that they are better than the others and cannot be done without (cf. *Commentary on 1 Tim, ad loc.*).

"Fall into the condemnation of the devil" or "fall into the same condemnation as the devil": the original text is not very clear. It may mean that it is the devil who is doing the condemning, in which case it would be the same as saying "fall into the power of the devil" or "fall into enslavement by the devil". At any rate it is fairly clear that St Paul wants to warn about the danger of committing the same sin as the fallen angel, that is, becoming proud and thereby earning damnation.

**7.** Another function of the "bishop" was to represent the Church to "outsiders", that is, non-Christians. All believers should give good example (cf. Mt 5:16; Col 4:5; 1 Pet 2:13; 3:1), but those who hold Church office have a special duty to avoid giving scandal or providing grounds for gossip.

for *slanderer*

#### Qualifications for deacons

Acts 6:3

1 Tim 5:22

[8]Deacons likewise must be serious, not double-tongued, not addicted to much wine, not greedy for gain; [9]they must hold the mystery of the faith with a clear conscience. [10]And let them also be tested first; then if they prove themselves

---

testimonium habere bonum ab his, qui foris sunt, ut non in opprobrium incidat et laqueum Diaboli. [8]Diaconos similiter pudicos, non bilingues, non multo vino deditos, non turpe lucrum sectantes, [9]habentes mysterium fidei in con- scientia pura. [10]Et hi autem probentur primum, deinde ministrent nullum crimen

---

**8-13.** Deacons were ministers under bishops and priests. The origin of the diaconate probably goes back to the "seven men of good repute" who were elected to help the Apostles (cf. Acts 6:1-6 and note); we do know that those men had an adminstrative role in aiding the poor and the sick (Acts 6:1); they also preached (Acts 6:8-14; 8:6) and administered Baptism (Acts 8:26-40). Later on mention is made of deacons alongside "bishops" in certain important communities (cf. Phil 1:1), which suggests that they were part of the Church hierarchy.

This letter shows them to be ministers subordinate to the "bishop"; in these verses, which some commentators call "the deacons' statute", their specific functions are not stated (they probably performed a wide range of tasks); however, it does appear that, unlike the bishop, they did not represent the Church to outsiders and they could be drawn from among recent converts.

The requirements given here are very like those for the "bishop": as ministers of the Church they would naturally be required to live exemplary lives. The Second Vatican Council is in line with this text when it says that deacons, "waiting upon the mysteries of Christ and of the Church, should keep themselves free from every vice, should please God and give a good example to all in everything" (*Lumen gentium*, 41).

**10.** "Let them also be tested first": it is up to bishops (then and now) to ensure that holy orders are conferred on suitable candidates; probably even in St Paul's time candidates had to undergo a period of training, in the course of which their suitability could be checked.

The Church always tries to see that only people who are really suitable are given Church office, even if that means fewer people are ordained, for "God never so abandons his Church that suitable ministers are not to be found sufficient for the needs of the people; provided the worthy are promoted and the unworthy are set aside" (*Summa theologiae*, Supplement, q. 36, a. 4 ad 1).

**11.** The text says so little that it is difficult to work out who these women were. Many authors, St Thomas among them, think that they were deacons' wives because the reference to them interrupts the list of qualifications for deacons. Many other commentators think that they were women who per-

blameless let them serve as deacons. [11]The women likewise Tit 2:3-5 must be serious, no slanderers, but temperate, faithful in all things. [12]Let deacons be the husband of one wife, and let 1 Tim 3:2 them manage their children and their households well; [13]for 1 Tim 3:1 those who serve well as deacons gain a good standing for themselves and also great confidence in the faith which is in Christ Jesus.

### The Church is God's household

[14]I hope to come to you soon, but I am writing these 1 Tim 4:13 instructions to you so that, [15]if I am delayed, you may know Eph 2:20

---

habentes. [11]Mulieres similiter pudicas, non detrahentes, sobrias, fideles in omnibus. [12]Diaconi sint unius uxoris viri, qui filiis suis bene praesint et suis domibus; [13]qui enim bene ministraverint, gradum sibi bonum acquirent et multam fiduciam in fide, quae est in Christo Iesu. [14]Haec tibi scribo sperans venire ad te cito; [15]si autem tardavero, ut scias quomodo oporteat in domo Dei

---

formed some function or ministry in the early Church; this would explain why nothing is said about the wife of the bishop (when the qualifications for bishops are given at the start of this chapter) and it would also explain why the comportment of the deacons and of these women is referred to using the same adverb—"likewise", similarly—in v. 8 and v. 11. We do know (from a fourth-century document, *Apostolic Constitutions*, 2, 26; 3, 15) that some women did help in the instruction of catechumens, in their Baptism, in care of the sick, etc. In the Letter to the Romans, Phoebe is described as a "deaconess" (cf. Rom 16:1) though she was not a sacred minister in the strict sense.

**13.** "Gain a good standing for themselves": this may mean that being a deacon could be a step towards the higher office of "bishop"; or it could mean the the diaconate itself is a noble position, just as the office of "bishop" is "a noble task" (v. 1). Perhaps St Paul uses this vague expression because it covers both these things: it is an honourable ministry and also it can be a step to a higher position in the service of the community.

"Great confidence": the original text uses a word which, in classical Greek, refers to the right of free citizens to speak at public assemblies—with full freedom, confident, afraid of no one, with self-assurance, etc. A good deacon should expound the doctrine of the faith in the same kind of way: he should be well versed in it, he should stress those aspects which are most apposite at the time, and he should not be affected by what others may think of him.

**15.** This verse contains three very evocative expressions which sum up the letter's ecclesiology or theology of the Church.

"The Church of the living God": St Paul usually uses "church of God" and (once) "church of Christ" (Rom 16:16), thereby implying continuity with the "assemblies of Yahweh" in the Old Testament. The Church, in other words, is

> how one ought to behave in the household of God, which
> is the church of the living God, the pillar and bulwark of
> the truth.

conversari, quae est ecclesia Dei vivi, columna et firmamentum veritatis. [16]Et

the true people of God, founded on the New Covenant, heir to the ancient
promises and trustee of the means of salvation (cf. *Lumen gentium*, 9). It is "the
church of the *living* God", that is, it receives from him supernatural life (grace)
and distributes it to all. "It pleased God to call men to share in his life and not
merely singly, without any bond between them, but he formed them into a
people, in which his children who had been scattered were gathered together"
(Vatican II, *Ad gentes*, 2).

"The household of God": in the original Greek the definite article does not
appear, thereby emphasizing the family character of the Church. St Paul
frequently described the Church as God's family: "you are fellow citizens with
the saints and members of the household of God" (Eph 2:19). The expression
"household of God" conveys the idea of family and also the idea of the cohesion
of Christians as parts of a holy building: the children of God, convoked by the
will of God, form the Church, a home and a temple, where God dwells in a
fuller way than he did in the ancient temple of Jerusalem (cf. 1 Kings 8:12-64).

This house or household of God is made up of all the believers; they are
living stones, as it were (1 Pet 2:5); its foundations are the Apostles (1 Cor
3:11), and Christ himself is its cornerstone (Mt 21:42); those who hold office
in it are not domineering overlords but conscientious stewards, who should rule
with the same dedication as a father does in his own household (1 Tim 3:4-5,
12).

"Pillar and bulwark of the truth": those aspects of the building would have
been very meaningful to Christians familiar with the great pillars of the temple
of Jerusalem (cf. 1 Kings 7:15-52) or the columns of the huge temple at Ephesus
dedicated to the goddess Artemis. They very graphically convey the idea of the
Church's solidity and permanence in the role of safeguarding and transmitting
the truth, for "the deposit of revelation [. . .] must be religiously guarded and
courageously expounded" (*Lumen gentium*, 25).

"The truth" which the Apostle mentions here is the Revelation God has
communicated to men. It is interesting to note that there are three closely
connected expressions in this chapter: deacons are exhorted to hold "the
mystery of faith" (v. 9); the Church is "the pillar and bulwark of the truth" (v.
15); and then "the mystery of our religion" is extolled (v. 16). These are three
ways of looking at the Church's reason-of-being—Jesus Christ. For our Lord,
who is the fulness of Revelation (cf. Heb 1:2), is the centre of our faith: he alone
is the supreme Truth (cf. Jn 14:6); and because he is the fullest expression of
God's love for men (making them children of God), he is "the mystery of our
religion" (cf. *Reconciliatio et paenitentia*, 19).

**16.** The *pietatis mysterium*, the mystery of (our) religion, as opposed to the

**The mystery of our religion**

[16]Great indeed, we confess, is the mystery of our religion:
He[h] was manifested in the flesh,
vindicated[i] in the Spirit,
seen by angels,
preached among the nations,
believed on in the world,
taken up in glory.

Jn 1:14
Jn 16:10
Rom 1:3f
Mk 16:19

omnium confessione magnum est pietatis mysterium: Qui manifestatus est in carne, iustificatus est in Spiritu, apparuit angelis, praedicatus est in gentibus, creditus est in mundo, assumptus est in gloria.

"mystery of lawlessness" (2 Thess 2:7) which includes the devil and his activity, refers first and foremost to Christ and his work of redemption and reconciliation. By describing it as the mystery of "piety", the virtue which characterizes parent/children relations, it includes the idea of God's paternal love for men, for it is through Christ that men become children of God.

"It is profoundly significant", John Paul II comments, "that when Paul presents this *mysterium pietatis* he simply transcribes, without making a grammatical link with what he has just written, three lines of a *Christological hymn* which—in the opinion of authoritative scholars—was used in the Greek-speaking Christian communities" (*Reconciliatio et paenitentia*, 20). The introduction itself ("we confess": by the confession of all), the rhythmic style, the fact that no articles are used in the original Greek, and even the vocabulary—all point to these verses having been taken from an early liturgical hymn (cf. 1 Cor 14:26; Eph 5:19). It may even have been a kind of counter to the idolatrous chants of pagan Ephesians: they used to shout "Great is Artemis of the Ephesians!" (Acts 19:34); St Paul exclaims, "Great is the mystery of our religion."

The order of ideas in this confession of faith is typical of the christological hymns in the New Testament (cf. Phil 2:6-11; Col 1:15-20; Heb 1:3), and probably reflects the oral preaching of the Apostles which took in the existence of the Word from all eternity, his incarnation and life on earth; his message of salvation for the whole world; his passion, death, resurrection and ascension into heaven. Each of the three parts of this short creed stresses the paradox of the mystery by using phrases involving contrasts (Semites were very fond of this device). The first sentence, professing belief in the Incarnation, uses a very early form of words—"manifested in the flesh" (cf. 1 Jn 4:2; 2 Jn 7). Pope John Paul II comments as follows: "he was made manifest in the reality of human flesh and was constituted by the Holy Spirit as the Just One who offers himself for the unjust" (*Reconciliatio et paenitentia*, 20).

The second phrase describes how Christ is manifested: the angels have direct

[h]Greek *Who*; other ancient authorities read *God*; others, *Which*
[i]Or *justified*

# PART FOUR

# PASTORAL DIRECTIVES

## 4

### False teachers

1 Jn 2:18
2 Thess 2:3
2 Pet 3:3

¹Now the Spirit expressly says that in later times some will depart from the faith by giving heed to deceitful spirits and doctrines of demons, ²through the pretensions of liars

---

¹Spiritus autem manifeste dicit quia in novissimis temporibus discedent quidam a fide, attendentes spiritibus seductoribus et doctrinis daemoniorum, ²in hypo-

---

sight of him, men come to know him through preaching. Christ is manifested to all, for just as he is seen by the angels (that part of creation nearest to God), so is he revealed to the Gentiles (whom the Jews regarded as most distanced from God): "he appeared to the angels, having been made greater than them, and he was preached to the nations, as the bearer of salvation" (*ibid.*).

The last words profess faith in the glorification of Christ at the extremes of creation—earth and heaven. On earth he is glorified because faith in him implies recognizing him as God; and he is glorified in heaven because the Ascension (which in Pauline teaching marks the definitive victory of Christ— cf. Phil 2:9-12 and note) is the definitive glorious revelation of his Person: "he was believed in, in the world, as the one sent by the Father, and by the same Father he was assumed into heaven as Lord" (*ibid.*).

And so the *mysterium pietatis* involves the reconciliation-union of man with God in Christ: he takes our flesh without ceasing to be God; the nations of the earth will recognise him, as will the angels in heaven, he dwells in the hearts of men through faith, but his mansion is in heaven at the Father's side.

**1-2.** From this point onwards the letter seems to take on an even more friendly tone; it is almost like conversation put in writing—which makes it difficult to analyse. However, in the midst of all the various digressions and pastoral advice there are a number of basic themes. In the fourth chapter St Paul's counsels hinge on Timothy himself and his deportment; the fifth has to do with his relationship with the faithful; and the last (chap. 6) deals with policy towards false teachers.

In the present chapter St Paul tells Timothy that deceitful teachers are having a harmful effect on the faithful (vv. 1-5) and that he needs to act like a good minister—doing everything he can to steer them away from unsound doctrine (vv. 6-11) and being exemplary and prudent in the performance of his duties (vv. 12-16).

"The Spirit expressly says . . .": the Church is the pillar of the truth (3:9) but

whose consciences are seared, [3]who forbid marriage and
enjoin abstinence from foods which God created to be
received with thanksgiving by those who believe and know
the truth. [4]For everything created by God is good, and
nothing is to be rejected if it is received with thanksgiving;
[5]for then it is consecrated by the word of God and prayer.

Gen 9:3
1 Cor 10:30f

Gen 1:31
Acts 10:15

---

crisi loquentium mendacium et cauteriatam habentium suam conscientiam,
[3]prohibentium nubere, abstinere a cibis, quos Deus creavit ad percipiendum
cum gratiarum actione fidelibus et his, qui cognoverunt veritatem. [4]Quia omnis
creatura Dei bona, et nihil reiciendum, quod cum gratiarum actione percipitur,
[5]sanctificatur enim per verbum Dei et orationem. [6]Haec proponens fratribus

---

we should not be surprised if deceitful teachers cause people to give up the
faith; we have been warned that this would happen; St Paul may be referring
to what Jesus said in his eschatological discourse (cf. Mt 24:24 and par.) or to
warnings repeatedly given by the Apostles (cf. 2 Thess 2:3-12; 4:3-4; 2 Pet 3:2;
Jude 18). The "later times" are the period between our Lord's first and second
comings; no indication is given as to their duration.

Hypocrisy (pretension) and obstinacy are marks of these heretics. Their
teachings are as wrong as the devil's, although they are superficially attractive:
"No one can deceive another", St Thomas Aquinas comments, "by naked lying;
the lying has to be disguised. These people could not have deceived others
unless they covered their lie with the veil of good intentions, pretence or false
authority" (*Commentary on 1 Tim, ad loc.*).

Their obstinacy is referred to by the simile of a searing iron. It was common
at that time to punish evildoers by branding them with a mark to identify them
for what they were. St Paul may also be referring to this custom, but at least he
is implying that the conscience of these people suffers from the same defect as
cauterized skin: it becomes rough and often insensitive to the touch.

People nowadays also run the risk of their conscience going to sleep,
particularly on ethical matters. Hence "the Church constantly implores from
God the grace that *integrity of human consciences* will not be lost, that their
healthy *sensitivity* with regard to good and evil will not be blunted. This
integrity and sensitivity are profoundly linked to the intimate action of the Spirit
of truth. In this light the exhortations of St Paul assume particular eloquence:
'Do not quench the Spirit'; 'Do not grieve the Holy Spirit' (1 Thess 5:19; Eph
4:30). But above all the Church constantly implores with the greatest fervour
*that there will be no increase* in the world of the sin that the Gospel calls
'blasphemy against the Holy Spirit'. Rather, she prays that it will *decrease* in
human souls—and consequently in the forms and structures of society itself—
and that it will make room for that openness of conscience necessary for the
saving action of the Holy Spirit" (John Paul II, *Dominum et Vivificantem*, 47).

**3-5.** Two serious errors of these false teachers involved forbidding marriage
and enforcing Jewish dietary laws. These errors continued to be promoted for

⁶If you put these instructions before the brethren, you
will be a good minister of Christ Jesus, nourished on the
words of the faith and of the good doctrine which you have
followed. ⁷Have nothing to do with godless and silly myths.

bonus eris minister Christi Iesu, enutritus verbis fidei et bonae doctrinae, quam
assecutus es; ⁷profanas autem et aniles fabulas devita. Exerce teipsum ad

a long time, particularly by second-century Gnostics, whose dualism viewed
everything material as bad and only spiritual things as good.

Christian teaching, on the contrary, on the basis of our Lord's words and the
Apostles' (cf. also 1 Cor 7:1-7 and Eph 5:21-23), has always maintained the
dignity of marriage; Jesus in fact raised marriage to the level of a sacrament
(cf. Council of Trent, sess. XXIV). The Church also teaches that all food is
good, but it does preach sobriety and encourages fasting: "It firmly believes,
professes and teaches that everything made by God is good and nothing is to
be rejected provided it is received with thanksgiving (1 Tim 4:4), for, as the
Lord says, what enters a man's mouth does not make him unclean (Mt 15:11),
and the distinction made by the Mosaic Law between clean and unclean food
belongs to a rite which has been superseded and which ceased to be effective
with the advent of the Gospel" (Council of Florence, *Pro Jacobitis*).

This is the first Christian evidence of grace before and after meals (alluded
to in v. 5); this was of course a custom in the Jewish tradition.

**6.** The specific advice to Timothy starts with the main point: he should be
a "good minister of Christ Jesus". For this, the first thing he must do is be a
good transmitter of the doctrine he himself has received.

"Good doctrine": the Greek word *didaskalia* occurs frequently in the
Pastoral Epistles and is usually translated as "doctrine" or "teaching" (cf. 1 Tim
1:10; 4:1, 6, 13, 16; 2 Tim 3:10-16; Tit 1:9; 2:7). Divine Revelation encompasses all the truths which must be passed on from one generation to the next;
however, doctrinal fidelity is not only a matter of guarding the deposit of faith
(cf. 2 Tim 1:14); it involves dedicated study and meditation of these truths,
which should provide nourishment for our interior life. And so the Second
Vatican Council says that "a sacred minister's knowledge ought to be sacred
in the sense of being derived from a sacred source and directed to a sacred
purpose. Primarily, then, it is drawn from the reading and meditation of Sacred
Scripture. It is also fruitfully nourished by the study of the Fathers and Doctors
of the Church and the other ancient records of Tradition" (*Presbyterorum
ordinis*, 19).

**7-11.** "Train yourself in godliness": that is, in what fidelity to Jesus requires.
Godliness, *pietas*, is a divine attribute insofar as it is God's infinite love
expressed in action; that is why Christ is "the mystery of our religion", *pietatis
mysterium* (cf. 1 Tim 3:16). In man, godliness is loving response to God's
initiative; it therefore encompasses all the various ways of increasing one's

Train yourself in godliness; [8]for while bodily training is of some value, godliness is of value in every way, as it holds promise for the present life and also for the life to come. [9]The saying is sure and worthy of full acceptance. [10]For to this end we toil and strive,[j] because we have our hope set on the living God, who is the Saviour of all men, especially of those who believe. [11]Command and teach these things.

**Pastoral advice to Timothy**

[12]Let no one despise your youth, but set the believers an

pietatem; [8]nam corporalis exercitatio ad modicum utilis est, pietas autem ad omnia utilis est promissionem habens vitae, quae nunc est, et futurae. [9]Fidelis sermo et omni acceptione dignus: [10]in hoc enim laboramus et certamus, quia sperantes sumus in Deum vivum, qui est salvator omnium hominum, maxime fidelium. [11]Praecipe haec et doce. [12]Nemo adulescentiam tuam contemnat, sed

union with God (cf. "Introduction to the Pastoral Epistles", above, pp. 84-86).

St Paul is very fond of comparing the Christian life to athletics (cf. 1 Cor 9:26-27; Gal 2:2; 5:7; Phil 3:13-14), and, especially in the Greco-Roman world, it is easy to understand why: like the godly man, the athlete needs to train regularly to be strong, courageous and single-minded; godliness is a deeply religious attitude, but one can only stay godly by continuous practice.

Just as the athlete does not lose sight of the prize he is aiming for, the Christian knows that the goal of his daily effort is God, the Saviour of all; godliness can promote our physical health, but the main thing it does is promote spiritual life and eternal life (and it helps us develop human virtues, in this life). "Look: what we have to try to do is to get to heaven. If we don't, nothing is worthwhile. Faithfulness to Christ's doctrine is absolutely essential to our getting to heaven. To be faithful it is absolutely essential to strive doggedly against anything that blocks our way to eternal happiness. I know that the moment we begin to talk about fighting we come face to face with our weakness and we foresee falls and mistakes [. . .]. We are creatures and full of defects. I would almost say that they will always have to be there. They are the shadow which shows up the light of God's grace and our resolve to respond to God's kindness" (J. Escrivá, *Christ is passing by*, 76).

**12-13.** A good minister should be a model of virtue. Timothy was obviously very young for the office he held; the Apostle therefore keeps telling him that he must give good example because virtues give a person more experience than age does.

"Reading, preaching, teaching": all three were done at the liturgical assemblies of the early Christians (and continue to be done during the Liturgy of the Word at Mass): some texts of Sacred Scripture were read and then the minister

[j]Other ancient authorities read *suffer reproach*

example in speech and conduct, in love, in faith, in purity.
<sup></sup>13Till I come, attend to the public reading of scripture, to

Acts 6:6
2 Tim 1:6

preaching, to teaching. 14Do not neglect the gift you have,
which was given you by prophetic utterance when the

Acts 20:28

elders laid their hands upon you. 15Practise these duties,
devote yourself to them, so that all may see your progress.

2 Tim 3:14

16Take heed to yourself and to your teaching; hold to that,

---

exemplum esto fidelium in verbo, in conversatione, in caritate, in fide, in
castitate. 13Dum venio, attende lectioni, exhortationi, doctrinae. 14Noli negle-
gere donationem, quae in te est, quae data est tibi per prophetiam cum im-
positione manuum presybterii. 15Haec meditare, in his esto, ut profectus tuus

---

gave a homily which would have included some words of encouragement and
some doctrinal instruction.

**14.** The gift referred to here is that of the sacrament of Order: it is a
permanent gift ("the gift you *have*") from God, bestowed by an external rite
consisting of liturgical prayer and the laying on of hands. This interpretation is
derived from the context: the "gift" (charism) is indelible (Timothy may neglect
it but he can never lose it); therefore, it does not refer to sanctifying grace but
to the priestly "character" or mark which the sacrament imprints along with the
grace of the sacrament itself.

The "prophetic utterances", which in the New Testament means "public
teaching" (cf. note on 1 Tim 1:18-19) or words spoken in God's name, here
refers to the prayers used in the ordination rite.

The "laying on of hands" is another technical expression. Jesus used this
gesture many times (cf. Mt 9:18-19; 19:15; Mk 6:5; 7:32; 8:23-25; 16:8; Lk
4:40; 13:13); the Apostles used it as a rite for bringing down the Holy Spirit
(Acts 8:17; 19:6). Here, as elsewhere in these letters, the laying on of hands is
the rite of priestly ordination (cf. 1 Tim 5:22; 2 Tim 1:6), whereby the mission
and powers of the person performing the rite are passed on, thereby ensuring
continuity of priesthood. In 2 Timothy 1:6, a parallel text, it says "through the
laying on of my hands"; whereas here it says "when the elders laid their hands
on you". The participles "through" and "when" imply that the action of im-
position of hands is an essential part of the sacrament.

The Church has preserved intact the essential elements of the sacrament of
Order—the laying on of hands and the consecrating words of the bishop (cf.
Paul VI, Apost. Const. *Pontificalis Romani recognitio*, 18 July 1968).

**15-16.** As well as being mindful of his grace of ordination, the Christian
minister must remain true to his obligations: "Take heed to yourself". Although
the calling to Church office does not demand exceptional qualities in the
candidate, he still needs to be exemplary and to put special effort into developing virtues or else his ministry will not be nearly as productive as it might

for by so doing you will save both yourself and your hearers.

# 5

**His approach to the faithful in general**

¹Do not rebuke an older man but exhort him as you would a father; treat younger men like brothers, ²older women like mothers, younger women like sisters, in all purity.

Lev 19:32

---

manifestus sit omnibus. ¹⁶Attende tibi et doctrinae; insta in illis; hoc enim faciens et teipsum salvum facies et eos, qui te audiunt.
¹Seniorem ne increpaveris, sed obsecra ut patrem, iuvenes ut fratres, ²anus ut matres, iuvenculas ut sorores in omni castitate. ³Viduas honora, quae vere

---

be. "Apostolic soul: first of all, yourself. Our Lord has said, through St Matthew: 'When the day of Judgment comes, many will say to me, Lord, Lord, did we not prophesy in your name, work many miracles in your name? Then I shall tell them to their faces: I have never known you; away from me, you evil men.' God forbid—says St Paul—that I, who have preached to others should myself be rejected" (J. Escrivá, *The Way*, 930).

"Hold to that", literally "hold to these things": probably a reference to the various points made in this chapter and perhaps also to things the Apostle had at different times told Timothy to keep an eye on. Perseverance is necessary for the minister himself and for the good of the people to whom he ministers.

**1-2.** In this part of the letter (5:1 - 6:2) the Apostle gives Timothy practical rules for the governance of the Christian community. Although these counsels are given for particular circumstances, the core of them is valid for all situations. St Paul's instructions have to do with widows (vv. 3-16), elders (vv. 17-25) and slaves (6:1-2); but first of all he gives a general principle of behaviour towards others: the pastor should treat them as if they were members of his own family (vv. 1-2).

Among these practical guidelines, prominence is given to refinement in correcting older persons, and basic rules of prudence in dealings with younger women. Taking someone to task can be difficult, especially if the person is older; but charity often leaves one no way out; when a pastor has to rebuke someone, St John Chrysostom recommends that he "sweeten the intrinsic severity by gentleness of manner, for one can rebuke someone without hurting him if one tries to do it in that way" (*Hom. on 1 Tim, ad loc.*). Young women should be treated with special refinement and gravity, "because spiritual love for women", St Thomas comments, "unless it is chaste, degenerates into carnal affection, and therefore in dealings with young women there is a special need for chastity" (*Commentary on 1 Tim, ad loc.*).

**Widows, their role and lifestyle**

³Honour widows who are real widows. ⁴If a widow has children or grandchildren, let them first learn their religious duty to their own family and make some return to their parents; for this is acceptable in the sight of God. ⁵She who is a real widow, and is left all alone, has set her hope on God and continues in supplications and prayers night and

viduae sunt. ⁴Si qua autem vidua filios aut nepotes habet, discant primum domum suam pie regere et mutuam vicem reddere parentibus, hoc enim acceptum est coram Deo. ⁵Quae autem vere vidua est et desolata, sperat in

**3-16.** In the social conditions of the time widows were often unprotected and exposed to poverty. In fact in the Old Testament rules are given for their protection (cf. Ex 22:22ff; Deut 10:18), and the prophets spoke out on their behalf because they (and orphans and aliens also) were often ill-treated in one way or another (cf. Is 1:17, 23; Jer 7:6; Mic 2:9). There is plenty of evidence in the New Testament of the solicitous treatment widows received (cf. Acts 6:1ff; Jas 1:27). The present letter is the one in which St Paul has most to say about widows; he instructs his disciple concerning the duty of the faithful and of the Church to look after widows (vv. 3-5, 16) and he also gives specific rules for the organized groups of widows charged with some particular mission within the Christian community.

**3.** "Honour": the Greek verb means both "honour" and "give material help to". So the Apostle is elaborating on the fourth commandment of the Law of God: "Honour your father and your mother" (Ex 20:12; Deut 5:16). This means that one must show them affection and respect, but it also covers material help when necessary. The Second Vatican Council reminds us that "widowhood, accepted courageously as a continuation of the calling to marriage, will be honoured by all" (*Gaudium et spes*, 48).

The Apostle seems to distinguish widows with close relatives who have a duty to look after them (vv. 4,8); those who live completely alone and have no resources and are dependent on help from the faithful (vv. 3, 5); and finally those who (independently of whether they have relatives or not) devote themselves to the service of the Christian community (vv. 9-16).

**4.** Christians have a special duty to keep the fourth commandment, because parents "are, so to say, images of the immortal God [. . .]; from them we have received existence, them God made use of to infuse into us a soul and reason, by them we were led to the sacraments, instructed in our religion, schooled in right conduct and holiness, and trained in civil and human knowledge" (*St Pius V Catechism*, III, 5, 9). In addition to loving and respecting their parents, children should be grateful for all kinds of things they have received from them, and should help them in their old age.

day; [6]whereas she who is self-indulgent is dead even while
she lives. [7]Command this, so that they may be without
reproach. [8]If any one does not provide for his relatives, and
especially for his own family, he has disowned the faith and
is worse than an unbeliever.

[9]Let a widow be enrolled if she is not less than sixty years
of age, having been the wife of one husband; [10]and she must
be well attested for her good deeds, as one who has brought
up children, shown hospitality, washed the feet of the
saints, relieved the afflicted, and devoted herself to doing
good in every way. [11]But refuse to enrol younger widows;

Rev 3:1

Jn 13:14
Rom 12:13

---

Deum et instat obsecrationibus et orationibus nocte ac die; [6]nam quae in deliciis
est vivens, mortua est. [7]Et haec praecipe, ut irreprehensibiles sint. [8]Si quis autem
suorum et maxime domesticorum curam non habet, fidem negavit et est infideli
deterior. [9]Vidua adscribatur non minus sexaginta annorum, quae fuerit unius
viri uxor, [10]in operibus bonis testimonium habens: si filios educavit, si hospitio
recepit, si sanctorum pedes lavit, si tribulationem patientibus subministravit, si
omne opus bonum subsecuta est. [11]Adulescentiores autem viduas devita; cum

---

**9-16.** This is the earliest evidence there is that widows were in some way
treated as a special group within the primitive Christian communities; through
St Ignatius of Antioch and St Polycarp we know about some of the activities
they were responsible for, particularly works of charity to relieve the poor (cf.
Acts 9:36-39). Like bishops (cf. 1 Tim 3:2-7) and deacons (cf. 1 Tim 3:8-13),
to be a member of the widows' group a woman had to have been married only
once and be of respectable character and noted for good works.

The main criterion for admission was mature age, probably because the
duties involved required that the person be exemplary. Also, some unhappy
experiences (v. 15) may lie behind the Apostle's directive that young widows
without children or special family commitments should marry again, thereby
avoiding the dangers of an idle life. See also note on v. 12.

The advice given in this passage concludes St Paul's thought on how women
should conduct themselves in the various states of life: he had earlier written
about virginity and about married women (cf., e.g., 1 Cor 7; Eph 5:22ff).

**11.** "When they grow wanton against Christ": the Greek verb used here
appears nowhere else in the New Testament and therefore it is difficult to say
exactly what it means. It is possible that St Paul is referring to sexual desires,
which are stronger in young people. But it is more likely that he means youthful
enthusiasm: if the young widow's readiness to enrol is due to a passing emotion,
this same romantic emotion (which is not necessarily sinful) may lead her away
from Christ and then she will want to marry again. He would thus be describing
the kind of depression and neglect of Christ which a person could experience
when she becomes lukewarm after initial enthusiastic commitment to good

Rev 2:4
2 Thess 3:11

1 Cor 7:9
1 Tim 2:15

for when they grow wanton against Christ they desire to marry, [12]and so they incur condemnation for having violated their first pledge. [13]Besides that, they learn to be idlers, gadding about from house to house, and not only idlers but gossips and busybodies, saying what they should not. [14]So I would have younger widows marry, bear children, rule their households, and give the enemy no occasion to revile us. [15]For some have already strayed after Satan. [16]If any believing woman[l] has relatives who are widows, let her assist them; let the church not be burdened, so that it may assist those who are real widows.

### Criteria for choosing elders
1 Thess 5:12

[17]Let the elders who rule well be considered worthy of

---

enim luxuriatae fuerint adversus Christum, nubere volunt, [12]habentes damnationem, quia primam fidem irritam fecerunt; [13]simul autem et otiosae discunt circumire domos, non solum otiosae sed et verbosae et curiosae, loquentes quae non oportet. [14]Volo ergo iuniores nubere, filios procreare, dominas domus esse, nullam occasionem dare adversario maledicti gratia; [15]iam enim quaedam conversae sunt retro Satanam. [16]Si qua fidelis habet viduas, subministret illis, et non gravetur ecclesia, ut his, quae vere viduae sunt, sufficiat. [17]Qui bene

---

works as a member of the widows' group. Their desire to marry is not the reason they abandon Christ; it is simply an attempt to fill the gap left in their hearts when they reject Love.

**12.** Not all the Christian widows were obliged to belong to the organized group of widows which engaged in charitable and service activities. However, those who chose to enrol in the group took on a commitment, and if they were unfaithful to that commitment they were committing a sin. Even though St Paul is talking about an *ad hoc* group, he has things of permanent value to say about the grave moral obligation to keep commitments made to God.

Fidelity is the moral virtue which includes determination to fulfil contractual commitments with a right intention, sincerity and exactitude. St Thomas says that a faithful person is one who keeps his promises (cf. *Summa theologiae*, II-II, q. 110, a. 3 ad 5). A person who acquires a commitment to God or others is *freely* taking on an *obligation*. Fidelity is the best channel for freedom (making it creative and not destructive) and a guarantee of its proper use.

**17-22.** St Paul's instructions to Timothy on how to oversee elders (priests) are clear and precise: elders are worthy of respect (cf. vv. 17-18), one must be very prudent when judging and rebuking them (cf. vv. 19-21) and candidates

[l]Other ancient authorities read *man or woman*; others, simply *man*

double honour, especially those who labour in preaching
and teaching; [18]for the scripture says, "You shall not muzzle
an ox when it is treading out the grain," and, "The labourer
deserves his wages." [19]Never admit any charge against an
elder except on the evidence of two or three witnesses. [20]As
for those who persist in sin, rebuke them in the presence of
all, so that the rest may stand in fear. [21]In the presence of
God and of Christ Jesus and of the elect angels I charge you
to keep these rules without favour, doing nothing from

Deut 25:4
Lk 10:7
1 Cor 9:9

Deut 19:15
Mt 18:16
2 Cor 13:1

praesunt presbyteri, duplici honore digni habeantur, maxime qui laborant in
verbo et doctrina; [18]dicit enim Scriptura: *"Non infrenabis os bovi trituranti"* et:
*"Dignus operarius mercede sua"*. [19]Adversus presbyterum accusationem noli
recipere, nisi *sub duobus vel tribus testibus.* [20]Peccantes coram omnibus argue,
ut et ceteri timorem habeant. [21]Testificor coram Deo et Christo Iesu et electis
angelis, ut haec custodias sine praeiudicio nihil faciens in aliquam partem

for the priesthood should be carefully screened (cf. v. 22). In these counsels the
emphasis tends to increase, the greatest stress being placed on not being hasty
in laying on hands.

**17.** "Double honour": the Greek word means "honour" and "honorarium"
(cf. v. 3); by describing it as "double" the Apostle may be indicating that he
means it to be taken in both senses, for priests have a right to both. It is also a
simple way of saying that other believers should show priests special respect
because they are sacred ministers. St Paul quotes Scripture (v. 18) to make it
very clear that the faithful should contribute to the support of their pastors.
However, the main point he is making is that proper respect should be shown
to priests.

**18.** In our Lord's preaching and in the New Testament writings, quotations
from the Old Testament (acknowledged as sacred by Christians as well as Jews)
are often adduced as an authority to back up particular teachings. Here St Paul
bases his remarks on two texts, one being Deuteronomy 25:4 and the other a
saying of Jesus, recorded in Luke 10:7. He describes both texts as "scripture"
and recognizes both as having the same authority. This is one of the earliest
passages to acknowledge the sacred character of the Gospel text.

**20.** St Paul is apparently referring to priests who commit grave faults,
thereby causing scandal. The fear referred to is, obviously, fear of God. Fear
of God is not something bad; it is a virtue, a gift of the Holy Spirit (cf. Is 11:2-3),
the beginning of wisdom (Prov. 1:7; 9:10), wisdom itself (Job 28:23).

**22.** The laying on of hands in this context cannot refer to the absolution of
sinful priests, as if St Paul were advising great rigorism in the administration

partiality. [22]Do not be hasty in the laying on of hands, nor participate in another man's sins; keep yourself pure.

[23]No longer drink only water, but use a little wine for the sake of your stomach and your frequent ailments.

---

declinando. [22]Manus cito nemini imposueris, neque communicaveris peccatis alienis; teipsum castum custodi. [23]Noli adhuc aquam bibere, sed vino modico

---

of the sacrament of Penance. Here, as elsewhere in the Pastoral Epistles, the laying on of hands means the conferring of priestly ordination (cf. 1 Tim 4:14; 2 Tim 1:6; Acts 14:23). In biblical and Jewish tradition the laying on of hands signifies the passing on of inheritance and powers to one's successor in an office (cf. Deut 34:9).

The Apostle does not mince his words, "but even heavier," says Pius XII, "is the responsibility indicated by what the great bishop of Milan, St Charles Borromeo says: 'On this point, even slight carelessness on my part can be the cause of very great sins' (*Homiliae*, 4, 270). Listen then to what Chrysostom counsels: 'It is not after the first test, or the second or the third, that you should lay on hands, but when you have thought deeply on the matter and studied it carefully' (*Hom. on 1 Tim, ad loc.*). This must be followed particularly in matters concerning the holiness of life of candidates to the priesthood. 'It is not enough', the holy doctor Alphonsus Mary de Liguori says, for the bishop not to know anything bad about the (candidate); he must satisfy himself that he is positively good.' Therefore, do not be afraid of seeming too severe if, in the exercise of your right and the fulfilment of your duty, you require such proofs in advance [. . .]. Indeed, if you carefully follow everything that is laid down […], you will save the Church many tears and the faithful people much scandal" (*Ad catholici sacerdotii*).

The Second Vatican Council, which laid such stress on the fostering of priestly vocations, also emphasized the need for selectivity: "Due strictness should always be brought to bear on the choice and testing of (seminary) students. God will not allow his Church to lack ministers if the worthy are promoted" (*Optatam totius*, 6).

**23.** This piece of pastoral advice breaks the flow of an otherwise more weighty paragraph. Some scholars have suggested that the verse could not be by the author of the letter because it seems out of place. But it is in all the Greek codexes and it is very much in keeping with St Paul's personality to be concerned about his "true child in the faith" (1 Tim 1:2).

Timothy may have been increasing his acts of penance without telling anyone; the Apostle's advice to him is an instance of the Christian teaching that personal mortification should not be so severe as to put one's health at risk. "Remember", Monsignor Escrivá writes, "that God loves his creatures to distraction. How can a donkey work if it is not fed or given enough rest, or if its spirit is broken by too many beatings? Well, your body is like a little donkey, and it was a donkey that was God's chosen throne in Jerusalem, and it carries

²⁴The sins of some men are conspicuous, pointing to judgment, but the sins of others appear later. ²⁵So also good Mt 5:16; 10:26 deeds are conspicuous; and even when they are not, they cannot remain hidden.

# 6

### Slaves, their moral obligations

¹Let all who are under the yoke of slavery regard their masters as worthy of all honour, so that the name of God and the teaching may not be defamed. ²Those who have

Eph 6:5
Tit 2:9f
1 Pet 2:18

Philem 16

utere propter stomachum et frequentes tuas infirmitates. ²⁴Quorundam hominum peccata manifesta sunt praecedentia ad iudicium, quosdam autem et subsequuntur; ²⁵similiter et facta bona manifesta sunt, et, quae aliter se habent, abscondi non possunt.

¹Quicumque sunt sub iugo, servi dominos suos omni honore dignos arbitrentur, ne nomen Dei et doctrina blasphemetur. ²Qui autem fideles habent dominos,

you along the divine pathways of this earth of ours. It has to be controlled so that it doesn't stray away from God's paths—and it has to be encouraged so that it can trot along with all the briskness that you would expect from a poor beast of burden" (*Friends of God*, 137).

**24-25.** These thoughts complete what the Apostle has being saying about prudence in the selection of candidates for the priesthood (v. 22). In its concern that the Church have good ministers, the Council of Trent decreed the establishment of seminaries, and the Church has done much to promote the good training of future priests.

**1-2.** It is reckoned that approximately half the population of Ephesus were slaves; so it is reasonable to assume that a sizeable proportion of the Christians there were slaves.

The Apostle does not tackle the social problem of slavery in a direct way; this does not mean that he was happy about the situation; he simply felt it was more urgent to make people appreciate the intrinsic dignity of all men and their equality in the order of grace (cf. Gal 3:29). Slaves too have been redeemed by Christ and called to be holy; therefore, upright conduct is required of them as of others (for other Pauline texts touching on slavery see, for example, Eph 6:5-9; Col 3:22 - 4:1; Tit 2:9-10; Philem 8-21 and the notes on same).

St Paul provides two criteria to guide slaves in their dealings with others—apostolate and fraternity. For many pagans the example of their slaves was their only way of learning about Christianity; therefore slaves should act in a way that reflected their faith and their Christian formation (v. 1). If their masters

believing masters must not be disrespectful on the ground that they are brethren; rather they must serve all the better since those who benefit by their service are believers and beloved.

### False teachers described

Gal 1:6-9
2 Tim 1:13

Teach and urge these duties. [3]If any one teaches otherwise and does not agree with the sound words of our Lord Jesus Christ and the teaching which accords with godliness,

2 Tim 2:23
Rom 1:29

[4]he is puffed up with conceit, he knows nothing; he has a morbid craving for controversy and for disputes about

---

non contemnant, quia fratres sunt, sed magis serviant, quia fideles sunt et dilecti, qui beneficii participes sunt. Haec doce et exhortare. [3]Si quis aliter docet et non accedit sanis sermonibus Domini nostri Iesu Christi et ei, quae secundum pietatem est, doctrinae, [4]superbus est, nihil sciens, sed languens circa quaestiones et pugnas verborum, ex quibus oriuntur invidiae, contentiones,

---

were believers, the fraternity between master and slave should not lessen the slaves' obligations: they should fulfil these obligations out of a deep sense of Christian love. If this policy is applied, the whole social structure will become imbued with a Christian spirit and eventually the permanent abolition of slavery will come about, for "the ferment of the Gospel has aroused and continues to arouse in the hearts of men an unquenchable thirst for human dignity" (Vatican II, *Gaudium et spes*, 26).

See also the note on Col 3:22 - 4:1.

**3-10.** What he has to say about unmasking false teachers shows he is writing from long experience. He twice describes them as knowing nothing. Their intentions are wrong, because they seek only personal gain (v. 5); the reason why they cause controversy and are forever arguing is to distract attention from their defects and lack of true wisdom (v. 4).

"Sound words": words which bring spiritual health, words of salvation (cf. note on 1:8-10). "The sacred words [words of salvation] of our Lord Jesus Christ" (v. 3): this phrase, and the quotation from Luke 10:7 in 1 Timothy 5:18, give grounds for thinking that at the time this letter was written there was in circulation among the Christians of Ephesus, a written Gospel, specifically that of St Luke. However, there is no other evidence to support this theory. The Apostle could be referring to words of our Lord accurately passed on in oral teaching.

"Teaching which accords with godliness" (v. 3). The term *eusebeia* (*pietas*), godliness/religion/piety, which appears in the New Testament only in the Second Epistle of St Peter and in the Pastoral Epistles, has a broad meaning. Sometimes it refers to Christian doctrine, not in the sense of abstract truths but as a revelation of God to man. Sometimes it means "religion" (cf. 1 Tim 6:5-6,

words, which produce envy, dissension, slander, base sus-
picions, 5and wrangling among men who are depraved in
mind and bereft of the truth, imagining that godliness is a
means of gain. 6There is great gain in godliness with con-
tentment; 7for we brought nothing into the world, andᵐ we
cannot take anything out of the world; 8but if we have food
and clothing, with these we shall be content. 9But those who
desire to be rich fall into temptation, into a snare, into many
senseless and hurtful desires that plunge men into ruin and
destruction. 10For the love of money is the root of all evils;
it is through this craving that some have wandered away
from the faith and pierced their hearts with many pangs.

2 Tim 3:8
1 Tim 4:8
Phil 4:11
Heb 13:5
Job 1:21
Eccles 5:14
Prov 30:8
Mt 6:11
Prov 23:4; 28:22
Mt 6:24

blasphemiae, suspiciones malae, 5conflictationes hominum mente corruptorum
et qui veritate privati sunt, existimantium quaestum esse pietatem. 6Est autem
quaestus magnus pietas cum sufficientia. 7Nihil enim intulimus in mundum,
quia nec auferre quid possumus; 8habentes autem alimenta et quibus tegamur,
his contenti erimus. 9Nam qui volunt divites fieri, incidunt in tentationem et
laqueum et desideria multa stulta et nociva, quae mergunt homines in interitum
et perditionem; 10radix enim omnium malorum est cupiditas, quam quidam

where it is translated as "godliness". In this passage (v. 3) it is the same as
"revealed truth" insofar as revealed truth is our link with God; if one does not
accept the truth, one breaks that link; if one makes use of it for financial gain
one perverts its inner meaning.

**10.** "The love of money is the root of all evils": probably a proverb accepted
even by pagans of the time, particularly the more educated ones. Christians
were well aware of the harmful effects of greed (cf. 1 Jn 2:17 and note). St Paul
uses this memorable phrase to get at the false teachers: the root cause of all
their errors is their greed for possessions. It is clearly a perverted thing to do to
turn godliness, religion, into a way of making money (v. 5). Those who try to
satisfy this ambition will end up unhappy and wretched.

"It hurts you to see that some use the technique of speaking about the Cross
of Christ only so as to climb and obtain promotion. They are the same people
who regard nothing as clean unless it coincides with their own particular
standards. All the more reason, then, for you to persevere in the rectitude of
your intentions, and to ask the Master to grant you the strength to say: 'Non
mea voluntas, sed tua fiat!—Lord, may I fulfil your Holy Will with love'" (J.
Escrivá, *Furrow*, 352).

These severe warnings show how much St Paul suffers over the harm being
done. "For many, of whom I have often told you and now tell you even with
tears, live as enemies of the cross of Christ" (Phil 3:18). Good teachers, on the

ᵐOther ancient authorities insert *it is certain that*

**An appeal to defend the faith**

2 Tim 2:22      ¹¹But as for you, man of God, shun all this; aim at
righteousness, godliness, faith, love, steadfastness, gentle-

---

appetentes erraverunt a fide et inseruerunt se doloribus multis. ¹¹Tu autem, o

contrary, are content with food and a roof over their head (v. 8); detachment
has always been a pre-condition of apostolic effectiveness: "The spirit of
poverty and charity is the glory and witness of the Church of Christ" (Vatican
II, *Gaudium et spes*, 88).

**11-16.** The letter's final piece of advice is given with special solemnity.
There are two reasons for constancy in the fight (v. 12) the call to eternal life,
and fidelity to the confession of faith made at Baptism. The second obligation,
to keep what is commanded (v. 14), is urged with an appeal to the presence of
two witnesses—God the Father, and Jesus Christ (v. 13), who firmly proclaimed his kingship to Pontius Pilate.

There is a very close connexion between perseverance and the eternal
sovereignty of God (v. 16): "The eternity of God", St Bernard teaches, "is the
source of perseverance [. . .]. Who hopes and perseveres in love but he who
imitates the eternity of his charity? Truly, perseverance reflects eternity in some
way; only to perseverance is eternity granted or, to put it better, only perseverance obtains eternity for man" (*Book of Consideration*, 5, 14).

**11.** "Man of God": this expression was used in the Old Testament of men
who performed some special God-given mission—for example, Moses (Deut
33:1; Ps 40:1), Samuel (1 Sam 9:6-7); Elijah and Elisha (1 Kings 17:18; 2 Kings
4:7, 27, 42). In the Pastoral Epistles (cf. also 2 Tim 3:17) it is applied to Timothy
insofar as ordination has conferred on him a ministry in the Church. Through
ordination "the priest is basically a consecrated man, a *man of God* (1 Tim 6:11)
[. . .]. The ministerial priesthood in the people of God is something more than
a holy public office exercised on behalf of the community: it is primarily a
configuration, a sacramental and mysterious transformation of the person of
the man-priest into the person of Christ himself, the only mediator (cf. 1 Tim
2:5)" (A. del Portillo, *On Priesthood*, pp. 44-45).

"Fight the good fight": St Paul often uses military comparisons to describe
the Christian life (cf., e.g., 2 Cor 10:3-6; Eph 6:10-17; Col 1:29; 2 Tim 2:3;
4:7), and they have found their way into the ascetical tradition of the Church
(cf. note on 1 Tim 1:17-19). Here and in 2 Timothy he is referring more to
keeping the truth unsullied, and to preaching: the "good fight of the faith" is of
great importance to everyone.

"Confession in the presence of many witnesses": in addition to the day of
his consecration (cf. 1 Tim 4:14), Timothy would have often had occasion to
make public confession of his faith. However, this phrase is couched in such
formal terms that it seems to refer rather to the profession of faith which has
been made at Baptism ever since the early years of the Church (cf. Acts
2:38-41).

ness. [12]Fight the good fight of the faith; take hold of the 2 Tim 4:7
eternal life to which you were called when you made the
good confession in the presence of many witnesses. [13]In the Jn 18:36-37
presence of God who gives life to all things, and of Christ
Jesus who in his testimony before Pontius Pilate made the
good confession, [14]I charge you to keep the commandment 2 Tim 4:1
unstained and free from reproach until the appearing of our
Lord Jesus Christ; [15]and this will be made manifest at the Deut 10:17<br/>Rev 17:14

---

homo Dei, haec fuge; sectare vero iustitiam, pietatem, fidem, caritatem, patientiam, mansuetudinem. [12]Certa bonum certamen fidei, apprehende vitam aeternam, ad quam vocatus es, et confessus es bonam confessionem coram multis testibus. [13]Praecipo tibi coram Deo, qui vivificat omnia, et Christo Iesu, qui testimonium reddidit sub Pontio Pilato bonam confessionem, [14]ut serves mandatum sine macula irreprehensibile usque in adventum Domini nostri Iesu Christi, [15]quem suis temporibus ostendet beatus et solus potens, Rex reg-

---

**13-14.** "Keep the commandments": the Greek may be referring to one specific commandment (as the RSV reflects); but it can also mean law as a whole and, more likely, the truths of Revelation, that is, the deposit of the faith professed at Baptism.

St Paul very formally calls in, as witnesses to this instruction, God the Father and Christ Jesus, "who in his testimony before Pontius Pilate made the good confession". Jesus' "testimony" includes his entire passion and the declaration he made to the Roman procurator about messianic kingship and his true identity (cf. Jn 18:36-37).

"Until the appearing of our Lord Jesus Christ": when referring to the second coming of Christ the New Testament often uses the term *parousia* (cf. 1 Cor 15:23; 2 Pet 3:4) or "revealing" (cf., e.g., 1 Cor 1:7); the Pastoral Epistles prefer "appearing", epiphany, manifestation (cf. 2 Tim 4:1, 8; Tit 2:13), which better reflect the coming of Christ in glory as Saviour (cf. 2 Tim 1:10). There is, of course, a wonderful continuity between the redemptive work of Christ, the action of the Church in conserving Revelation and passing it on, and the final coming of Christ at the end of time.

**15-16.** This doxology or hymn of praise, one of the richest and most beautiful in the New Testament, may have been taken from the Church's liturgy (which may also be the case with the other hymns in this letter: cf. 1:17 and 3:15-16). It was possibly a reply to pagan hymns honouring rulers and emperors as Gods. However, it is more likely that this particular hymn was inspired by the Old Testament, which speaks of God in similar language. Whatever its origin, the important thing about the hymn is that it expresses faith in God who merits all praise.

At a time known only to him (cf. Mt 24:36), God the Father will bring about the glorious manifestation of Jesus Christ. The text refers to four attributes

1 Tim 1:17
Ex 33:20
Jn 1:18

proper time by the blessed and only Sovereign, the King of kings and Lord of lords, [16]who alone has immortality and dwells in unapproachable light, whom no man has ever seen or can see. To him be honour and eternal dominion. Amen.

### The right way to use wealth

Rom 12:16
Jas 1:10
Ps 62:11
Lk 12:20

[17]As for the rich in this world, charge them not to be haughty, nor to set their hopes on uncertain riches but on God who richly furnishes us with everything to enjoy.

---

nantium et Dominus dominantium, [16]qui solus habet immortalitatem, lucem habitans inaccessibilem, quem vidit nullus hominum nec videre potest; cui honor et imperium sempiternum. Amen. [17]Divitibus huius saeculi praecipe non

---

which show the power and sublimity of God: he is the *only Sovereign*, from whom all lawful rulers on earth receive their authority (cf. Jn 19:11). He is the *King of kings and Lord of lords* (literally, "the King of those who reign and the Lord of those who wield lordship"); this is not, then, a merely honorific title: he does actually exercise sovereignty over those who claim to possess it (cf. Rev 17:14; 19:16). He is *immortal*, for immortality is proper to God, who is Life (cf. Jn 1:4); angels and souls are immortal only by virtue of the nature given them by God. Finally, he is *light* and brightness: these are attributed to God (cf. Ps 104:2) to show his sublimity: God transcends all created things and cannot be fully comprehended by man. St Thomas explains that an object can be invisible on two counts—either because it lacks brightness, as occurs with things which are dark and opaque, or because it is too bright, as occurs in the case of the sun, which is so bright that the human eye cannot look at it; God is so far beyond the capacity of the human mind that man cannot entirely take him in—even though what we can learn about him by the right use of reason and through revelation is true and accurate (cf. *Commentary on 1 Tim, ad loc.*). The conclusion of the hymn, which is liturgical and pedagogical in style, is similar to that found in 1:17: there it says "honour and glory", here "heaven and eternal dominion", putting more stress on God's sovereignty.

This and the other hymns which appear in the letter show that the first Christians were fully aware that man's true purpose in life is to give glory to God. "We do not live for the world, or for our own honour, but for the honour of God, for the glory of God, for the service of God. That is what should motivate us!" (J. Escrivá, *The Forge*, 851).

**17-19.** Material things, which God gives in abundance (cf. Mt 25:14), are not bad in themselves, nor is it forbidden to enjoy them (v. 17); but they need to be used with a sense of social responsibility, with detachment, because true wealth is that which never perishes (cf. Lk 12:33)—virtue: "Let all see that they direct their affections rightly, lest they be hindered in their pursuit of perfect love by the use of worldly things and by an adherence to riches which is contrary to the spirit of evangelical poverty, following the Apostle's advice: Let those

[18]They are to do good, to be rich in good deeds, liberal and generous, [19]thus laying up for themselves a good foundation for the future, so that they may take hold of the life which is life indeed.

Mt 6:20

### Epilogue

[20]O Timothy, guard what has been entrusted to you. Avoid the godless chatter and contradictions of what is falsely called knowledge, [21]for by professing it some have missed the mark as regards the faith.
Grace be with you.

2 Tim 1:12, 14;
4:7

1 Tim 1:6

---

superbe sapere neque sperare in incerto divitiarum, sed in Deo, qui praestat nobis omnia abunde ad fruendum, [18]bene agere, divites fieri in operibus bonis, facile tribuere, communicare, [19]thesaurizare sibi fundamentum bonum in futurum, ut apprehendant veram vitam. [20]O Timothee, depositum custodi, devitans profanas vocum novitates et oppositiones falsi nominis scientiae, [21]quam quidam profitentes circa fidem aberraverunt. Gratia vobiscum.

---

who use this world not fix their abode in it, for the form of this world is passing away (cf. 1 Cor 7:31)" (*Lumen gentium*, 42).

On Christian poverty, see the notes to Mt 5:3 and 6:11.

**20-21.** This is a summary of the letter: as minister of the Christian community of Ephesus, Timothy should guard and pass on the faith he has received, and reject false doctrine which can do harm to the faithful.

"What has been entrusted", sometimes translated as the "deposit". According to Roman law, a "deposit" was something one entrusted to someone who was then under an obligation to protect it so as to be able to return it to the depositor when the latter so required; usually a deposit consisted of money or some other form of property. St Paul applies the term to Revelation and the faith (cf. 2 Tim 1:12-14) and it has passed into the language of theology. St Vincent of Lerins explains all this very well: "What does 'Guard the deposit' mean? St Paul said 'Guard it', against thieves, against enemies, to ensure that while men were asleep no one sowed weeds among the good wheat sown by the Son of Man in his field. And so he said, 'Guard the deposit.' But, what is the 'deposit'? It is what you must believe, not what you invented; what you received, not what you thought up yourself; it is the outcome of teaching, not the result of ingenuity; what comes from public tradition, not from private plundering. It is something which has come down to you, but which you have not produced; something of which you are not the author but the guardian; not the leader but the one led. 'Guard the deposit', the Apostle says; keep inviolate and spotless the talent of the catholic faith. What you have believed hold fast to, and pass it on to another" (*Commonitorium*, 22).

# Introduction to the Second Epistle to Timothy

The information contained in this epistle leads one to think that it was the Apostle's last letter, written as it was from gaol in Rome shortly before his death (cf. 1:8, 16-17; 2:9; 4:6); for this very good reason it is usually regarded as his spiritual testament.

The tone is more personal, more from the heart, than that of 1 Timothy; it is a letter with many personal references: Paul twice presses Timothy to join him, as if he felt the need of his company (4:9, 21); he laments the fact that certain disciples have deserted the cause (4:9, 14); he asks him to do him the favour of bringing his cloak and books (4:11); etc. Given the circumstances in which he found himself, St Paul's counsels are his "last word". He repeatedly exhorts Timothy to persevere in his preaching and ministry (1:6 - 2:13; 4:1-5), never minding physical suffering or mental fatigue. To counter the work of those who spread false doctrine, Timothy must be tireless—a good "workman who has no need to be ashamed" (2:15); even if there are difficult times ahead (3:1), false teachers will never gain the upper hand—just as they failed to do so in Moses' time (3:8, 9). Two pieces of advice stand out: Timothy should stay true to the Apostle's teaching and the example he has set him (3:10), and he must keep Sacred Scripture as his point of reference because it is inspired by God and useful for teaching and for defending the truth (3:16).

The letter makes frequent reference to being faithful to God-given responsibilities: God will "judge the living and the dead" (4:1); he will punish those who desert him (4:14) and will give the crown "to all who have loved his appearing" (4:8). The fact that we will be judged should not make us afraid or depressed; rather it should give us hope and serenity; these words, probably the last the Apostle ever wrote, are particularly expressive and show his greatness of soul and his total trust in God: "The Lord will rescue me from every evil and save me for his heavenly kingdom. To him be glory for ever and ever. Amen."

# The Second Epistle to Timothy

ENGLISH AND LATIN VERSIONS, WITH NOTES

# 1

## Greeting

¹Paul, an apostle of Christ Jesus by the will of God according to the promise of the life which is in Christ Jesus, ²To Timothy, my beloved child: Grace, mercy, and peace from God the Father and Christ Jesus our Lord.

³I thank God whom I serve with a clear conscience, as did my fathers, when I remember you constantly in my

1 Cor 1:1
Rom 1:1

Acts 16:1
1 Tim 1:2

Rom 1:9
Phil 3:5

¹Paulus apostolus Christi Iesu per voluntatem Dei secundum promissionem vitae, quae est in Christo Iesu, ²Timotheo carissimo filio: gratia, misericordia, pax a Deo Patre et Christo Iesu Domino nostro. ³Gratias ago Deo, cui servio a

**1-2.** The greeting is like that of 1 Timothy, although now St Paul adds a specific reference to the purpose of his God-given call to the apostolate—"according to the promise of the life which is in Christ Jesus". Christ fulfils all the promises of happiness given to Abraham and the other Old Testament patriarchs. The purpose of the Gospel message is to let men know that they have been called to enjoy a new life in Christ, that is, the divine life whose germ we receive at Baptism. That sacrament initiates the life of grace in the soul, and ultimately that life will blossom into eternal life (cf. 1 Tim 1:16; 6:12; Tit 1:2; 3:9).

On the exact meaning of the expression "in Christ Jesus", see the note on 1 Tim 1:14.

**3.** "I thank God": this is not a spontaneous expression of gratitude but rather a permanent disposition of Paul's soul.

St Paul makes the point that his attitude of service and worship is the same as that of his ancestors, the righteous of the Old Testament, for although the Gospel is something new it does not involve a break with the earlier revelation; rather it brings that revelation to fulfilment. The Apostle pays tribute to the chosen people, not hiding his satisfaction at being a Jew himself (cf. Rom 9:3; 11:1; Gal 2:15). "The Church of Christ acknowledges", Vatican II states, "that in God's plan of salvation the beginning of her faith and election is to be found in the patriarchs, Moses and the prophets [. . .]. The Church cannot forget that she received the revelation of the Old Testament by way of that people with whom God in his inexpressible mercy established the ancient covenant [. . .]. She is mindful, moreover, that the Apostles, the pillars on which the Church stands, were of Jewish descent, as were many of those early disciples who proclaimed the Gospel of Christ to the world" (*Nostra aetate*, 4).

**4-5.** These first lines show the Apostle's deep affection for his disciple; he remembers him all the time and longs to see him; they are reminiscent of the elders' farewell to Paul at Miletus (cf. Acts 20:37). The mention of Timothy's

135

prayers. [4]As I remember your tears, I long night and day to see you, that I may be filled with joy. [5]I am reminded of your sincere faith, a faith that dwelt first in your grandmother Lois and your mother Eunice and now, I am sure, dwells in you.

## PART ONE

# PREACHING THE GOSPEL MESSAGE

### Response to grace

[6]Hence I remind you to rekindle the gift of God that is

---

progenitoribus in conscientia pura, quod sine intermissione habeo tui memoriam in orationibus meis nocte ac die [4]desiderans te videre, memor lacrimarum tuarum, ut gaudio implear, [5]recordationem accipiens eius fidei, quae est in te non ficta, quae et habitavit primum in avia tua Loide et matre tua Eunice, certus sum autem quod et in te. [6]Propter quam causam admoneo te, ut resuscites

---

mother and grandmother also shows the intimate tone of the letter and the warm friendship the first Christians had for one another.

On this occasion the Apostle, while expressing gratitude to God, reminds Timothy that he owes a large part of his vocation to the upbringing he received. His mother—a practising Jew (cf. Act 16:1)—and possibly his grandmother also, taught him Sacred Scripture from childhood on (cf. 2 Tim 3:15); and the atmosphere of faith in his home played a major part in his religious education.

The family is the natural context in which children learn all the basic values (including spiritual ones) which help to shape their character and steer them in the right direction. Therefore, "the family must educate the children for life in such a way that each one may fully perform his or her role according to the vocation received from God. Indeed, the family that is open to transcendent values, that serves its brothers and sisters with joy, that fulfils its duties with generous fidelity, and is aware of its daily sharing in the mystery of the glorious Cross of Christ, becomes the primary and most excellent seedbed of vocations to a life of consecration to the Kingdom of God" (John Paul II, *Familiaris consortio*, 53).

**6.** "The gift of God" is the priestly character which Timothy received on the day of his ordination. St Paul is using very graphic and precise language: by the sacrament of Order a divine gift is conferred on the priest; it is like an ember which needs to be revived from time to time in order to make it glow and give forth the warmth it contains. St Thomas Aquinas comments that "the grace of God is like a fire, which does not glow when it is covered by ashes;

within you through the laying on of my hands; [7]for God did
not give us a spirit of timidity but a spirit of power and love
and self-control.

2 Tim 3:14f

### St Paul, herald of the Gospel

[8]Do not be ashamed then of testifying to our Lord, nor
of me his prisoner, but take your share of suffering for the
gospel in the power of God, [9]who saved us and called us
with a holy calling, not in virtue of our works but in virtue

1 Tim 4:14
Rom 8:15

Rom 1:16
Lk 9:26

---

donationem Dei, quae est in te per impositionem manuum mearum; [7]non enim
dedit nobis Deus Spiritum timoris sed virtutis et dilectionis et sobrietatis. [8]Noli
itaque erubescere testimonium Domini nostri neque me vinctum eius, sed
collabora evangelio secundum virtutem Dei, [9]qui nos salvos fecit et vocavit
vocatione sancta, non secundum opera nostra sed secundum propositum suum

---

the same thing happens when grace is covered over in a person by sluggishness
or natural fear" (*Commentary on 2 Tim, ad loc.*).

The gifts which God confers on the priest "are not transitory or temporary
in him, but stable and permanent, attached as they are to an indelible character,
impressed on his soul, by which he is made a priest forever (cf. Ps 109:4), in
the likeness of Him in whose priesthood he has been made to share" (Pius XI,
*Ad catholici sacerdotii*, 17).

"The laying on of my hands": see the note on 1 Tim 4:14.

7. The gift of God, received in the sacrament of Order by the laying on of
hands, includes sanctifying grace and sacramental grace, and the actual graces
needed for performing ministerial functions in a worthy manner. The Council
of Trent uses this text (vv. 6-7) when it solemnly defines that Priestly Order is
a sacrament instituted by Jesus Christ (cf. *De Sacram. Ordinis*, chap. 3).

The minister, then, must be courageous in performing his office: he should
preach the truth unambiguously even if it clashes with the surroundings; he
should do so with love, and be open to everyone despite their faults; with
sobriety and moderation, always seeing the good of souls, not his own
advantage. Since the days of the Fathers the Church has urged priests to develop
these virtues: "Priests should be compassionate", St Polycarp warns; "they
should show mercy to all; they should try to reclaim those who go astray, visit
the sick, and care for the poor, the orphan and the widow. They should be
concerned always to do what is honourable in the sight of God and men. They
should avoid any show of anger, any partiality or trace of greed. They should
not be over-ready to believe ill of anyone, not too severe in their censure, being
well aware that we all owe the debt of sin" (*Letter to the Philippians*, chap. 6).

9-10. There is a theological basis for courageously confronting the difficulties the Gospel brings with it—the fact that we have been called by God,
who has revealed himself as our Saviour. As elsewhere in these letters (cf. 1

Tit 3:5
Eph 1:11

Rom 16:25f
1 Tim 6:11

of his own purpose and the grace which he gave us in Christ Jesus ages ago, [10]and now has manifested through the appearing of our Saviour Christ Jesus, who abolished death and brought life and immortality to light through the gospel. [11]For this gospel I was appointed a preacher and apostle and teacher, [12]and therefore I suffer as I do. But I am not

---

et gratiam, quae data est nobis in Christo Iesu ante tempora saecularia, [10]manifestata autem nunc per illustrationem salvatoris nostri Iesu Christi, qui destruxit quidem mortem, illuminavit autem vitam et incorruptionem per evangelium, [11]in quo positus sum ego praedicator et apostolus et doctor. [12]Ob quam causam

---

Tim 3:15ff; Tit 3:5-7). St Paul here speaks a succinct hymn in praise of salvation, probably using expressions based on some liturgical hymn or confession of faith.

The salvation which God brings about is viewed in this passage as it applies to Christians (v. 9) and is manifested in the incarnation of Christ (v. 10). Four essential aspects of salvation are identified: 1) God has already accomplished salvation for everyone; 2) it is God, too, who calls all men to avail of it; 3) it is entirely a gift: man cannot merit it (cf. Tit 3:5; Eph 2:8-9); and 4) God's plan is an eternal one (cf. Rom 8:29-30; Eph 1:11).

"The appearing of our Saviour Jesus Christ" (v. 10) refers in the first place to his incarnation (cf. Tit 2:11; 3:4) but it includes his entire work of redemption, which culminates in his appearing in glory and majesty (cf. 1 Tim 6:14; 2 Tim 4:1, 8). The Redemption has two wonderful effects—victory over death (physical and spiritual) and the abundant and luminous gift of everlasting life. "He is the true Lamb who took away the sins of the world. By dying he destroyed our death; by rising he restored our life" (*Preface of Easter*, I).

"Ages ago": literally, "from the times of the ages", a primitive expression meaning the same thing as "eternity".

**12.** "I know whom I have believed": through the virtue of faith we assent to the truths God has revealed, not on the intrinsic evidence they provide but on the authority of God, who can neither deceive nor be deceived (cf. Vatican I, *Dei Filius*, chap. 3). The response of faith is basically a trusting abandonment of oneself into God's hands: "By faith man freely commits his entire life to God, making 'the full submission of his intellect and will to God who reveals', and willingly assenting to the Revelation given by him. Before this faith can be exercised, man must have the grace of God to move and assist him; he must have the interior helps of the Holy Spirit, who moves the heart and converts it to God, who opens the eyes of the mind and 'makes it easy for all to accept and believe the truth'" (Vatican II, *Dei Verbum*, 5).

"What has been entrusted to me": some commentators think that this "deposit" is the sum total of the good works and merits the Apostle has built up over his lifetime. However, it is more likely that he is referring to the body

ashamed, for I know whom I have believed, and I am sure
that he is able to guard until that Day what has been
entrusted to me.a 13Follow the pattern of the sound words    1 Tim 2:7
which you have heard from me, in the faith and love which
are in Christ Jesus; 14guard the truth that has been entrusted    2 Tim 1:5
to you by the holy Spirit who dwells within us.    1 Tim 6:3

### Attitudes towards certain disciples

15You are aware that all who are in Asia turned away    1 Tim 6:20

etiam haec patior, sed non confundor; scio enim, cui credidi, et certus sum quia
potens est depositum meum servare in illum diem. 13Formam habe sanorum
verborum, quae a me audisti, in fide et dilectione, quae sunt in Christo Iesu;
14bonum depositum custodi per Spiritum Sanctum, qui habitat in nobis. 15Scis
hoc quod aversi sunt a me omnes, qui in Asia sunt, ex quibus est Phygelus et

of doctrine which he strives to guard and to teach to others. It is in that sense
that St John Chrysostom interprets it: "What does this 'deposit' mean? Faith,
preaching. He himself who has entrusted the deposit to me knows how to keep
it intact. I suffer as may be to ensure that this treasure is not snatched away
from me. I do not try to escape whatever evils I have to undergo; I am happy
as long as the deposit is preserved pure and intact" (*Hom. on 2 Tim, ad loc.*).
See also the note on 1 Tim 6:20.

"That Day": the day of judgment, when he will be called to give an account
to God. It can refer to both the particular judgment and the last judgment.

**13-14.** In guarding what has been entrusted to him (cf. notes on 1 Tim 6:20
and 2 Tim 1:12), Timothy, like all the pastors of the Church, receives the
supernatural help of the Holy Spirit. "Guiding the Church in the way of all truth
(cf. Jn 16:13) and unifying her in communion and in the works of ministry, (the
Spirit) bestows upon her varied hierarchic and charismatic gifts, and in this way
directs her; and he adorns her with his fruits (cf. Eph 4:11-12; 1 Cor 12:4; Gal
5:22)" (Vatican II, *Lumen gentium*, 4).

The Holy Spirit has been with the Church since the day of Pentecost,
ever-active in the sanctification of all believers. His action includes guaran-
teeing the faithful transmission of the entire body of teaching revealed by God,
ensuring that it be unchanged in any way. The First Vatican Council teaches
that the Holy Spirit "was not promised to the successors of St Peter so that they
by their own revelation might make known some new teaching; he was
promised so that by means of his help they might reverently guard and faithfully
expound the revelation transmitted by the Apostles, that is, the deposit of faith"
(*Pastor aeternus*, chap. 4).

**15-18.** St Paul tells his disciple about being deserted by Christians from
Asia (that is, the Roman province of that name, now western Turkey); he gives

aOr *what I have entrusted to him*

from me, and among them Phygelus and Hermogenes. [16]May the Lord grant mercy to the household of Onesiphorus, for he often refreshed me; he was not ashamed of my chains, [17]but when he arrived in Rome he searched for me eagerly and found me—[18]may the Lord grant him to find mercy from the Lord on that Day—and you well know all the service he rendered at Ephesus.

## 2

### How Timothy should face hardships

[1]You then, my son, be strong in the grace that is in Christ Jesus, [2]and what you have heard from me before many

---

Hermogenes. [16]Det misercordiam Dominus Onesiphori domui, quia saepe me refrigeravit et catenam meam non erubuit, [17]sed cum Romam venisset, sollicite me quaesivit et invenit [18]—det illi Dominus invenire misercordiam a Domino in illa die—et quanta Ephesi ministravit, melius tu nosti.

[1]Tu ergo, fili mi, confortare in gratia, quae est in Christo Iesu; [2]et quae audisti

---

the names of two of them, who must have been well known to the Ephesians, but this is the only reference to them we have. Against this he praises the fidelity of an Ephesian, Onesiphorus. This man, when he arrived in Rome, visited St Paul regularly—which involved inconvenience and risk, given the conditions of the Apostle's second imprisonment (he was being harshly treated, like a criminal). St Paul prays for him and in doing so makes a play on words: just as Onesiphorus "searched" eagerly for Paul, God will be good enough to let him "find" mercy on the day of judgment, thanks to his kind action (which reminds us that visiting those in prison is one of the works of mercy which the Lord will reward on the last day: cf. Mt 25:36).

**1-2.** The grace referred to is that of priestly ordination. In addition to making us like Christ through the infusing of "sanctifying" grace, every sacrament confers its own specific "sacramental" grace which provides the necessary "actual" graces which enable the person to keep the obligations which derive from the sacrament. The sacramental grace of the sacrament of Order equips priests to be good stewards of the mysteries of God and to help men attain salvation.

Timothy will discover in the sacramental grace of Order all the strength he needs to guard the deposit of faith and to train his helpers and successors to do the same. The transmission of Christian doctrine from the Apostles to Christians right down the ages is what is known as "Tradition". This living Tradition

witnesses entrust to faithful men who will be able to teach others also. [3]Take your share of suffering as a good soldier of Christ Jesus. [4]No soldier on service gets entangled in civilian pursuits, since his aim is to satisfy the one who enlisted him. [5]An athlete is not crowned unless he competes according to the rules. [6]It is the hard-working farmer who ought to have the first share of the crops. [7]Think over what I say, for the Lord will grant you understanding in everything.

2 Tim 1:8

1 Cor 9:25
2 Tim 4:8

1 Cor 9:7, 10
Prov 2:6

---

a me per multos testes, haec commenda fidelibus hominibus, qui idonei erunt et alios docere. [3]Collabora sicut bonus miles Christi Iesu. [4]Nemo militans implicat se saeculi negotiis, ut ei placeat, qui eum elegit; [5]si autem certat quis agone, non coronatur nisi legitime certaverit. [6]Laborantem agricolam oportet primum de fructibus accipere. [7]Intellege, quae dico; dabit enim tibi Dominus

---

together with Sacred Scripture constitutes the sacred deposit of the Word of God which has been placed in the Church's keeping. "The apostolic preaching, which is expressed in a special way in the inspired books, was to be preserved in a continuous line of succession until the end of time. Hence the Apostles, in handing on what they themselves had received, warn the faithful to maintain the traditions which they had learned either by word of mouth or by letter (cf. 2 Thess 2:15); and they warn them to fight hard for the faith that had been handed on to them once and for all (cf. Jude 3). What was handed on by the Apostles comprises everything that serves to make the people of God live their lives in holiness and increase their faith. In this way the Church, in her doctrine, life and worship, perpetuates and transmits to every generation all that she herself is, all that she believes" (Vatican II, *Dei Verbum*, 8).

"Faithful men": in the military world (from which St Paul takes this expression), fidelity has always been seen as a necessary virtue for those who are assigned to be on guard, on watch. Therefore, bishops (*episkopos* in Greek means "watchman") have a special need of this virtue. But they also need "to be able to teach others". "What good would it do the bishop to be faithful", St John Chrysostom asks himself, "if he were unable to pass the faith on to others, or if, settling for not betraying the faith, he was unable to awake it in other believers? So, both conditions are necessary in the training of teachers—to be faithful and to have a capacity to teach" (*Hom. on 2 Tim, ad loc.*).

**3.** Military metaphors, applied to Christian living, are a feature of St Paul's writing (cf. Rom 6:13; 13:12; 2 Cor 6:7; 10:4; Eph 6:11-18; Phil 2:25; 1 Tim 1:18; etc.).

**4-7.** The soldier, the athlete and the farmer are three examples of people who work hard and responsibly. In the Greco-Roman world each general was responsible for recruiting and paying his own soldiers; the men who enlisted

**Jesus, the apostle's model**

⁸Remember Jesus Christ, risen from the dead, descended from David, as preached in my gospel, ⁹the gospel for

in omnibus intellectum. ⁸Memor esto Iesum Christum resuscitatum esse a mortuis, ex semine David, secundum evangelium meum, ⁹in quo laboro usque

in those armies undertook to follow the orders of the man who contracted them. The commitment required for athletics was (and is) also very considerable because it meant a person had to be in top physical form and keep within the rules in order to achieve victory. A farmer also had to be working all the year round at one thing or another. In each of these examples stress is put on the eventual reward.

"Think over what I say": St Paul has used these examples to make Timothy realise that his work as a minister of the Church calls for effort if it is to produce results. A priest must be noted for his total, disinterested commitment to his office; as Pius XI writes, "he must be untainted by any selfishness and look with holy disdain on any sordid desire for earthly gain; he must seek souls, not riches; the glory of God, not his own. He is not a wage-earner doing a job for a temporal reward [. . .]; he is the good soldier of Christ who avoids becoming entangled in civil affairs to please whoever engaged him; he is the minister of God and father of souls, and he realizes that his work, his interests, have no adequate compensation in terms of earthly honours and riches" (*Ad catholici sacerdotii*, 39).

**8.** "Jesus Christ, risen from the dead": the Resurrection is the climax of our faith (cf. 1 Cor 15) and the fixed reference point for Christian living, for we know that "Christ being raised from the dead will never die again; death no longer has dominion over him" (Rom 6:9). Therefore, Christ lives on in a glorified condition: "Christ is alive. He is not someone who has gone, someone who existed for a time and then passed on, leaving us a wonderful example and a great memory. No, Christ is alive. Jesus is Emmanuel: God with us. His resurrection shows us that God does not abandon his own" (J. Escrivá, *Christ is passing by*, 102).

"As preached in my gospel": literally, "according to my gospel"; Jesus' glorious resurrection and his descent from David were key points in St Paul's preaching.

**9-10.** The trials which St Paul was experiencing in prison on account of his preaching of the Gospel constitute an entitlement to heaven, for "martyrdom makes the disciple like his master, who willingly accepted death for the salvation of the world, and through it he is conformed to him by the shedding of blood" (*Lumen gentium*, 42). This is a shining example of the Communion of Saints at work, for, when a Christian links his suffering to Christ's passion, that suffering contributes to the Redemption: "Therefore he is carrying out an irreplaceable service. In the Body of Christ, which is ceaselessly born of the

which I am suffering and wearing fetters like a criminal. But the word of God is not fettered. [10]Therefore I endure everything for the sake of the elect, that they also may obtain the salvation which in Christ Jesus goes with eternal glory.

Phil 1:7 / Col 1:24

[11]The saying is sure:

If we have died with him, we shall also live with him; [12]if we endure, we shall also reign with him; if we deny him, he also will deny us; [13]if we are faithless, he remains faithful— for he cannot deny himself.

*Rom 6:3, 8*

*Mt 10:33*

*Rom 3:3 / 1 Cor 10:13*

---

ad vincula quasi male operans, sed verbum Dei non est alligatum! [10]Ideo omnia sustineo propter electos, ut et ipsi salutem consequantur, quae est in Christo Iesu cum gloria aeterna. [11]Fidelis sermo: Nam si commortui sumus, et convivemus; [12]si sustinemus, et conregnabimus; si negabimus, et ille negabit nos; [13]si non credimus, ille fidelis manet, negare enim seipsum non potest. [14]Haec

Cross of the Redeemer, it is precisely suffering permeated by the spirit of Christ's sacrifice that is *the irreplaceable mediator and author of the good things* which are indispensable for the world's salvation. It is suffering, more than anything else, which clears the way for the grace which transforms human souls. Suffering, more than anything else, makes present in the history of humanity the powers of the Redemption" (John Paul II, *Salvifici doloris*, 27).

Throughout history many pastors of the Church have suffered persecution on account of their fidelity to Christ. St John Chrysostom, shortly before going into exile, expressed his feelings in this way: "For me, this world's evils are something I despise; and its good things are an object of scorn. I am not afraid of poverty nor do I have any desire for riches; I am not afraid of death nor do I have any desire to live unless it be to your advantage" (*Ante exilium hom.*, 1).

**11-13.** "The saying is sure": this is a technical expression used a number of times in the Pastoral Epistles to attract attention to especially important statements (cf. note on 1 Tim 1:15). Here it introduces a poetic section in the form of a hymn of four verses, each consisting of a pair of contrasting phrases (of the type the Semitic mind loves). It is quite possible that this hymn was used in very early baptismal liturgy, given that it has to do with the intimate union of the baptized person with Christ, who died and is now risen; it also encourages Christians to stay faithful in the face of adverse circumstances even if that means martyrdom.

Thus, the first verse deals with the beginning of Christian life. Dying to sin and rising to the life of grace are Pauline expressions (cf. Rom 6:3-4) which point to the fact that in Baptism the Christian becomes a sharer in the passion, death and burial of the Lord, and also in the glory of his resurrection. Grace is the source of supernatural life and that life will attain its full form in heaven.

# PART TWO

# DEFENDING THE GOSPEL

**Avoiding useless argument**

1 Tim 1:4
Tit 3:9
[14]Remind them of this, and charge them before the Lord[b] to avoid disputing about words, which doeş no good, but 2 Tim 1:8 only ruins the hearers. [15]Do your best to present yourself to God as one approved, a workman who has no need to be 1 Tim 4:7 ashamed, rightly handling the word of truth. [16]Avoid such

commone testificans coram Deo verbis non contendere: in nihil utile est, nisi ad subversionem audientium. [15]Sollicite cura teipsum probabilem exhibere Deo, operarium inconfusibilem, recte tractantem verbum veritatis. [16]Profana

The two following verses deal with the stark choice the Christian has to make in the face of difficulties—endurance, or denial of the faith (cf. Mt 10:33; Lk 12:9); the hymn puts special emphasis on endurance, using as it does terminology proper to athletics (cf. Heb 12:1-3); also, the verb used in the second part of each phrase is in the future tense, as if an unlikely possibility were being discussed: "In the event of our denying him ...". And (what is most important) the Christian's faithfulness is orientated towards Christ: "we shall reign with him." "To persevere is to persist in love, 'per Ipsum et cum Ipso et in Ipso ...'. Indeed we can also interpret that as: He himself, with me, for me and in me" (J. Escrivá, *Furrow*, 366).

The last verse breaks the pattern because it does not counterpose attitude and result but rather man's infidelity and Christ's fidelity: "If we are faithless, he remains faithful." This paradox of our Lord's love marks the climax of the hymn, which is a kind of poem extolling Christian endurance based on our Lord's eternal faithfulness. "We Christians have the right to proclaim the royalty of Christ. Although injustice abounds, although many do not desire the kingdom of love, the work of salvation is taking place in the same human history as harbours evil" (J. Escrivá, *Christ is passing by*, 186).

**14-16.** False teachers were in a position to do harm to the still immature Christian community of the time; apparently they were not teaching things which were directly heretical; but they were involving the believers in controversy to such an extent that there was a danger of turning the truth of faith into rational deductions in a complicated philosophical system. The Apostle advises that the best way to deal with all that dangerous wordiness is to expound revealed truth in a simple, straightforward way.

"Rightly handling": the original means "cutting straight", the way a mason cuts a stone or a farmer ploughs a furrow. Similarly, preaching and teaching the Gospel should be done in direct, simple language accessible to all. The

[b]Other ancient authorities read *God*

godless chatter, for it will lead people into more and more ungodliness, [17]and their talk will eat its way like gangrene. Among them are Hymenaeus and Philetus, [18]who have swerved from the truth by holding that the resurrection is past already. They are upsetting the faith of some. [19]But

1 Tim 1:20
1 Cor 15:19, 22
Num 16:5, 26
Is 26:13

---

autem inaniloquia devita, magis enim proficient ad impietatem, [17]et sermo eorum ut cancer serpit; ex quibus est Hymenaeus et Philetus, [18]qui circa veritatem aberraverunt dicentes resurrectionem iam factam, et subvertunt quorundam fidem. [19]Sed firmum fundamentum Dei stat habens signaculum

---

teacher should not simply recommend views, attitudes and feelings: his function is to pass on the certainties which "the word of truth" (that is, revealed teaching) provides. Paul VI taught that one "sign of love will be the effort to transmit to Christians, not doubts and uncertainties born of an erudition poorly assimilated but certainties that are solid because they are anchored in the Word of God. The faithful need these certainties for their Christian life" (*Evangelii nuntiandi*, 79).

**17-18.** The Pastoral Epistles frequently describe true teaching as "sound" or healthy, and see false teaching as unhealthy (cf. 1 Tim 6:3; Tit 1:13); here the latter is compared with gangrene because of the way it gradually corrupts the faithful. The possible damage people who spread false doctrine can do to the Church from within is something which it had to face from very early on. St Augustine has this to say about sowers of confusion: "They are more numerous than we might expect, and when they are not refuted they lead others astray and their sect grows, so I do not know where they are going to end up. I would prefer to see them cured in the body of the Church than cut off from that body as incurable members, unless there is an urgent need to do that. The danger is that they will infect others, if we ignore their infection. However, the mercy of the Lord is well able to set them free from their disease" (*Letter* 157, 23).

Hymenaeus and Philetus are an example of the kind of people who sow confusion by lots of subtle arguments. They were saying that "the resurrection is past already". Because the idea of the resurrection of the dead was difficult to accept (especially in a Hellenic culture: cf. Acts 17:32; 1 Cor 15:12), they were interpreting it in a purely spiritual sense. It is true that we have been reborn to a new life at Baptism, but they glossed over the central meaning of the dogma of the resurrection of the dead: a day will come when we will rise again with our own bodies (cf. *Athanasian Creed*). Possibly because, even in apostolic times, some were trying to reduce this resurrection to something entirely spiritual, the early creeds included this article of faith: "we expect the resurrection of the dead" (*Nicene-Constantinopolitan Creed*).

**19.** To counter errors and misunderstandings, St Paul emphasizes the stability of the Church, using a building simile already employed by our Lord (cf. Mt 16:18 and par.) and one of his own favourites (cf. 1 Tim 3:15). There was

God's firm foundation stands, bearing this seal: "The Lord knows those who are his," and, "Let every one who names the name of the Lord depart from iniquity." <sup></sup>

[20]In a great house there are not only vessels of gold and silver but also of wood and earthenware, and some for noble use, some for ignoble. [21]If any one purifies himself from what is ignoble, then he will be a vessel for noble use, consecrated and useful to the master of the house, ready for any good work.

---

hoc: *Cognovit Dominus, qui sunt eius,* et: *Discedat ab iniquitate omnis, qui nominat nomen Domini.* [20]In magna autem domo non solum sunt vasa aurea et argentea sed et lignea et fictilia, et quaedam quidem in honorem, quaedam autem in ignominiam; [21]si quis ergo emundaverit se ab istis, erit vas in honorem,

---

a custom (still followed in some places) of attaching a "foundation document" to the first stone; in the case of a temple or some religious building the foundation document would indicate the building's origin and purpose. St Paul develops his building simile by envisaging two inscriptions on the foundation stone. The first, taken from the Book of Numbers, shows that God looks after his chosen ones, to save them from straying and being lost like Moses' opponents (cf. Num 6:15); this solicitude on God's part is the basis of the Church's infallibility (cf. *Lumen gentium,* 25). The second inscription, taken from the prophet Isaiah (cf. Is 26:13) is an assurance of holiness—the holiness of the individual Christian, who should flee from sin, given that he invokes the name of God; and particularly that of the Church as a whole, because even if its members are sinners, it is preserved from all sin.

**20-21.** These verses continue the metaphor of the Church as a temple or mansion. In the temple of Jerusalem, as in pagan temples, there were all kinds of vessels. On great occasions and for public events, vessels of precious metals were used; cheaper vessels were used for lesser, ordinary, purposes but that did not in any way take from the dignity and holiness of the temple. The same held good for the private houses of noble families. Therefore, no one should be scandalized to find that the Church contains sinners or people who do not conduct themselves very well; the Church is "unfailingly holy. This is because Christ, the Son of God, who with the Father and the Spirit is hailed as 'alone holy', loved the Church as his Bride, giving himself up for her so as to sanctify her with the gift of the Holy Spirit for the glory of God" (Vatican II, *Lumen gentium,* 39).

Therefore "it would be a sign of very little maturity if, in view of the defects and miseries of someone who belongs to the Church (no matter how highly placed he be by virtue of his function), anyone should feel his faith in the Church and in Christ lessened [. . .]. If we love the Church, there will never arise in us a morbid interest in airing, as the faults of the Mother, the weaknesses of some

**Patience towards those in error**

<sup>22</sup>So shun youthful passions and aim at righteousness, faith, love, and peace, along with those who call upon the Lord from a pure heart. <sup>23</sup>Have nothing to do with stupid, senseless controversies; you know that they breed quarrels. <sup>24</sup>And the Lord's servant must not be quarrelsome but kindly to every one, an apt teacher, forbearing, <sup>25</sup>correcting his opponents with gentleness. God may perhaps grant that they will repent and come to know the truth, <sup>26</sup>and they may escape from the snare of the devil, after being captured by him to do his will.<sup>c</sup>

1 Tim 6:11

1 Tim 6:4

1 Tim 3:2
Tit 1:7; 3:2
Gal 6:1

sanctificatum, utile Domino, ad omne opus bonum paratum. <sup>22</sup>Iuvenilia autem desideria fuge, sectare vero iustitiam, fidem, caritatem, pacem cum his, qui invocant Dominum de corde puro. <sup>23</sup>Stultas autem et sine disciplina quaestiones devita, sciens quia generant lites; <sup>24</sup>servum autem Domini non oportet litigare, sed mansuetum esse ad omnes, aptum ad docendum, patientem, <sup>25</sup>cum mansuetudine corripientem eos, qui resistunt, si quando det illis Deus paenitentiam ad cognoscendam veritatem, <sup>26</sup>et resipiscant a Diaboli laqueo, a quo capti tenentur ad ipsius voluntatem.

of her children. The Church, the spouse of Christ, does not have to intone any *mea culpa*. But we do: *mea culpa, mea culpa, mea maxima culpa"* (J. Escrivá, *In Love with the Church*, 7).

All believers, even if they be stained by personal sin, can be cleansed by penance and become a vessel for noble use. St John Chrysostom makes this point about St Paul himself: "Paul was an earthenware vessel but he became one of gold" (*Hom. on 2 Tim, ad loc.*).

**22-26.** This passage contains valuable pastoral advice, especially for those who tend to make everything a matter of debate and thereby sow confusion among the faithful. They are an appeal for patience and serenity; when faced with error one should try to bring the other person round to the truth, and do everything one can to avoid a break and the consequent danger of people being lost to the Church.

In his homily on this text, St John Chrysostom calls for patience, even if opponents are slow to listen to correction: "It very often happens that, if teaching is kept up, one's words do manage to reach the centre of a person's soul, the way the plough enters the soil, and cut the very roots of the passion which was preventing it from being fertile. Through hearing the word, results will come. It cannot be that the word of the Gospel, if listened to continuously, will fail to work. If one did not take that into account, (the teacher) could easily give up his effort in a moment of dejection and lose everything" (*Hom. on 2 Tim, ad loc.*).

<sup>c</sup>Or *by him, to do his* (that is, God's) *will*

**Preventing error from doing harm**

1 Tim 4:1
2 Pet 3:3
Rom 1:29-31

¹But understand this, that in the last days there will come times of stress. ²For men will be lovers of self, lovers of money, proud, arrogant, abusive, disobedient to their parents, ungrateful, unholy, ³inhuman, implacable, slanderers, profligates, fierce, haters of good, ⁴treacherous, reckless, swollen with conceit, lovers of pleasure rather Tit 1:16
Mt 7:15 than lovers of God, ⁵holding the form of religion but denying the power of it. Avoid such people. ⁶For among them

---

¹Hoc autem scito, quod in novissimis diebus instabunt tempora periculosa. ²Erunt enim homines seipso amantes, cupidi, elati, superbi, blasphemi, parentibus inoboedientes, ingrati, scelesti, ³sine affectione, sine foedere, criminatores, incontinentes, immites, sine benignitate, ⁴proditores, protervi, tumidi, voluptatum amatores magis quam Dei, ⁵habentes speciem quidem pietatis, virtutem autem eius abnegantes; et hos devita. ⁶Ex his enim sunt, qui penetrant

---

**1-5.** "The last days": strictly speaking, this means the time immediately prior to the second coming of our Lord; but because it has not been revealed to us exactly when that will be (cf. Mt 24:3ff), the "last days" can be taken to mean the entire period between the Incarnation (cf. Heb 1:2) and our Lord's coming in glory: these are the times when the vices mentioned will afflict mankind.

As many as eighteen types of sin are listed here. Elsewhere in the Pastoral Epistles (cf. 1 Tim 1:9-10; 6:4-5; Tit 3:3; 2 Tim 3:2-5) the vices mentioned have to do mainly with doctrinal aberrations; but here they are more the result of selfishness and are more serious because they strike at the basis of the moral order.

The morality of human acts is measured in terms of their conformity to the eternal law of God, that is, the moral order established by the Creator to guide us to our individual goal and to the universal goal of Creation, the glory of God. When man allows himself to be dictated to by his passions and fails to respect the order desired by God, he does grave harm to himself and to society, because he opens the door to every type of moral disorder. The last vice named by the Apostle is especially dangerous to the Church: it is that of people who project themselves as being godly and concerned about others but who are empty on the inside, devoid of grace and of love for God.

**6-9.** Of all those burdened with vice (vv. 2-5) the most dangerous are people who go about spreading ideas contrary to the truth and harmful to faith. They claim to have new insights, new wisdom, and lead astray those who listen to them out of idle curiosity.

According to Jewish tradition, Jannes and Jambres were the names of the Egyptian magicians summoned by Pharoah to perform miracles in answer to

are those who make their way into households and capture weak women, burdened with sins and swayed by various impulses, [7]who will listen to anybody and can never arrive at a knowledge of the truth. [8]As Jannes and Jambres opposed Moses, so these men also oppose the truth, men of corrupt mind and counterfeit faith; [9]but they will not get very far, for their folly will be plain to all, as was that of those two men.

[10]Now you have observed my teaching, my conduct, my aim in life, my faith, my patience, my love, my steadfastness, [11]my persecutions, my sufferings, what befell me

Ex 7:11

2 Tim 3:13

Acts 13:50;
14:2ff
Ps 34:18

domos et captivas ducunt mulierculas oneratas peccatis, quae ducuntur variis concupiscentiis, [7]semper discentes et numquam ad scientiam veritatis pervenire valentes. [8]Quemadmodum autem Iannes et Iambres restiterunt Moysi, ita et hi resistunt veritati, homines corrupti mente, reprobi circa fidem; [9]sed ultra non proficient, insipientia enim eorum manifesta erit omnibus, sicut et illorum fuit. [10]Tu autem assecutus es meam doctrinam, institutionem, propositum, fidem, longanimitatem, dilectionem, patientiam, [11]persecutiones, passiones, qualia

the prodigies Moses and Aaron worked in his presence (cf. Ex 7:11). Like them, false teachers oppose the truth of the Gospel, but they too will ultimately fail because human ingenuity is no match for God.

This passage carries a strong note of sarcasm: the only thing these people manage to do is to convince a few dim-witted and weak-willed women. They "will not get very far", so Timothy should not be pessimistic, nor should he be cowed. "At times I think that a few enemies of God and his Church live off the fear of many good people, and I am filled with shame" (J. Escrivá, *Furrow*, 115).

One of the primary responsibilities of the pastors of the Church is to try to prevent the faithful being exposed to teachings harmful to their faith. St Ignatius of Antioch advises St Polycarp to this effect: "Do not let yourself be upset by those who seem to be very reliable and yet put forward strange teachings. Stand your guard, like an anvil under the hammer. The mark of a good athlete is to win despite taking blows. Accept trials of all kinds for God's sake and we will be accepted by him. Be even more diligent than you are now" (*Letter to Polycarp*, 3, 1).

**10-13.** Unlike those who were opposing St Paul's teachings, Timothy is commended for his faithfulness and is offered practical advice on how to cope with difficulties. To encourage him, Paul recalls his own experience (with which Timothy, a native of Lystra, was very familiar). In his first letter (cf. 1 Thess 3:2-3 and note) he already made the point and now he repeats it: "all who desire to live a godly life in Christ Jesus will be persecuted." Thanks to suffering we can obtain a share in the victory won by Christ. "Christ has overcome the

at Antioch, at Iconium, and at Lystra, what persecutions I endured; yet from them all the Lord rescued me. ¹²Indeed all who desire to live a godly life in Christ Jesus will be persecuted, ¹³while evil men and impostors will go on from bad to worse, deceivers and deceived.

**Staying true to Scripture**

¹⁴But as for you, continue in what you have learned and have firmly believed, knowing from whom you learned it
¹⁵and how from childhood you have been acquainted with

mihi facta sunt Antiochiae, Iconii, Lystris, quales persecutiones sustinui; et ex omnibus me eripuit Dominus. ¹²Et omnes, qui volunt pie vivere in Christo Iesu, persecutionem patientur; ¹³mali autem homines et seductores proficient in peius in errorem mittentes et errantes. ¹⁴Tu vero permane in his, quae didicisti et credita sunt tibi, sciens a quibus didiceris, ¹⁵et quia ab infantia Sacras Litteras

world definitively by his Resurrection. Yet, because of the relationship between the Resurrection and his Passion and death, he has at the same time overcome the world by his suffering [. . .]. Through the Resurrection, he manifests *the victorious power of suffering*, and he wishes to imbue with the conviction of this power the hearts of those whom he chose as Apostles and those whom he continually chooses and sends forth" (John Paul II, *Salvifici doloris*, 25).

**14-15.** "Continue in what you have learned and firmly believed": this is sound advice—that Timothy should not relinquish the truth which he learned from his mother and from the Apostle: "Religion, of its nature, must be passed on in its entirety to children with the same fidelity as it has been received by the parents themselves; we have no right to take religion and do with it what we will; rather, it is we who must follow religion wherever it leads us" (St Vincent of Lerins, *Commonitorium*, 5).

Assiduous meditation on the Word of God and reflection on our experience in the light of faith make for deeper understanding of revealed truth; but the essential meaning of the truths of faith does not change, because God does not contradict himself. Progress in theology consists in obtaining this deeper understanding of the content of Revelation and relating it to the needs and the insights of people in each culture and period of history. In this connexion Paul VI wrote: "We also insisted on the grave responsibility incumbent upon us, but which we share with our Brothers in the Episcopate, of preserving unaltered the content of the Catholic faith which the Lord entrusted to the Apostles. While being translated into all expressions, this content must be neither impaired nor mutilated. While being clothed with the outward forms proper to each people, and made explicit by theological expression which takes account of different cultural, social and even racial milieux, it must remain the content of the Catholic faith just exactly as the ecclesial Magisterium has received it and transmits it" (*Evangelii nuntiandi*, 65).

the sacred writings which are able to instruct you for salvation through faith in Christ Jesus. <sup>16</sup>All scripture is inspir-

---

nosti, quae te possunt instruere ad salutem per fidem, quae est in Christo Iesu.
<sup>16</sup>Omnis Scriptura divinitus inspirata est et utilis ad docendum, ad arguendum,

**16.** Due to the conciseness of the Greek language (which often omits the verb *to be*), this verse can also be translated as "All scripture inspired by God *is* profitable"; cf. the RSV note. Paul is explicitly stating here that all the books of the Bible are inspired by God, and are therefore of great help to the Church in its mission.

The books of Sacred Scripture enjoy special authority because "the divinely revealed realities, which are contained and presented in the text of Sacred Scripture, have been written down under the inspiration of the Holy Spirit. For Holy Mother Church, relying on the faith of the apostolic age, accepts as sacred and canonical the books of the Old and the New Testaments, whole and entire, with all their parts, on the grounds that, written under the inspiration of the Holy Spirit they have God as their author, and have been handed on as such to the Church herself. To compose the sacred books, God chose certain men who, all the while he employed them in this task, made full use of their powers and faculties so that, though he acted in them and by them, it was as true authors that they consigned to writing whatever he wanted written, and no more. Since, therefore, all that the inspired authors, or sacred writers, affirm should be regarded as affirmed by the Holy Spirit, we must acknowledge that the books of Scripture, firmly, faithfully and without error, teach that truth which God, for the sake of our salvation, wished to see confided to the Sacred Scripture" (Vatican II, *Dei Verbum*, 11).

Therefore, the Bible is very useful in preaching and teaching, in theological research and for one's own spiritual advancement and that of others. Referring to the training of future priests, the Second Vatican Council recommends that they "receive a most careful training in Holy Scripture, which should be the soul, as it were, of all theology" (*Optatam totius*, 16).

St Gregory the Great has this to say about Scripture's usefulness "for teaching": "Anyone preparing to preach in the right way needs to take his points from the Sacred Scriptures in order to ensure that everything he says is based on divine authority" (*Moralia*, 18, 26). And the same Father says elsewhere: "What is Sacred Scripture if not a kind of letter from almighty God to his creature? [. . .] Therefore, please study and reflect on the words of your Creator every day. Learn what the will of God is by entering deep into the words of that God, so as to desire divine things more ardently and set your soul aflame with great yearning for heavenly delights" (*Epistula ad Theodorum medicum*, 5, 31).

Scripture is also profitable "for reproof", St Jerome writes: "Read the divine Scriptures very often, or, to put it better, never let sacred reading matter out of your hands. Learn what it has to teach, keep a firm hold on the word of faith which accords with doctrine, so as to be able to exhort others with sound doctrine and win over your opponents" (*Ad Nepotianum*, 7).

ed by God and[d] profitable for teaching, for reproof, for correction, and for training in righteousness, [17]that the man of God may be complete, equipped for every good work.

## 4

### Dedication to preaching

[1]I charge you in the presence of God and of Christ Jesus who is to judge the living and the dead, and by his appearing

---

ad corrigendum, ad erudiendum in iustitia, [17]ut perfectus sit homo Dei, ad omne opus bonum instructus.

[1]Testificor coram Deo et Christo Iesu, qui iudicaturus est vivos ac mortuos, per

---

**17.** "Man of God": see the note on 1 Tim 6:11. This description shows the basis of a priest's dignity. "The priestly vocation is invested with a dignity and greatness which has no equal on earth. St Catherine of Siena put these words on Jesus' lips: 'I do not wish the respect which priests should be given to be in any way diminished; for the reverence and respect which is shown them is not referred to them but to Me, by virtue of the Blood which I have given to them to administer. Were it not for this, you should render them the same reverence as lay people, and no more. . . . You must not offend them; by offending them you offend Me and not them. Therefore I forbid it and I have laid it down that you shall not touch my Christs'" (J. Escrivá, *In Love with the Church*, 38).

**1.** The last chapter of the letter, summing up its main themes, is in fact St Paul's last will and testament and has the features of that type of document: it begins in a formal manner (vv. 1-5), protests the sincerity of his dedicated life (vv. 6-8) and concludes with some very tender, personal messages (vv. 9-22).

The opening is couched in a solemn form (also found in 1 Tim 5:21) similar to a Greco-Roman will, laying on the heirs an obligation to carry out the testator's wishes: "I charge you"; a series of imperatives follows. To underline the importance of what the testator is requesting, God the Father and Jesus Christ are invoked as witnesses, guarantors of the commitments which will devolve on the heirs. By swearing this document the testator is performing an act of the virtue of religion, because he is acknowledging God as Supreme Judge, to whom we must render an account of our actions.

"Christ Jesus who is to judge the living and the dead": a graphic, catechetical expression (cf. Acts 10:42; 1 Pet 4:5), confessing belief in the truth that all men without exception will undergo judgment by Jesus Christ, from whose decision there is no appeal. This has become part of the Creed; in a solemn profession of faith, the *Creed of the People of God*, Pope Paul VI elaborated on this article of faith as we have seen in the commentary on 2 Thessalonians 1:5 above.

[d]Or *Every scripture inspired by God is also*

and his kingdom: ²preach the word, be urgent in season and
out of season, convince, rebuke, and exhort, be unfailing in
patience and in teaching. ³For the time is coming when
people will not endure sound teaching, but having itching
ears they will accumulate for themselves teachers to suit
their own likings, ⁴and will turn away from listening to the
truth and wander into myths. ⁵As for you, always be steady,

Acts 20:20, 31

1 Tim 4:1
2 Tim 1:13

1 Tim 4:7
2 Thess 2:11

2 Tim 2:3

---

adventum ipsius et regnum eius: ²praedica verbum, insta opportune, importune,
argue, increpa, obsecra in omni longanimitate et doctrina. ³Erit enim tempus,
cum sanam doctrinam non sustinebunt, sed ad sua desideria coacervabunt sibi
magistros prurientes auribus, ⁴et a veritate quidem auditum avertent, ad fabulas
autem convertentur. ⁵Tu vero vigila in omnibus, labora, opus fac evangelistae,

**2.** "Preach the word": that is, the message of the Gospel, which includes all
the truths to be believed, the commandments to be kept and the sacraments and
other supernatural resources to be availed of. In the life of the Church the
ministry of the word has special importance; it is the channel God has established whereby man can partake of the Gospel; priests have a special duty to
preach the word: "The people of God is formed into one in the first place by
the Word of the living God, which is quite rightly sought from the mouth of
priests. For since nobody can be saved who has not first believed, it is the first
task of priests as co-workers of the bishops to preach the Gospel of God to all
men. In this way they carry out the Lord's command, 'Go into all the world and
preach the Gospel to the whole creation' (Mk 16:15) and thus set up and
increase the people of God" (Vatican II, *Presbyterorum ordinis*, 4).

"In season and out of season", that is, even in adverse circumstances (cf. v.
3), or when hearers are disinclined to accept the Christian message. Timothy
and, like him, all other sacred ministers, ought to behave towards the faithfull
in accordance with the demands of Christian life and doctrine. "What do men
want, what do they expect of the priest, the minister of Christ, the living sign
of the presence of the Good Shepherd? We would venture to say that, although
they may not explicitly say so, they need, want and hope for a priest-priest, a
priest through and through, a man who gives his life for them, by opening to
them the horizons of the soul; a man who unceasingly exercises his ministry,
whose heart is capable of understanding, and a man who gives simply and
joyfully, in season and even out of season, what he alone can give—the richness
of grace, of divine intimacy which, through him, God wishes to distribute
among men" (A. del Portillo, *On Priesthood*, p. 66).

**3-5.** With sadness in his heart and with no little irony St Paul unmasks those
who prefer smooth talk to the truth. Earlier Cicero criticized certain Greeks
who by skilful use of words managed to delude their listeners even though they
had really nothing to say, or were misleading them. However, where Christian
doctrine is at stake, the danger that can be done to souls is much more grave:

153

endure suffering, do the work of an evangelist, fulfil your ministry.

### The crown of righteousness

Phil 2:17
Acts 20:24
1 Tim 1:18
1 Cor 9:24
1 Cor 9:25
1 Tim 6:14

[6]For I am already on the point of being sacrificed; the time of my departure has come. [7]I have fought the good fight, I have finished the race, I have kept the faith. [8]Henceforth there is laid up for me the crown of righteousness,

ministerium tuum imple. [6]Ego enim iam delibor, et tempus meae resolutionis instat. [7]Bonum certamen certavi, cursum consummavi, fidem servavi; [8]in reliquo reposita est mihi iustitiae corona, quam reddet mihi Dominus in illa die,

"Do not be afraid, or surprised, to see the resistance of some people's minds. There will always be stupid people who deck out the armour of their ignorance with a display of culture" (J. Escrivá, *Furrow*, 934).

As an antidote to empty talk, the Apostle recommends solid teaching, constancy in the face of difficulty, and commitment to the ministry. St John Chrysostom called for fidelity to the Gospel in these words: "What you should fear is not that people might malign you but that you should be regarded as tainted with the same hypocrisy as your detractors. For if that were the case you would become tasteless and people would trample you underfoot. But if you offer the salt in all sobriety and are criticized on that account, do not be dismayed; for that is what salt is for—to irritate and disturb the corrupt. People will continue to speak evil of you, but they will do you no harm; they will only prove your reliability" (*Hom. on St Matthew*, 15, 7).

**6-8.** Conscious of his closeness to death, St Paul writes in poetic strain about his life in the service of the Gospel, about the meaning of death and his hope of heaven. The imagery he uses shows how he interprets his experience in the light of faith. "On the point of being sacrificed": literally "poured out in sacrifice": death is an offering to God, like the libations of oil poured on the altar of sacrifices. Death is the beginning of a journey: "the point of my departure has come", the anchor is being weighed, the sails unfurled.

The Christian life is like magnificent Games taking place in the presence of God, who acts as the judge. In Greece the Games had close connexions with religious worship; St Paul presents the Christian life as a type of spiritual sport: "races" indicates the continuous effort to achieve perfection (cf. Phil 3:14); training for athletics indicates the practice of self-denial (cf. 1 Cor 9:26-27); fighting stands for the effort required to resist sin even if that means death, as can happen in the event of persecution (cf. Heb 12:4). It is well worthwhile taking part in this competition, because, as St John Chrysostom points out, "the crown which it bestows never withers. It is not made of laurel leaves, it is not a man who places it on our head, it has not been won in the presence of a crowd made up of men, but in a stadium full of angels. In earthly competitions a man fights and strives for days and the only reward he receives is a crown which

which the Lord, the righteous judge, will award to me on that Day, and not only to me but also to all who have loved his appearing.

## PART THREE

## FINAL ADVICE

**News and messages**

⁹Do your best to come to me soon. ¹⁰For Demas, in love

2 Tim 4:21; 1:4<br>Col 4:14

iustus iudex, non solum autem mihi sed et omnibus, qui diligunt adventum eius. ⁹Festina venire ad me cito. ¹⁰Demas enim me dereliquit diligens hoc saeculum

withers in a matter of hours [. . .]. That does not happen here: the crown he is given is a glory and honour whose brilliance lasts forever" (*Hom. on 2 Tim, ad loc.*).

All Christians who "have loved his appearing", that is, who stay true to Christ, share St Paul's expectation of eternal life. "We who know about the eternal joys of the heavenly fatherland should hasten to reach it by the more direct route" (St Gregory the Great, *In Evangelia homiliae*, 16).

**9-18.** In his letters St Paul often asks people to do things for him; his messages here are particularly moving, given as they are on the eve of his martyrdom. He is following the example of Christ: he puts his trust in God even though his friends desert him (vv. 10-12, 16); his enemies harass him more than ever, yet he forgives them (vv. 14, 16); in the midst of his sufferings he praises the Lord (v. 18). His mention of Thessalonica, Galatia, Dalmatia, Ephesus, Troas, Corinth and Miletus show how warmly he remembers places which were very receptive to the Christian message. These few verses constitute a mini-biography.

His generosity of spirit is shown by the fact that he mentions so many disciples by name; to all he gave of his best; some of them fell by the wayside but most of them stayed faithful; some are mentioned in the Acts of the Apostles or in other letters, but for others this is the only mention in the New Testament. However, all without exception must have been very present to the Apostle who became "all things to all men, that I might by all means save some" (1 Cor 9:22).

**10.** Demas was one of St Paul's companions during his first Roman imprisonment (cf. Col 4:14; Philem 24); but now, when the Apostle is near to death and in a harsher prison than before, he has left him alone.

"That passage of the Second Epistle to Timothy makes me shudder, when the Apostle laments that Demas has fallen in love with this present world and

Acts 12:12;
15:37

Acts 20:4
Eph 6:21
Tit 3:12
1 Tim 1:20
Ps 28:4
Prov 24:12
Rom 2:6

2 Tim 1:15
Acts 23:11
Ps 22:22

with this present world, has deserted me and gone to Thessalonica; Crescens has gone to Galatia,[e] Titus to Dalmatia. [11]Luke alone is with me. Get Mark and bring him with you; for he is very useful in serving me. [12]Tychicus I have sent to Ephesus. [13]When you come, bring the cloak that I left with Carpus at Troas, also the books, and above all the parchments. [14]Alexander the coppersmith did me great harm; the Lord will requite him for his deeds. [15]Beware of him yourself, for he strongly opposed our message. [16]At my first defence no one took my part; all deserted me. May it not be charged against them! [17]But the

et abiit Thessalonicam, Crescens in Galatiam, Titus in Dalmatiam; [11]Lucas est mecum solus. Marcum assumens adduc tecum, est enim mihi utilis in ministerium. [12]Tychicum autem misi Ephesum. [13]Paenulam, quam reliqui Troade apud Carpum, veniens affer, et libros, maxime autem membranas. [14]Alexander aerarius multa mala mihi ostendit. Reddet ei Dominus secundum opera eius; [15]quem et tu devita, valde enim restitit verbis nostris. [16]In prima mea defensione nemo mihi affuit, sed omnes me dereliquerunt. Non illis reputetur; [17]Dominus

gone to Thessalonica. For a trifle, and for fear of persecution, this man, whom St Paul had quoted in other epistles as being among the saints, had betrayed the divine enterprise. I shudder when I realize how little I am: and it leads me to demand from myself faithfulness to the Lord even in situations that may seem to be indifferent—for if they do not help me to be more united to Him, I do not want them" (J. Escrivá, *Furrow*, 343).

**13.** The cloak he refers to was a sleeveless cape used for protection against rain and cold. The "books" were probably less important documents usually written on sheets of papyrus, whereas the parchments would probably have contained more important texts, such as Sacred Scripture. This message does indicate that St Paul was fond of study and reading. And the fact that the letter goes into details like this speaks in favour of its being written by Paul.

**16-17.** St Paul points to the contrast between the way men treat him and the way God does. Because of the hazards involved in staying with Paul or defending him, some of his friends, even some of his closest friends, have deserted him; whereas God stays by his side.

"You seek the company of friends who, with their conversation and affection, with their friendship, make the exile of this world more bearable for you. There is nothing wrong with that, although friends sometimes let you down. But how is it you don't frequent daily with greater intensity the company, the conversation, of the great Friend, who never lets you down?" (J. Escrivá, *The Way*, 88).

[e]Other ancient authorities read *Gaul*

Lord stood by me and gave me strength to proclaim the word fully, that all the Gentiles might hear it. So I was rescued from the lion's mouth. [18]The Lord will rescue me from every evil and save me for his heavenly kingdom. To him be the glory for ever and ever. Amen.

### Farewells and final good wishes
[19]Greet Prisca and Aquila, and the household of Onesiphorus. [20]Erastus remained at Corinth: Trophimus I left ill at Miletus. [21]Do your best to come before winter. Eubulus sends greetings to you, as do Pudens and Linus and Claudia and all the brethren.

2 Tim 1:16
Acts 18:2
Acts 19:22; 21:29

2 Tim 4:9

---

autem mihi astitit et confortavit me, ut per me praedicatio impleatur, et audiant omnes gentes, et liberatus sum de ore leonis. [18]Liberabit me Dominus ab omni opere malo et salvum faciet in regnum suum caeleste; cui gloria in saecula saeculorum. Amen. [19]Saluta Priscam et Aquilam et Onesiphori domum. [20]Erastus remansit Corinthi, Trophimum autem reliqui infirmum Mileti. [21]Festina ante

---

**18.** "The Lord will rescue me from every evil": literally "every evil work". He is not saying that God will protect him from the martyrdom which he sees is imminent. He is expressing his conviction that God will enable him to fight any temptation, and will grant him salvation in heaven. Final perseverance is a grace which man cannot merit (cf. Council of Trent, *De iustificatione*, chap. 13); it is also a truth of faith that in order to reach heaven one needs to be in the grace of God at the moment of death (cf. Mt 24:13).

**19-21.** These words of farewell are more intimate than those in other Pauline letters: St Paul mentions many disciples by name, gives information about Trophimus and advises Timothy to travel before winter, when sea travel is safer, etc. It all shows how deeply committed St Paul was to his apostolate and the great regard he had for everyone who followed Christ.

**22.** "The Lord be with your spirit": an early Christian greeting invoking God's help, protection and blessing. Although this may be a Semitic turn of phrase meaning "The Lord be with you", some Fathers interpreted it, in this context, as alluding to the grace conferred by the sacrament of Order; with this meaning it would have passed into the liturgy, where only sacred ministers (bishop, priests and deacons) speak the greeting "The Lord be with you", and the faithful reply, "And also with you" (in Latin: "*Et cum spiritu tuo*": "And with your spirit"). According to this interpretation, St Paul is calling on God to help Timothy in his pastoral work.

In a letter to St Polycarp, St Ignatius of Antioch reminds him of his special responsibilities as pastor: "Have special concern for unity, for there is nothing

<sup>22</sup>The Lord be with your spirit. Grace be with you.

---

hiemem venire. Salutat te Eubulus et Pudens et Linus et Claudia et fratres omnes. <sup>22</sup>Dominus cum spiritu tuo. Gratia vobiscum.

---

more important than this. Make yourself the support of all, as the Lord is to you, and continue to bear with them lovingly, as you are doing at present. Pray constantly, and ask for an increase in wisdom. Be watchful and unsleeping in spirit. Speak to each one personally, as God does. Carry the infirmities of all on your shoulders, as a good champion should" (*Letter to Polycarp*, 2, 1).

# Introduction to the Epistle to Titus

The content of this letter is very reminiscent of that of the First Letter to Timothy, probably because both were written around the same time. Titus, the son of Gentile parents, must surely have been baptized by St Paul, to judge from the affection the Apostle shows him (cf. Tit 1:4). He went to Jerusalem with Paul and Barnabas for the first Council, without having been circumcised (cf. Gal 2:1-5); he is not mentioned in Acts but we do know that, towards the end of the third missionary journey, he was sent to Corinth on two delicate missions, first to deliver a letter (cf. 2 Cor 2:13; 7:12-14), and then for the collection and to deliver the Second Letter to the Corinthians (cf. 2 Cor 8:6, 16-23; 12:18). We have no evidence that he was with the Apostle during his first Roman imprisonment, but we do know that St Paul later left him in Crete to continue the missionary work they both had been doing there (cf. Tit 1:5). Titus must have stayed in Crete until Artemas and Tychicus relieved him (cf. Tit 3:12). As in 1 Timothy, the Apostle in this letter is advising his co-worker on how the community should be organized and on the need to protect the flock from the unsound ideas some people were beginning to spread.

In the early years of the Church it was particularly important that suitable people should be chosen for the priestly ministry: they should be strong in the faith and morally irreproachable (cf. 1:5-9). Other Christians too—older people, the young, women, slaves—should be exemplary (cf. 2:2-10); their lives should be in line with the faith they profess, to edify pagans, particularly the authorities (cf. 3:1-2). That was how Jesus acted, manifesting in his life the love of God the Father (cf. 2:11-15).

In defending the truth, Titus must do everything he can (cf. Tit 1:10-16), even to the point of "silencing" false teachers (cf. Tit 1:11); and he should not become embroiled in unprofitable and futile controversies (cf. 3:9-11). However, his first priority should be to be a "model of good deeds" (cf. 2:7) and a model preacher, so that no Christian could disregard him, no opponent have grounds to criticize him (2:8, 15).

# The Epistle to Titus

ENGLISH AND LATIN VERSIONS, WITH NOTES

# 1

### Greeting

Rom 1:1
1 Tim 2:4

¹Paul, a servant[a] of God and an apostle of Jesus Christ, to

¹Paulus servus Dei, apostolus autem Iesu Christi secundum fidem electorum

**1-4.** The heading is particularly long and formal. It contains, as usual (cf. Rom 1:1-2; 1 Cor 1:13; etc.), the sender's name—Paul; the addressee's—Titus; and the greeting—"Grace and peace". In this case, however, Paul's title (Apostle), and the prerogatives of his authority and his God-given mandate to preach are given special emphasis (v. 3). This has led some scholars to argue that the epistle was in fact written by a disciple of St Paul—who would have put in all this about the Apostle's authority in order to give the letter more weight. However, it is more reasonable to suppose that when St Paul was writing the letter he had Titus very much in mind and also the community in Crete, whom false teachers were beginning to unsettle; the solemn, official tone would be due to the serious nature of their doctrinal aberrations and to the need to ensure that the church in Crete was properly organized.

These introductory verses provide a very succinct definition of the mission of an Apostle: it derives from God himself, the Saviour of all (vv. 1, 3); the Apostle has a mandate from God, he is God's representative (v. 3); the purpose of his mission is to communicate the word of God, which is true, which "accords with godliness" and leads to eternal life (v. 2). His letter is addressed to the believers, who have been endowed with faith (v. 1) and whom he has to lead to heaven (v. 2).

**1.** "Servant of God": in the language of the Bible, serving God means rendering him the worship that is his due. While keeping this basic meaning, "servant of God" means one who fulfils the task his Lord gives him. Like the Old Testament prophets (who were conscious of having a sacred mission, which they could not avoid: cf. Amos 3:7; Jer 7:25), St Paul knows that he has a God-given mission which he has a duty to perform.

"To further the faith of God's elect": God sends his apostles to instruct people in the faith so that they know the truth that saves and view their lives and the world from a supernatural vantage-point. As the Church's Magisterium has reminded us, evangelization begins by teaching the essential revealed truths: "It is not superfluous to recall the following points: to evangelize is first of all to bear witness, in a simple and direct way, to God revealed by Jesus Christ, in the Holy Spirit; to bear witness that in his Son God has loved the world—that in his Incarnate Word he has given being to all things and has called men to eternal life" (Paul VI, *Evangelii nuntiandi*, 26).

"The truth that accords with godliness". The virtue of godliness or "piety"

[a] Or *slave*

2 Tim 2:13

further the faith of God's elect and their knowledge of the
truth which accords with godliness, [2]in hope of eternal life
which God, who never lies, promised ages ago [3]and at the

Dei et agnitionem veritatis, quae secundum pietatem est [2]in spem vitae aeternae,
quam promisit, qui non mentitur, Deus ante tempora saecularia, [3]manifestavit

includes, particularly, openness to God, docility to his commandments and
recognition of his divinity—in a word, religion. Godliness and truth are very
closely connected: to acquire a solid, well-grounded piety one needs to have a
good grasp of the truth. St Teresa of Avila explains this in her inimitable way:
"I should prefer spirituality to be unaccompanied by prayer than not to be
founded upon the truth. Learning is a great thing, for it instructs those of us
who have little knowledge, and enlightens us, so that when we are faced with
the truth of Holy Scripture, we act as we should. From foolish devotions may
God deliver us!" (*Life*, 13, 16).

2. In doing the work given him, the Apostle always keeps before his eyes
the "hope of eternal life"; this determines the content and purpose of his
preaching—eternal beatitude for himself and for all who accept the word of
God, the attainment of the indescribable joy which is God's reward to those
who love him: "What words can describe what is to come—the pleasure, the
good fortune, the joy of being with Christ? It is impossible to explain the
blessedness and the advantage the soul has when it is returned to its noble self
and can from then on contemplate its Lord. And it is not only that he enjoys
good things to hand: his joy is permanent because these good things will never
cease to be his" (St John Chrysostom, *Ad Theod. lapsum*, 1, 13).

"In hope of eternal life": hope of eternal life should imbue our devout life,
and it should also inspire the truth we teach, the faith we profess and the
apostolic ministry itself.

Promised "ages ago": this ambiguous Semitic expression (it can also be
translated as "from all eternity") refers to God's promise of salvation made in
ancient times to the patriarchs and prophets of the Old Testament; but it refers
mainly to God's eternal plan: from all eternity God decided to save men. This
decision of his is the basis of the theological virtue of hope; we place our hope
in God "who never lies", who cannot deceive or be deceived.

3-4. "At the proper time": salvation (God's plan for all eternity, communicated in a veiled way to the prophets) has been manifested in the fulness
of time by the advent of the Son of God (cf. Heb 1:1); preaching concerns itself
exclusively with this message of salvation. The Apostle preaches "by command
of God our Saviour", not on his personal initiative. It is worth pointing out that
this whole passage is very dense and very typical of Pauls's style: lots of ideas
are crammed into very few words. The key factor is the divine plan of salvation;
but the way that plan is communicated is also important, as is the way it is
carried out; the word of God, in addition to making the plan of salvation known,

proper time manifested in his word through the preaching
with which I have been entrusted by command of God our
Saviour; <sup>4</sup>To Titus, my true child in a common faith: Grace
and peace from God the Father and Christ Jesus our
Saviour.

# PART ONE

## TITUS' MISSION IN CRETE

**Qualifications for elders**

<sup>5</sup>This is why I left you in Crete, that you might amend

autem temporibus suis verbum suum in praedicatione, quae credita est mihi
secundum praeceptum salvatoris nostri Dei, <sup>4</sup>Tito, germano filio secundum
communem fidem: gratia et pax a Deo Patre et Christo Iesu salvatore nostro.
<sup>5</sup>Huius rei gratia reliqui te Cretae, ut ea, quae desunt, corrigas et constituas per

is itself salvific, it is an effective instrument of salvation. The Apostle is very
conscious that his mission is divine, for God keeps urging him on; he chose
him for this very purpose and granted him the title of "servant of God" (cf. v.
1).

On the meaning of the greeting "Grace and peace", see the note on 1 Tim
1:2 and Rom 1:7.

**5-9.** The qualities of Church pastors described here agree with those recommended in the First Letter to Timothy (cf. 1 Tim 3:2-7 and note). In neither
instance is St Paul trying to give a complete list; he is simply urging that
ministers be a model for their flock. Emphasis is laid on four aspects which
seem to be particularly important: a minister should be of irreproachable
conduct (vv. 6-7); his family should be exemplary Christians (v. 6); he should
be an upright and welcoming person (vv. 7-8); and finally, he should have a
grasp of Christian doctrine (v. 9). The Church has always tried to have people
of this calibre as minsters; the last ecumenical council, for example, reminded
pastors that, in the pursuit of holiness, they have a special obligation to give
good example to others: "they should abound in every spiritual good and bear
a living witness of God to all" (*Lumen gentium*, 41).

**5.** St Paul seems to have given Titus two jobs to do. One, which is implied
here, was to complete the catechetical instruction of the young community in
Crete; there is a lot of emphasis throughout the letter on firmness in the truth,
on counteracting false teachers, and on the need for all believers, particularly
pastors, to have a well-grounded faith.

The second job is to complete the hierarchical structuring of the Church.
The elders mentioned here perform the same role as that of the bishops in the

1 Tim 3:2-4

2 Tim 2:24
Rom 12:13

1 Tim 1:10

what was defective, and appoint elders in every town as I directed you, ⁶if any man is blameless, the husband of one wife, and his children are believers and not open to the charge of being profligate or insubordinate. ⁷For a bishop, as God's steward, must be blameless; he must not be arrogant or quick-tempered or a drunkard or violent or greedy for gain, ⁸but hospitable, a lover of goodness, master of himself, upright, holy, and self-controlled; ⁹he must hold firm to the sure word as taught, so that he may be able to give instruction in sound doctrine and also to confute those who contradict it.

---

civitates presbyteros, sicut ego tibi disposui, ⁶si quis sine crimine est, unius uxoris vir, filios habens fideles, non in accusatione luxuriae aut non subiectos. ⁷Oportet enim episcopum sine crimine esse sicut Dei dispensatorem, non superbum, non iracundum, non vinolentum, non percussorem, non turpis lucri cupidum, ⁸sed hospitalem, benignum, sobrium, iustum, sanctum, continentem, ⁹amplectentem eum, qui secundum doctrinam est, fidelem sermonem, ut potens

---

First Letter to Timothy, and they are all required to have the same qualities (on the as yet unfixed bishop/priest terminology, see the note on 1 Tim 3:1). St Paul's insistence on appointing successors is a pointer to the Apostolicity of the Church: not only do bishops have the same mission as the Apostles; that mission comes to them from the Apostles: "In fact, not only had (the Apostles) various helpers in their ministry, but, in order that the mission entrusted to them might be continued after their death, they consigned, by will and testament, as it were, to their immediate collaborators the duty of completing and consolidating the work they had begun, urging them to tend to the whole flock, in which the Holy Spirit had appointed them to shepherd the Church of God (cf. Acts 20:28)" (*Lumen gentium*, 20).

Very little information is available as to when St Paul visited Crete and evangelized it. When he was being brought as a prisoner to Rome in the autumn of the year 60, he probably evangelized some Cretans (cf. Acts 27:7-12); there may also have been some Christians there ever since St Peter preached for the first time in Jerusalem (cf. Acts 2:11). It could be that the Apostle spent a while on the island at some stage and established a Christian community there. Crete was fairly important, being a necessary port of call on the Greece-Asia Minor sea route.

**10-11.** As in the First Epistle to Timothy, St Paul unmasks the enemies of the faith; in Crete, as in Ephesus (cf. 1 Tim 1:6) certain philosophers were beginning to make headway with their sophistry and fallacious arguments. The main problem was that many well-meaning but naive Christians were letting themselves be taken in by these professional teachers, who were really only out

**Attitudes towards false teachers**

<sup>10</sup>For there are many insubordinate men, empty talkers and deceivers, especially the circumcision party; <sup>11</sup>they must be silenced, since they are upsetting whole families by teaching for base gain what they have no right to teach. <sup>12</sup>One of themselves, a prophet of their own, said, "Cretans are always liars, evil beasts, lazy gluttons." <sup>13</sup>This testimony is true. Therefore rebuke them sharply, that they may

1 Tim 1:6
2 Tim 3:13

2 Tim 3:6

2 Tim 4:2
1 Tim 5:20

---

sit et exhortari in doctrina sana et eos, qui contradicunt, arguere. <sup>10</sup>Sunt enim multi et non subiecti vaniloqui et seductores, maxime qui de circumcisione sunt, <sup>11</sup>quibus oportet silentium imponere, quia universas domos subvertunt docentes, quae non oportet, turpis lucri gratia. <sup>12</sup>Dixit quidam ex illis, proprius ipsorum propheta: "Cretenses semper mendaces, malae bestiae, ventres pigri". <sup>13</sup>Testimonium hoc verum est. Quam ob causam increpa illos dure, ut sani sint

---

for personal gain. St Paul warns Titus particularly about false teachers of "the circumcision party", "from Judaism", probably because there was quite a large Jewish population on the island (we know this from Jewish writers such as Flavius Josephus and Philo); some of them, members of influential families, were mixing their ancient traditions with decadent Greek philosophy and putting forward theories that sounded attractive but lacked depth.

**12-14.** St Paul's reference to the character of Cretans includes a hard-hitting quotation from some early poet (perhaps Epimenides, sixth century B.C.); seemingly the Cretans had a reputation for telling lies; the verb *krethizein* (coming from the Greek for "Crete") means to deceive. The false teachers' arguments must have been very self-contradictory if St Paul resorts to combatting them in this way. He prefers to make them look ridiculous, in the hope that that will "silence them" (v. 11).

As pastor of those Christians, Titus' aim should be to keep their faith sound, that is, uncontaminated by myths (cf. 1 Tim 1:4; 4:7) or outdated rules (cf. 1 Tim 4:3); this reference to "the commands of men" may refer to detailed rules about "clean" and "unclean" food. Over the centuries the Church has shown her maternal concern by protecting and consolidating Christians' faith. "She seeks", writes Paul VI, "to deepen, consolidate, nourish and make ever more mature the faith of those who are already called the faithful or believers, in order that they may be so still more. This faith is nearly always today exposed to secularism, even to militant atheism. It is a faith exposed to trials and threats and, even more, a faith besieged and actively opposed. It runs the risk of perishing from suffocation or starvation if it is not fed and sustained each day. To evangelize must therefore very often be to give this necessary food and sustenance to the faith of believers, especially through a catechesis full of Gospel vitality and in a language suited to people and circumstances" (*Evangelii nuntiandi*, 54).

1 Tim 4:7; 1:4
Mt 15:11
Rom 14:14-20

be sound in the faith, [14]instead of giving heed to Jewish myths or to commands of men who reject the truth. [15]To the pure all things are pure, but to the corrupt and unbelieving nothing is pure; their very minds and consciences

2 Tim 3:5

are corrupted. [16]They profess to know God, but they deny him by their deeds; they are detestable, disobedient, unfit for any good deed.

# 2

## PART TWO

# MORAL DEMANDS OF THE CHRISTIAN FAITH

### Duties of Christians in different situations

1 Tim 6:3
2 Tim 1:13

[1]But as for you, teach what befits sound doctrine. [2]Bid the

---

in fide, [14]non intendentes Iudaicis fabulis et mandatis hominum aversantium veritatem. [15]Omnia munda mundis; coinquinatis autem et infidelibus nihil mundum, sed inquinatae sunt eorum et mens et conscientia. [16]Confitentur se nosse Deum, factis autem negant, cum sint abominati et inoboedientes et ad omne opus bonum reprobi.

[1]Tu autem loquere, quae decent sanam doctrinam. [2]Senes, ut sobrii sint, pudici,

---

**15-16.** "To the pure all things are pure": this principle of Christian freedom contrasts sharply with the hypocrisy of trying to combine Christian faith and reprehensible moral conduct (v. 16). Jesus himself emphasized that inner purity was what mattered (cf. Mt 23:25-26) rather than purely external rites. It was important then, and will always be, for Christians to live in a manner consistent with the faith they profess.

**1-10.** To counter the fallacies of those whose depraved conduct is at odds with what they profess to believe, Titus is urged to be sincere in everything he does and always to act in accordance with the faith. A key feature of Christian morality is that it can never be reduced to an abstract ethical code with no theological basis; rather, it flows directly from the deep truth one professes: doctrinal orthodoxy leads to upright conduct—and upright conduct equips one to understand and accept revealed truth. As the Second Vatican Council teaches, faith is meant to shape the Christian's life: "Bishops should be especially concerned about catechetical instruction. Its function is to develop in men a living, explicit and active faith, enlightened by doctrine. It should be very carefully imparted, not only to children and adolescents but also to young

older men be temperate, serious, sensible, sound in faith, in 1 Tim 5:1
love, and in steadfastness. ³Bid the older women likewise 1 Tim 3:11
to be reverent in behaviour, not to be slanderers or slaves
to drink; they are to teach what is good, ⁴and so train the 1 Tim 5:14
young women to love their husbands and children, ⁵to be

prudentes, sani fide, dilectione, patientia. ³Anus similiter in habitu sanctae, non
criminatrices, non vino multo deditae, bene docentes, ⁴ut prudentiam doceant
adulescentulas, ut viros suos ament, filios diligant, ⁵prudentes sint, castae,

people and even to adults. In imparting this instruction the teachers must
observe an order and method suited not only to the matter in hand but also to
the character, the ability, the age and the lifestyle of their audience. This
instruction should be based on holy Scripture, tradition, liturgy, and on the
teaching authority and life of the Church" (*Christus Dominus*, 14).

In this section of the letter St Paul reminds Titus about the obligations and
the virtues people have (depending on their age, state-in-life, social position,
etc.); this advice is very like that given to Timothy in 1 Timothy (cf. 1 Tim 5:1
- 6:2).

**2-3.** "Sound in faith . . .": in the Pastoral Epistles physical health is often
used metaphorically in connexion with Christian doctrine and its transmission
(cf. 1 Tim 6:3; 2 Tim 1:13; 4:3; Tit 1:9; 2:8); it is also applied to people: as the
years go on their interior life should grow stronger and stronger.

"Be reverent in behaviour": older women are given special mention (cf. 1
Tim 5:2-16); they must be exemplary, because younger women have to learn
from them.

**4-5.** All members of the Church are responsible for the formation and
Christian life of their juniors; this general principle applies to adult women:
they have to show younger women that their role as mothers, their place in the
home, is so important that it must be given priority over outside activities (in
which they do have a right to engage). In connexion with the role of women in
society and in the family Pope John Paul II says: "the mentality which honours
women more for their work outside the home than for their work within the
family must be overcome. This requires that men should truly esteem and love
women with total respect for their personal dignity, and that society should
create and develop conditions favouring work in the home" (*Familiaris consortio*, 23).

"That the word of God may not be discredited": an expression very similar
to that used by St Paul when advising slaves to be submissive (cf. 1 Tim 6:1).
The Apostle is not approving behaviour which women or slaves find obnoxious;
what he is saying is that obedience and humility is the best way to do God
honour and to offer others a testimony of love, following the example of the
Master, who "humbled himself and became obedient unto death" (cf. Phil
2:6-11).

Eph 5:22
Col 3:18
1 Cor 14:34

1 Tim 4:12
1 Pet 5:3
1 Pet 2:15; 3:16

Eph 6:5
Col 3:22
1 Tim 6:1

sensible, chaste, domestic, kind, and submissive to their husbands, that the word of God may not be discredited. ⁶Likewise urge the younger men to control themselves. ⁷Show yourself in all respects a model of good deeds, and in your teaching show integrity, gravity, ⁸and sound speech that cannot be censured, so that an opponent may be put to shame, having nothing evil to say of us. ⁹Bid slaves to be submissive to their masters and to give satisfaction in every respect; they are not to be refractory, ¹⁰nor to pilfer, but to show entire and true fidelity, so that in everything they may adorn the doctrine of God our Saviour.

### The Incarnation, the basis of Christian ethics and piety

¹¹For the grace of God has appeared for the salvation of

---

domus curam habentes, benignae, subditae suis viris, ut non blasphemetur verbum Dei. ⁶Iuvenes similiter hortare, ut sobrii sint. ⁷In omnibus teipsum praebens exemplum bonorum operum, in doctrina integritatem, gravitatem, ⁸in verbo sano irreprehensibilem, ut is, qui ex adverso est, vereatur, nihil habens malum dicere de nobis. ⁹Servos dominis suis subditos esse in omnibus, placentes esse, non contradicentes, ¹⁰non fraudantes, sed omnem fidem bonam ostendentes, ut doctrinam salutaris nostri Dei ornent in omnibus. ¹¹Apparuit

**6-8.** The model for the younger men should be Titus himself; as in the case of Timothy in Ephesus (1 Tim 4:12), Titus' duty to be exemplary derives from the fact that pastors have an obligation to reflect Jesus' life in their own life: "Be imitators of me, as I am of Christ" (1 Cor 11:1; cf. Phil 3:17; 2 Thess 3:9). *"The priestly personality* must be *for others* a clear and plain *sign and indication.* This is the first condition for our pastoral service. The people from among whom we have been chosen and for whom we have been appointed want above all to see in us such a sign and indication, and to this they have a right" (John Paul II, *Letter to All Priests*, 8 April 1979).

**9-10.** The fact that there are these references to the duties of slaves (and others in 1 Tim 6:1-2) shows that slaves were very much taken account of in the early Christian community. Christianity has been responsible for an enormous amount of social change, because being a Christian means that, whatever one's position in society, one should give honour and glory to God and recognize the innate dignity of everyone, without exception.

**11-14.** This section is almost like a hymn in praise of saving grace and God's loving kindness as manifested in Christ. The terse, sober style, with phrases piled on one another, and very few verbs, is typical of St Paul. The duties just described (2:1-10)—of older men, women, young people and slaves—all point to Christians' having a common lifestyle, which is the fruit of grace. God is the

all men, [12]training us to renounce irreligion and worldly
passions, and to live sober, upright, and godly lives in this
world, [13]awaiting our blessed hope, the appearing of the
glory of our great God and Saviour[c] Jesus Christ, [14]who
gave himself for us to redeem us from all iniquity and to
purify for himself a people of his own who are zealous for
good deeds.

1 Jn 2:16

Rom 5:2
1 Tim 6:14

Eph 2:10
1 Tim 2:6
Ps 130:8
Ex 19:5

enim gratia Dei salutaris hominibus [12]erudiens nos, ut abnegantes impietatem
et saecularia desideria sobrie et iuste et pie vivamus in hoc saeculo, [13]exspec-
tantes beatam spem et adventum gloriae magni Dei et salvatoris nostri Iesu
Christi, [14]qui dedit semetipsum pro nobis, ut nos redimeret ab omni iniquitate

source of that grace, and salvation its goal, and it is given to us through Jesus
Christ.

Thus, divine grace manifested in the Incarnation is actively at work to
redeem us; it brings salvation; it sanctifies us, enabling us to live godly lives;
and it is the basis of our hope in the second coming of the Lord. All these
dimensions of the action of grace summarize revealed doctrine on righteousness
(justification) in Jesus Christ. Thus, in the Incarnation, God's salvific will,
embracing all men, is manifested in a special way (cf. 1 Tim 2:4); in the
Redemption, Christ, the only Mediator and Saviour (cf. 1 Tim 2:5) obtains for
us the gift of grace, whereby man becomes a sharer in the good things of
salvation. Jesus is our model; by means of grace he instructs the Christian on
how to control his defects and grow in virtue. The instruction we receive is not
only an external one: God inwardly moves us to seek holiness (cf. Rom 5:1-5
and note). Grace also channels our hope, for Christians are motivated not only
by the memory of a past event (our Lord's life on earth) but also, and especially,
by the fact that Jesus is in the glory of heaven even now and that we are invited
to share his inheritance (cf. 2 Pet 3:12-13).

**13.** "The glory of our great God and Saviour Jesus Christ": an explicit
confession of faith in the divinity of Jesus Christ, who is stated at one and at
the same time (with only one article in the original Greek) to be God and
Saviour. This expression is the hinge on which the entire hymn turns: Jesus
Christ our God is the one who came at the Incarnation, who will manifest
himself fully at his second coming, and who through his work of redemption
has made it possible for man to live a life pleasing to God.

This verse is reminiscent of Romans 9:5, where St Paul wrote: "to them
belong the patriarchs, and of their race according to the flesh is the Christ, who
is God over all, blessed for ever. Amen."

**14.** The mention of Jesus Christ at the end of the previous verse leads St
Paul to summarize the doctrine of the Redemption in this lovely passage. Four

---

[c]*Or of the great God and our Saviour*

1 Tim 4:12

¹⁵Declare these things; exhort and reprove with all authority. Let no one disregard you.

## 3

1 Pet 2:13
Rom 13:1-7
1 Tim 2:2

**Respect for lawful authority**

¹Remind them to be submissive to rulers and authorities, to

et mundaret sibi populum peculiarem, sectatorem bonorum operum. ¹⁵Haec loquere et exhortare et argue cum omni imperio. Nemo te contemnat!

¹Admone illos principibus, potestatibus subditos esse, dicto oboedire, ad omne

essential elements in redemption are listed: Christ's self-giving; redemption from all iniquity; purification; and Christ's establishment of a people of his own dedicated to good deeds. The reference to Christ's self-giving clearly means his voluntary sacrifice on the Cross (cf. Gal 1:4; 2:20; Eph 5:2; 1 Tim 2:6), whereby we are set free from the slavery of sin; Christ's sacrifice is the cause of the freedom of the children of God (analogously, God's action during the Exodus liberated the people of Israel). Purification, a consequence of redemption, enables a man to become part of God's own people (cf. Ezek 37:23). The expression "a people of his own" is a clear allusion to Exodus 19:5: through the covenant of Sinai God made Israel his own people, different from other nations; through the New Covenant of his blood Jesus forms his own people, the Church, which is open to all nations: "As Israel according to the flesh which wandered in the desert was already called the Church of God, so, too, the new Israel, which advances in this present era in search of a future and permanent city, is called also the Church of Christ. It is Christ indeed who has purchased it with his own blood; he has filled it with his Spirit; he has provided means adapted to its visible and social union [. . .]. Destined to extend to all regions of the earth, it enters into human history, though it transcends at once all times and all racial boundaries" (*Lumen gentium*, 9).

**1-8.** In the last part of the epistle St Paul deals with the way believers conduct themselves in society at large (vv. 1-8); he warns Titus to see that the Church does not become a place where people argue (vv. 9-11); and finally he gives him some little personal commissions and messages (vv. 12-14) and ends with the usual words of farewell (v. 15).

The scheme of the first section (vv. 1-8), like the previous chapter, is as follows: first he describes the requirements of Christian living, specifically the attitude towards civil authority and one's fellow-citizens (vv. 1-2); then he gives the theological reasoning behind it (vv. 3-8): for a Christian, moral behaviour is a consequence of faith.

**1-2.** Respect for lawful authority (cf. Rom 13:1-7; 1 Tim 2:2; 1 Pet 2:13-14)

be obedient, to be ready for any honest work, [2]to speak evil of no one, to avoid quarrelling, to be gentle, and to show perfect courtesy toward all men.

### Renewal of the Christian life in the Holy Spirit

[3]For we ourselves were once foolish, disobedient, led astray, slaves to various passions and pleasures, passing our days in malice and envy, hated by men and hating one another; [4]but when the goodness and loving kindness of

---

opus bonum paratos esse, [2]neminem blasphemare, non litigiosos esse, modestos, omnem ostendentes mansuetudinem ad omnes homines. [3]Eramus enim et nos aliquando insipientes, inoboedientes, errantes, servientes concupiscentiis et voluptatibus variis, in malitia et invidia agentes, odibiles, odientes invicem.

---

was particularly difficult and meritorious in the situation in Crete, where the local population (many of them Jews) were not at all happy with their Roman overlords. However, the freedom of the children of God (cf. Rom 8:21) which the Christian acquires at Baptism does not mean he has to be opposed to existing structures: the main thing it leads him to is personal improvement: "The acute need for radical reforms of the structures which conceal poverty and which are themselves forms of violence, should not let us lose sight of the fact that the source of injustice is in the hearts of men. Therefore it is only by making an appeal to the *moral potential* of the person and to the constant need for inner conversion, that social change will be brought about which will truly be in the service of man. For it will only be in the measure that they collaborate freely in these necessary changes through their own initiative and solidarity, that people, awakened to a sense of their responsibility, will grow in humanity" (SCDF, *Libertatis nuntius*, 11, 8).

Gentleness and courtesy are expressions of the new commandment of love; they show that a person is spiritually mature, and they are very effective in drawing souls closer to Christ. "To criticize, to destroy, is not difficult; any unskilled labourer knows how to drive his pick into the noble and finely-hewn stone of a cathedral. To construct: that is what requires the skill of a master" (J. Escrivá, *The Way*, 456).

**3-7.** The main subject of the chapter is the theological basis of social obligations (vv. 1-2); every Christian should bear witness to salvation history, to the change from sin to grace, and the change from an era of slavery and error to the era of freedom and rebirth ushered in by Christ.

The "old regime" is sketched out in a very vivid way (v. 3), showing the effects of sin on man in his three dimensions: in relation to himself, sin makes a person foolish, rebellious, wayward, a slave; in respect of God, he becomes hateful in his rebellious pride; and as far as others are concerned he becomes their enemy—"hating one another".

Eph 5:26
2 Tim 1:9
Jn 3:5

Rom 5:5
Joel 3:1
Acts 2:17
Rom 3:24

God our Saviour appeared, [5]he saved us, not because of deeds done by us in righteousness, but in virtue of his own mercy, by the washing of regeneration and renewal in the Holy Spirit, [6]which he poured out upon us richly through Jesus Christ our Saviour, [7]so that we might be justified by

---

[4]Cum autem benignitas et humanitas apparuit salvatoris nostri Dei, [5]non ex operibus iustitiae, quae fecimus nos, sed secundum suam misericordiam salvos nos fecit per lavacrum regenerationis et renovationis Spiritus Sancti, [5]quem effudit super nos abunde per Iesum Christum salvatorem nostrum, [7]ut iustificati

However, the coming of Christ has opened up a new panorama (vv. 4-7). As elsewhere in these letters (cf. 1 Tim 3:15; Tit 2:11-14), we have here a hymn to Christ which may well have come from primitive Christian liturgy or from a confession of faith. It summarizes Christian teaching on the Incarnation, the Redemption and the application of salvation to the individual.

According to this text, the Incarnation is the revelation of God our Saviour, who makes known his goodness ("benignity", a word which often occurs in the Old Testament and sometimes in the New: cf. Rom 2:4; 11:22; Gal 5:22; Eph 2:7) and "loving goodness" (literally "philanthropy", a word taken from Greek). The Redemption is referred to in Old Testament language: "he saved us in virtue of his own mercy."

Finally, the Christian's access to salvation is something gratuitous: without any prior merit on our part, God's mercy has sought us out (v. 5; cf. note on Rom 3:27-31); Baptism is the door to salvation, for it is the sacrament of "regeneration and renewal" (cf. Eph 5:26); the Holy Spirit sent by Christ (cf. Jn 14:26) makes the waters of Baptism effective; his grace gives life to the soul and entitles it to eternal life (cf. Gal 4:7; Rom 8:16-17). The Council of Trent specified that "justification is not only the remission of sins, but sanctification and renovation of the interior man through the voluntary reception of grace and gifts whereby a man becomes just instead of unjust and a friend instead of an enemy, that he may be an heir in the hope of life everlasting" (*De iustificatione*, chap. 7).

The magnificent resume of faith in Christ contained in Titus 3:3-7 also helps Christians see how to approach their work and social involvement; the Second Vatican Council has reminded us once again that "the promised and hoped-for restoration has already begun in Christ. It is carried forward in the sending of the Holy Spirit and through him continues in the Church in which, through our faith, we learn the meaning of our earthly life, while we bring to term, with hope of future good, the task allotted to us in the world by the Father, and so work out our salvation" (*Lumen gentium*, 48).

**8.** St Paul presses Titus to be firm in the faith so as to encourage the faithful to practise good works. As against the proverbial laziness of the Cretans (cf. 1:12), Christians must apply themselves to the pursuit of virtue. Here again we

his grace and become heirs in hope of eternal life. ⁸The
saying is sure.
I desire you to insist on these things, so that those who
have believed in God may be careful to apply themselves
to good deeds;ᵈ these are excellent and profitable to men.

### Other advice

⁹But avoid stupid controversies, genealogies, dissen-    1 Tim 4:7
sions, and quarrels over the law, for they are unprofitable    2 Tim 2:23
and futile. ¹⁰As for a man who is factious, after admon-    Mt 18:15-17
ishing him once or twice, have nothing more to do with him,    Rom 16:17
¹¹knowing that such a person is perverted and sinful; he is
self-condemned.

---

gratia ipsius heredes simus secundum spem vitae aeternae. ⁸Fidelis sermo, et
volo te de his confirmare, ut curent bonis operibus praeesse, qui crediderunt
Deo. Haec sunt bona et utilia hominibus; ⁹stultas autem quaestiones et
genealogias et contentiones et pugnas circa legem devita, sunt enim inutiles et
vanae. ¹⁰Haereticum hominem post unam et secundum correptionem devita,
¹¹sciens quia subversus est, qui eiusmodi est, et delinquit, proprio iudicio

---

can see that morality is based on faith, and that the pastor has a special duty to
build up people's knowledge of the faith: "When they exercise their teaching
role, bishops should proclaim the gospel of Christ to men. This is one of the
principal duties of bishops. Fortified by the Spirit they should call on men to
believe or should strengthen them when they already have a living faith. They
should expound to them the whole mystery of Christ, that is, all those truths
ignorance of which means ignorance of Christ. They should show them,
likewise, the way, divinely revealed, to give glory to God and thus attain eternal
beatitude" (*Lumen gentium*, 12).

9. As in 1 Tim 1:3-4 Paul's advice is to avoid controversy and argument
(very popular in certain Jewish circles). Debate may not be heterodox exactly
(cf. 1:10-16); but at best it is a waste of time and energy which can be better
employed in doing the job a pastor of souls is supposed to do (cf. note on 1 Tim
1:3-4).

10-11. "As for a man who is factious" (*airetikos* in Greek; *haereticus* in
Latin): literally, a heretic. This is the only time this word appears in the New
Testament; it did not yet have the technical negative meaning of someone who
denies a revealed truth; it simply meant someone who followed his own
erroneous ideas, even if that did not involve a direct attack on the Church. Here
it refers to those false teachers who rejected Titus' teaching, even if they did

---

ᵈOr *enter honourable occupations*

**Final advice**

2 Tim 4:12
Acts 20:4

Acts 18:24
3 Jn 6

¹²When I send Artemas or Tychicus to you, do your best to come to me at Nicopolis, for I have decided to spend the winter there. ¹³Do your best to speed Zenas the lawyer and Apollos on their way; see that they lack nothing. ¹⁴And let our people learn to apply themselves to good deeds,ᵈ so as to help cases of urgent need, and not to be unfruitful.

---

condemnatus. ¹²Cum misero ad te Artemam aut Tychicum, festina ad me venire Nicipolim; ibi enim statui hiemare. ¹³Zenam legis peritum et Apollo sollicite instrue, ut nihil illis desit. ¹⁴Discant autem et nostri bonis operibus praeesse ad

---

not do so in any formal or organized way. If they do not listen to fraternal correction as Jesus taught (cf. Mt 18:15-17). they must be treated as estranged from the Church. It should be noted that it is not the Church who condemns them; it is they who have gone astray and the Church simply states its position to show the faithful where error lies. "The bishops are heralds of the faith, who draw new disciples to Christ; they are authentic teachers, that is, teachers endowed with the authority of Christ, who preach the faith to the people assigned to them; [. . .] they make it bear fruit and with watchfulness they ward off whatever errors threaten their flock" (*Lumen gentium*, 25).

**12-14.** The very personal and specific little messages given at the end of the letter are typical of Paul's capacity to take an interest in quite small things. We do not know all the people mentioned or what positions they had in the Church, so the significance of the messages is rather lost on us.

"Nicopolis", which means "the city of victory", was the name of a number of Greek towns; the one referred to here may have been that near the Adriatic, in Epirus. Artemas and Tychicus were two co-workers of the Apostle; this is the only time Artemas is mentioned, but we know that Tychicus accompanied St Paul on his third missionary journey (cf. Acts 20:4) and delivered letters to the Ephesians and the Colossians (cf. Eph 6:21-22 and Col 4:7-9).

Two other people are mentioned—Zenas and Apollos. This is the only New Testament mention of Zenas; Apollos, however, is mentioned as a cultured and eloquent man (cf. Acts 18:24-26); in addition to his evangelizing work in Ephesus, he contributed a lot in Corinth (cf. 1 Cor 1:12; 3:4-6, 22; 4:6; 16:12).

These instructions show the important part hospitality played among the first Christians; Titus should also be a model for others as regards help to those in need. St Thomas Aquinas comments: "The people of God, the vineyard of the Lord, should yield not only spiritual fruit but also material fruit, and the latter it should use to meet needs as they arise; otherwise Christians would be unfruitful" (*Commentary on Tit, ad loc.*).

---

ᵈOr *enter honourable occupations*

¹⁵All who are with me send greetings to you. Greet those
who love us in the faith.
Grace be with you all.

---

usus necessarios, ut non sint infructuosi. ¹⁵Salutant te, qui mecum sunt, omnes.
Saluta, qui nos amant in fide. Gratia cum omnibus vobis!

---

**15.** St Paul sends farewell greetings first to Titus (the original addressee)
and then to the other Christians.

"Those who love us in the faith", or less literally, "our friends in the faith",
meaning the Christians, whose love for one another stems from God's love. St
Jerome comments: "If everyone who loves loved in the faith, St Paul would not
have added faith to love; mothers love their children and are ready to give their
lives for them, but that kind of love is not necessarily love in the faith; and
wives love their husbands and often even die for them, yet that is not love in
the faith. Only saints love in the faith, for their love embraces also unbelievers;
indeed, they love even their enemies; that is love in the faith, for it is a love
based on Him who has promised the reward to those who keep the *new
commandment*" (*Comm. on Tit, ad loc.*).

# Headings added to the text of the Epistles for this edition

## 1 THESSALONIANS

**Chap.**
1   Greeting

PART ONE: THANKSGIVING

Thanksgiving for the Thessalonians' fidelity

2   First Gospel preaching in Thessalonica
Their patience
Paul's anxiety

3   Timothy's mission to Thessalonica
Paul rejoices over the good reports brought by Timothy
He prays for the Thessalonians

4   PART TWO: A CALL TO VIRTUE

He calls for holiness and purity
Charity and the good use of time
The second coming of the Lord

5   Various counsels
Closing prayer and farewell

## 2 THESSALONIANS

**Chap.**
1   Greeting

PART ONE: GOD IS JUST

Thanksgiving
Prayer for perseverance

2   The coming of the Lord
The need for steadfastness

3   PART TWO: A CALL TO VIRTUE

Paul asks for prayers
Avoiding idleness. Earning one's living
Prayer and farewell wishes

## 1 TIMOTHY

**Chap.**
1   Greeting

PART ONE: SOUND DOCTRINE

False teachers to be admonished
The purpose of the Law
Paul recalls his own conversion
Timothy's responsibilities

2   PART TWO: REGULATIONS ABOUT PRAYER

God desires the salvation of all
Men at prayer, women at prayer

3   PART THREE: CHURCH OFFICE

Qualifications for bishops
Qualifications for deacons
The Church is God's household
The mystery of our religion

4   PART FOUR: PASTORAL DIRECTIVES

False teachers
Pastoral advice to Timothy

5   His approach to the faithful in general
Widows, their role and lifestyle
Criteria for choosing elders

6   Slaves, their moral obligations
False teachers described
An appeal to defend the faith
The right way to use wealth
Epilogue

## 2 TIMOTHY

**Chap.**
1   Greeting

PART ONE: PREACHING THE GOSPEL MESSAGE

Response to grace
St Paul, herald of the Gospel
Attitudes towards certain disciples

2   How Timothy should face hardships
Jesus, the apostle's model

PART TWO: DEFENDING THE GOSPEL

Avoiding useless argument
Patience towards those in error

3   Preventing error from doing harm
Staying true to Scripture

4   Dedication to preaching
The crown of righteousness

PART THREE: FINAL ADVICE

News and messages
Farewells and final good wishes

179

# TITUS

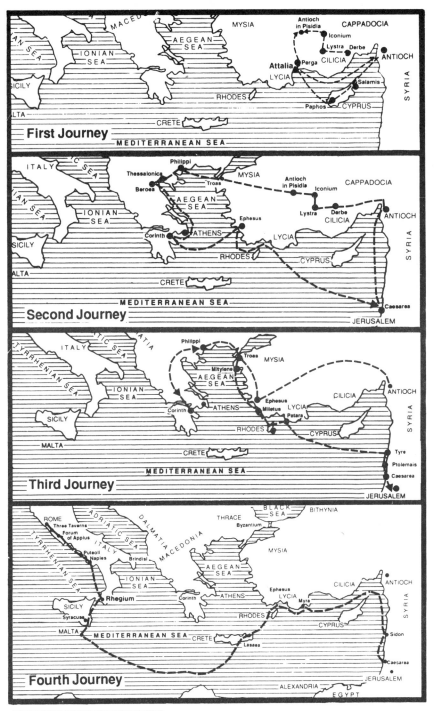

**MISSIONARY JOURNEYS OF SAINT PAUL**

# The Navarre Bible (New Testament)

St Matthew's Gospel
St Mark's Gospel
St Luke's Gospel
St John's Gospel
Acts of the Apostles
Romans and Galatians
Corinthians
Captivity Epistles
Thessalonians and Pastoral Epistles
Hebrews
Catholic Epistles
Revelation

## ESSAYS ON BIBLICAL SUBJECTS

In addition to special introduction(s) in each volume, the following essays etc. are published in the series:

| | |
|---|---|
| *St Mark* | General Introduction to the Bible; Introduction to the Books of the New Testament; Introduction to the Holy Gospels; and The Dates in the Life of our Lord Jesus Christ |
| *St Luke* | Index to the Four Gospels |
| *Acts* | The History of the New Testament Text |
| *Romans & Galatians* | Introduction to the Epistles of St Paul |
| *Corinthians* | Divine Inspiration of the Bible |
| *Captivity Epistles* | The Canon of the Bible |
| *Thessalonians* | The Truth of Sacred Scripture |
| *Hebrews* | Interpretation of Sacred Scripture and the Senses of the Bible; Divine Worship in the Old Testament |
| *Catholic Epistles* | Rules for Biblical Interpretation |
| *Revelation* | Index to the New Testament |